CAMBRIDGE LIBRARY COLLECTION

Books of enduring scholarly value

Travel and Exploration

The history of travel writing dates back to the Bible, Caesar, the Vikings and the Crusaders, and its many themes include war, trade, science and recreation. Explorers from Columbus to Cook charted lands not previously visited by Western travellers, and were followed by merchants, missionaries, and colonists, who wrote accounts of their experiences. The development of steam power in the nineteenth century provided opportunities for increasing numbers of 'ordinary' people to travel further, more economically, and more safely, and resulted in great enthusiasm for travel writing among the reading public. Works included in this series range from first-hand descriptions of previously unrecorded places, to literary accounts of the strange habits of foreigners, to examples of the burgeoning numbers of guidebooks produced to satisfy the needs of a new kind of traveller - the tourist.

Expeditions into the Valley of the Amazons

The publications of the Hakluyt Society (founded in 1846) made available edited (and sometimes translated) early accounts of exploration. The first series, which ran from 1847 to 1899, consists of 100 books containing published or previously unpublished works by authors from Christopher Columbus to Sir Francis Drake, and covering voyages to the New World, to China and Japan, to Russia and to Africa and India. This 1859 volume contains three accounts of the Amazon area, all translated from the Spanish and covering the century 1539–1639: 'The Expedition of Gonzalo Pizarro to the Land of Cinnamon'; 'The Voyage of Francisco de Orellana down the River of the Amazons'; and the 'New Discovery of the Great River of the Amazons', by Cristoval de Acuña. Their stories are full of revealing insights into the suffering of the Spaniards, afflicted as much by greed, in-fighting and treachery as by the difficult terrain and the hostility of the native Amazonians. An editorial introduction provides a context for the narratives, and an appendix lists the principal tribes of the Amazon, with the sources of this information.

T0370867

Expeditions into the Valley of the Amazons

1539, 1540, 1639

Edited by Clements R. Markham

CAMBRIDGE
UNIVERSITY PRESS

CAMBRIDGE UNIVERSITY PRESS

Cambridge, New York, Melbourne, Madrid, Cape Town, Singapore,
São Paolo, Delhi, Dubai, Tokyo, Mexico City

Published in the United States of America by Cambridge University Press, New York

www.cambridge.org
Information on this title: www.cambridge.org/9781108008174

© in this compilation Cambridge University Press 2010

This edition first published 1859
This digitally printed version 2010

ISBN 978-1-108-00817-4 Paperback

WORKS ISSUED BY

The Hakluyt Society.

EXPEDITIONS INTO THE VALLEY OF
THE AMAZONS.

M.DCCC.LIX.

EXPEDITIONS

INTO THE

VALLEY OF THE AMAZONS,

1539, 1540, 1639.

TRANSLATED AND EDITED, WITH NOTES,

BY

CLEMENTS R. MARKHAM, F.R.G.S.,

AUTHOR OF " CUZCO AND LIMA."

LONDON:

PRINTED FOR THE HAKLUYT SOCIETY.

M.DCCC.LIX.

THE HAKLUYT SOCIETY.

CONTENTS.

—

INTRODUCTION.

THE early expeditions into the great valley of the river of Amazons, during the sixteenth century, are, perhaps, the most romantic episodes in the history of Spanish discovery. The first that is deserving of notice was sent by the conqueror Pizarro, under the command of his youngest brother Gonzalo, " who was held to be the best lance that ever went to those countries, and all confess that he never showed his back to the enemy."[1]

I have translated the narrative of the expedition to the land of Cinnamon, undertaken by Gonzalo Pizarro, from the royal commentaries of Garcilasso Inca de la Vega. This chronicler had excellent opportunities of collecting information respecting the expedition, and, as we have no account actually written by one who was concerned in it, Garcilasso's narrative may be considered to be the best that is now procurable. His father was intimate with Gonzalo Pizarro ; the younger Garcilasso had himself seen him when a boy,[2]

[1] *Varones Illustres del Nuevo Mundo*, by Don F. Pizarro y Orellana, which contains an eulogistic life of Gonzalo Pizarro.

[2] When Gonzalo Pizarro entered Cuzco, after the bloody battle

he had conversed with several persons who were engaged in the expedition, and had consulted the accounts of Zarate and Gomara. The Inca historian has frequently been accused of exaggeration; but in narrating the terrible sufferings endured by Gonzalo and his followers, their heroic endurance, and final escape from the dismal forests, I cannot see that he outsteps the bounds of probability in any single instance.

The base desertion of Orellana, which added so much to the sufferings of Gonzalo's people, was the means of discovering the course of the mightiest river in the world. I have translated the account of Orellana's voyage from Antonio de Herrera's "Historia general de las Indias occidentales;" and it forms a sequel to the expedition of Gonzalo Pizarro. Herrera held the post of historiographer of the Indies for many years, during the reigns of Philip II and Philip III, and died in 1625. He had the use of all public documents, and his account of the expedition of Orellana is the best that has come to my knowledge.

After the disastrous termination of these enterprizes, no attempt was made to penetrate far into the

of Huarina in 1547, the young Garcilasso went out as far as Quispicanchi (about three leagues) to meet his father, who was then serving under the rebel chief. Garcilasso describes all the events of this day, which seem to have. been deeply impressed on his mind. He tells us that he walked part of the way, and was carried by Indians towards the end of his journey, but that he got a horse to come back on. He remembered these trifles, " porque la memoria guarda mejor lo que viò en su niñez, que lo que pasa en su edad mejor."—*Com. Real.*, ii, lib. v, cap. 27.

valley of the Amazons for several years, with one notable exception. I allude to the escape of some of the followers of the younger Almagro into the forests of Caravaya, after the final overthrow of the young adventurer at the battle on the heights of Chupas in 1542. A few scattered notices respecting these fugitives have alone come within my reach. It appears that they crossed the snowy range of the Andes to the eastward of the city of Cuzco, and descended into the great tropical forests of Colla-huaya ; where they discovered rivers, the sands of which were full of gold.[1] On the banks of these rivers they built the towns of Sandia, San Gaban, and San Juan del Oro ; large sums of gold were sent home to Spain ;[2] and the last named settlement received the title of a royal city from Charles V. But eventually the wild Chuncho Indians, of the Sirineyri tribe, fell upon them, burnt the towns, and massacred every Spaniard to the eastward of the Andes. Until within the last few years no further attempt was made to settle in these forests of Caravaya ; but it is said that the *Cascarilleros*, or

---

[1] Don Manuel Guaycochea, the obliging Cura of Sandia, supplied me with some of the above information. The province of Colla-huaya (now called Caravaya), in the Peruvian department of Puno, is becoming important, both on account of its gold washings, and of the number of valuable cinchona trees in its forests. The village of Sandia is on the eastern slope of the Cordillera, and on the verge of the boundless forests, which extend for hundreds of miles to the north and east.

[2] *Comm. Real.*, ii, lib. iii, cap. 19. "La provincia de Colla-huaya, donde sacaron muy mucho oro finisimo, de viento y quatro quilates, y hoy se saca todavia, aunque no en tanta abundancia."

collectors of Peruvian bark, sometimes stumble upon
ruined walls almost hidden in the dense underwood:
—the crumbling remains of San Gaban, or San Juan
del Oro.

Beyond this settlement in Caravaya, no attempt
was made to penetrate into the valley of the Amazons,
after the return of Gonzalo Pizarro, for about fourteen years. In 1555, however, the Marquis of Cañete,
a scion of the noble house of Mendoza, was appointed
viceroy of Peru.

On arriving in Lima, he found that the disgraceful
feuds of the Pizarros, the Almagros, and their followers, had just been concluded by the death of the rebel
Hernandez Giron, at Pucara. It was his care to
punish all traitors with severity, and to turn the rest-
lessness of the turbulent adventurers into another
channel, by promoting expeditions of discovery.

Thus it was that Juan Alvarez Maldonado was sent
to explore the forests east of Cuzco, and that Pedro
de Ursua started in search of El Dorado, and the
kingdom of the Omaguas.

Juan Alvarez Maldonado was, says Garcilasso, "one
of the fattest and most corpulent men that I have ever
seen;" but at the same time he was brave and active.
Throughout Cuzco he was famous for having escaped death in a most unusual way. When fighting
against Gonzalo Pizarro, a bullet struck him full on
the chest, and knocked him down ; but the ball happened to strike upon the breviary which was in his
bosom, and so, by the miraculous interposition of the
blessed Virgin, as it was said, his life was preserved.

Ever afterwards he hung the book outside his clothes, as a charm against the evil eye.

This cavalier had heard that a number of the Incas, with forty thousand followers, had assembled together, with great store of gold and silver, and had fled far away into the forests to the eastward of Cuzco ;[1] to escape from the oppression of their conquerors. He intended, therefore, to pursue them with a chosen band of soldiers, spoil them of their treasure, and proceed also to explore the great river which was reported to take its rise in those forests.[2] Maldonado, however, had cause for alarm in the knowledge that another adventurer named Tordoya also intended to chase the Incas; and it was probable that the two parties of Spanish wolves would rend each other over the carcasses of their prey.

Maldonado crossed the snowy range of the eastern Cordillera, penetrated some distance into the forests, along the banks of the Tono, (a tributary of the Purus), and encountered his rival Gomez de Tordoya, who was waiting to receive him. They fought for three successive days, until nearly every man, on both sides, was killed. The wild Indians, called

[1] M. Rodriguez, lib. vi, cap. iv, p. 384.

[2] This is the river Amaru-mayu, Madre de Dios, or Purus (the Cuchivara of Acuña and Samuel Fritz), one of the largest tributaries of the Amazons, which remains unexplored to this day. In mentioning this flight of the Incas into the valley of the Amazons, Velasco, in his *Historia de Quito*, enumerates eight powerful Amazonian tribes as being descended from them, namely, the Cingacuchuscas, Campas, Comavas, Cunivas, Pirras, Jibitos, Panos, and Chunchos.

Chunchos, finished off the remainder, three only escaping out of the whole number, among whom was Maldonado himself, who eventually made his escape alone, through the forests of Caravaya, to Cuzco. Such an adventure must have reduced the size of this lucky old soldier.

Thus did these exploring expeditions to the eastward of Cuzco destroy each other; and we know less now concerning the vast territory along the banks of the Purus, and its tributaries, than was known in the days of the Marquis of Cañete, three hundred years ago.[1]

The other expedition, mentioned above, under Don Pedro de Ursua, led to more important results; and the story of his murderer, the pirate Lope de Aguirre, is one of the most extraordinary which even that age of wonderful adventures can furnish.

The enterprize was organized, by order of the Marquis of Cañete, to search for the nation of Omaguas, of whose fabulous wealth most exciting rumours had reached Peru. Felipe de Utre, a German who had started from Coro, in Venezuela, in search of El

---

[1] Lieutenant Gibbon, U.S.N., in 1852, reached the banks of the Purus; and, in 1853, I followed the course of the Tono as far as its junction with that great tributary of the Amazons. No one has yet explored the whole course of the Purus.

In a report from the Deputy of Caravaya to the Minister of Public Works at Lima, on the improvement of the roads in that district, dated December 11th, 1858, it is proposed to send an expedition to the confluence of the rivers San Gaban and Ynambari, to ascertain if the united streams could be made available for navigation, as far as the river Purus, or Madre de Dios.— *Commercio*, Dec. 18th, 1858.

Dorado, in 1541, returned with a story that, after many days journey, he had come to a village whence he saw a vast city, with a palace in the centre, belonging to the Omaguas. At about the same time, information respecting this wealthy nation reached Peru from an equally reliable source. Father Pedro Simon gives the following account of the way in which these wonderful stories were disseminated.

" Certain brave rumours," he says, " prevailed in those times, both in the city of Lima, and throughout the provinces of Peru, which were spread by Indians from Brazil, respecting the rich provinces which they declared they had seen, when on their road from the east coast. These Indians, more than two thousand in number, left their homes with the intention of settling in other lands, as their own were too crowded ; but others declare that the Indians undertook this journey, to enjoy human food in those parts. At length, after travelling for ten years, with two Portuguese in their company, they reached the province of the Motilones in Peru, by way of a famous river which flows thence, and enters the Marañon.[1] These Indians brought news respecting the provinces of the Omaguas, in which El Dorado was said to reside. This so excited the minds of those restless spirits in Peru, who were ever ready to give credit to these rumours, that the Viceroy thought it prudent to seek some way, by which to give them employment."[2]

[1] The *Huallaga*.
[2] *Sexta Noticia de las Conquistas de Tierra Firme*, cap. i, p. 402.

The expedition in search of Omaguas and El
Dorado was, therefore, organized ; and the Marquis
of Cañete selected Don Pedro de Ursua to command
it. This cavalier was a native of a small town near
Pampluna, in the kingdom of Navarre, from which
he took his name. He had already served with some
distinction, both in New Granada and against the
Cimarrones, or rebellious negroes, on the Isthmus
of Panama.

Ursua collected his forces at a little village of
Motilones Indians, called Lamas, on the banks of the
river Moyobamba, a tributary of the Huallaga ; and
began to build vessels capable of containing four
hundred men. He sent forward a party under Juan
de Vargas, and followed himself with the main body,
in September 1560.[1] The expedition descended the
river Huallaga, entered the Marañon, and passed
the mouth of the Ucayali ; where Ursua appointed
Vargas to be his lieutenant, and Don Fernando de
Guzman to be " Alferez Mayor."

But Ursua soon found that he had with him a
number of desperate wretches, who were prepared
for any atrocity ; and a mutinous spirit was raised
by a villain named Lope de Aguirre, who desired to
return to Peru, and restore the days of anarchy
and civil war. Others set their eyes upon Ursua's

---

[1] The second expedition which descended the river Moyobamba
to the Huallaga, was made in 1650, by General Don Martin de la
Riba Aguero, who subjugated the territory of Lamas. He was
governor of Lamas for thirty years ; and, on his death, the government of the Motilones or Lamistas Indians was annexed to the
jurisdiction of Chachapoyas.

mistress, a beautiful widow, named Inez de Atienza.

Guzman, who was an unprincipled young man, of a good Andalusian family, was won over by the conspirators ; and they agreed to assassinate their general. On a dark night, when the explorers were encamped on the great river of Amazons, and every one seemed wrapped in sleep, a figure passed in front of Ursua's tent, exclaiming : " Pedro de Ursua, governor of Omagua and El Dorado, may God have mercy upon thee!" The following day the expedition arrived off a village called Machiparo.[1] It was new year's day, 1561, when the conspirators entered Ursua's tent and murdered him. Vargas was killed at the same time.

The assassins then elected Guzman to be their general, and Aguirre to be master of the camp. The latter had been the chief instigator to the mutiny ; and his extraordinary career, and the number of atrocious crimes of which he was guilty, give him a pre-eminence in villainy over all the adventurers who flocked to the new world, during the sixteenth century.

Lope de Aguirre was born at Oñate, in Biscay, of noble but poor parents. He had proceeded to the new world when very young, and plunged into all the turmoil of the civil wars amongst the conquerors of Peru, often serving in the lowest employments. He was hideously ugly, and lame in one foot, from a

[1] Near the mouth of the river Putumayu. See pages 27 and 29 of this volume.

wound received when fighting against the rebel Giron, at Coquimbo.

This audacious monster took the lead in the revolt, and induced the soldiers to renounce their allegiance to King Philip, and to elect Guzman as their new sovereign. All who refused were murdered. Meanwhile they continued their voyage down the river; and a bloody voyage it was. Every one, whom Aguirre and his blood-hounds suspected of disliking their proceedings, was murdered, amongst others the unfortunate mistress of Ursua, Doña Inez de Atienza. Finally they slaughtered Guzman, the puppet king, and Aguirre caused himself to be proclaimed commander of the expedition. A half blood named Carrion, the murderer of Doña Inez, was made chief magistrate, and the piratical crew were christened Marañones by their leader, after the great river which they were navigating. These villains committed every kind of atrocity on the unfortunate Indians whom they encountered, and their crimes were not unfrequently varied by a murder amongst themselves. Thus they continued their bloody course towards the Atlantic.

Padre Simon, Acuña, and Rodriguez, believe that the Marañones ascended the Rio Negro, and reached the ocean, by following the streams of the Cassiquiari and Orinoco. They eventually reached the island of Margarita, which they got possession of, committing the most horrible atrocities on the inhabitants, and murdering all the officers of the Spanish government. Aguirre then landed with his Marañones, at Burbu-

rata in Venezuela, with the intention of conquering
New Granada; whence he dispatched a letter to
Philip II, a most extraordinary production, part of
which was published by Baron Humboldt in his
Personal Narrative.[1] It is addressed to " King Philip,
native of Spain, son of Charles the invincible," and
continues :—

"I, Lope de Aguirre, thy vassal, a christian of
poor but noble parents, and native of the town of
Oñate in Biscay, went over young to Peru, to labour
lance in hand. I fought for thy glory : but I recom-
mend to thee to be more just to the good vassals
whom thou hast in this country ; for I and mine,
weary of the cruelties and injustice which thy viceroy, thy governors, and thy judges exercise in thy
name, have resolved to obey thee no more. We re-
gard ourselves no longer as Spaniards. We make a
cruel war on thee, because we will not endure the
oppression of thy ministers. I am lame in the left
foot from two shots of an arquebuss, which I received
fighting against Francisco Hernandez Giron, who was
then a rebel, as I am at present, and always shall
be : for since thy Viceroy, the Marquis of Cañete, a
cowardly, ambitious, and effeminate man, has hanged
our bravest warriors, I care no more for thy pardon
than for the books of Martin Luther.

" Remember, King Philip, that thou hast no right
to draw revenues from these provinces, the conquest
of which has been without danger to thee." He then
describes his exploits with cool effrontery,—and goes

---

[1] Humboldt, *Reise*, iii, p. 220.

on to say,—"We navigated for eleven months, till we reached the mouth of the river. We sailed more than fifteen hundred leagues. God knows how we got through that great mass of water. I advise thee, O great king, never to send Spanish fleets into that cursed river." Thus he concluded this remarkable document, which was dispatched under the care of a captive monk.

Aguirre and his Marañones then advanced into the interior of Venezuela ; but their career was drawing to a close. They were met by a Spanish force under Gutierrez de la Peña, and entirely defeated.[1] The pirate chief murdered his own daughter, who had accompanied him from Peru, " that she might never be called the daughter of a traitor," and then delivered himself into the hands of the king's officers ; and he was put to death, on the spot, by two of his own Marañones. His head was exposed for many years at Tocuyo, in an iron cage. In Peru, and most of the other countries in South America, this monster is always known as the " tyrant Aguirre."

Fray Pedro Simon, in his sixth historical notice of the conquest of Tierra Firme, has left us a long and detailed account of this piratical voyage down the river of Amazons, and his information appears to have been derived from some person who was actually in the expedition.[2]

[1] The poet Ercilla, then on his way home from Chilé, was present at this battle.

[2] I have not dwelt at any length on this extraordinary voyage, because I hope, at some future time, to translate the sixth histori-

Lope de Aguirre was the second leader who descended from the eastern slopes of the Cordilleras to
the Atlantic, by water. It was upwards of seventy
years before any European performed a similar feat.

Expeditions, however, continued to be sent into
the valley of the Amazons, in different directions.

The first attempts, after the catastrophe which
befell Don Pedro de Ursua, were made in the direction of the " Gran Chacu," that extensive region in
the extreme south of the valley of the Amazons,
where the tributaries of the river Madeira, as well as
those of the Paraguay, take their rise.[1]

The tribe, in Gran Chacu, which wandered nearest
to the confines of Peru, was that of the Chirihuanas,
who were described by Padre Machoni in 1733, as a
quarrelsome and drunken race, living together in

cal notice of Pedro Simon, for the Hakluyt Society. I regret that
circumstances should have prevented me from inserting Simon's
account of the expedition of Aguirre, in the present volume, according to my original intention.

[1] " Gran Chacu" is a vast territory between the provinces of
Paraguay, Tucuman, Charcas, and Sta. Cruz de la Sierra. The
etymology of the name indicates the multitude of nations in this
region. When the Incas went out hunting, the animals were collected together from various parts, and this congregated multitude
was called " Chacu" in the Quichua language. On account of the
number of tribes inhabiting this region, it is called, with reference
to this assemblage of animals, " Gran Chacu."

The chief rivers are the Pilco-mayu, Bermejo, and Salado, all
tributaries of the Paraguay ; but the northern part of Gran Chacu
is drained by streams which form the rivers Itenez and Mamoré,
two of the principal feeders of the Madeira.—*Gran Chacu por
Pedro Lozano*, Cordova, 1733.

small villages, and amounting to about thirty thousand men, besides women and children.

In the year 1572 Don Francisco de Toledo, then Viceroy of Peru, attempted the conquest of the Chirihuanas. He organized a small army, and, accompanied by a number of cows and horses, entered their territory; but he was not prepared for the difficulties of those untrodden forests. Leaving all his baggage and live stock behind, his forces retreated in disorder, suffering great losses on the way. The Viceroy himself was carried in a litter; and the Chirihuanas hung upon his rear, shouting, jeering, and crying out: "Tumble that old woman out of the basket, that we may eat her alive."[1]

Though the Viceroy with his soldiers could not penetrate into the Gran Chacu; many solitary priests, cross in hand, descended from the lofty plateau of the Andes, and fearlessly mingled with the wild Indians, preaching and baptizing.

San Francisco Solano was the first Christian missionary who entered the Gran Chacu.[2] In 1589 Padre Juan Fonte, accompanied only by a boy to

---

[1] *Com. Real.*, i, lib. vii, cap. 17. The Viceroy Toledo had cruelly put to death young Tupac Amaru, the last of the Incas, during the preceding year; and I therefore dwell with peculiar pleasure on his ludicrous discomfiture by the Chiriguanas. He was a cousin of the butcher Duke of Alva, and second son of the Count of Oropesa.

[2] *Lozano*, p. 108. Solano is one of the four Peruvian saints. The others are San Toribio de Mogrovejo, third archbishop of Lima; San Martin de Poras, a Dominican negro; and Santa Rosa of Lima.

assist at mass, preached amongst the savage Lules
Indians; and in 1591 Alonzo de Barzana, a Jesuit,
also entered the Chacu, and married three thousand
couples "in facie Ecclesiæ". In 1592 Padre Gaspar
de Monroy ventured amongst the indomitable Chiriguanas, and, says the chronicler of these pious
achievements, "the devil was much enraged at his
success".[1] Thus, while the Indians remained independent of Spanish rule, numbers of Christian priests
continued, from time to time, to explore the vast
forest covered plains of the Chacu.

While these intrepid missionaries were penetrating
into the Gran Chacu, attempts continued to be made
to explore the valley of the Amazons in other directions; and especially from the province of Quito.

The first European who reached the banks of the
main stream of the Amazons, subsequent to the
piratical voyage of Aguirre, was Don Rafael Ferrer,
a Jesuit priest. This devoted missionary entered the
forests to the eastward of Quito, in the year 1602,
and, descending the Napo, reached the banks of the
Marañon in 1608. He was eventually murdered by
the Cofanes Indians.[2] But previous to this single-
handed attempt of the fearless Jesuit, some steps had

---

[1] *Lozano*, p. 120. The Viceroy of Peru (the Count of Mon-
terey) in 1607, gave fresh vigour to missionary enterprize in the
Gran Chacu, and numbers of priests continued to go forth into
those wilds, during the seventeenth and eighteenth centuries.

[2] The territory of the Cofanes Indians was discovered by Don
Gonzalez Diaz de Pineda in 1536; and was more fully explored
by Don Francisco Perez de Quesada in 1557, who was appointed
governor of that country by the Viceroy of Peru.

been taken to secure the territory which was discovered by Gonzalo Pizarro. In 1551 the Marquis
of Cañete sent Don Egidio Ramirez Davalos to establish a government in the land of Cinnamon, and he
founded the settlement of Quijos in 1552, on the
river of the same name. This cavalier was succeeded
in the command of these forests by his brother, Don
Gil Ramirez Davalos, in 1558; an officer who had
already distinguished himself by subjugating the
Cañares Indians, and founding the city of Cuença.

Don Gil Ramirez seems to have entered upon his
command with great energy, and his former popu-
larity induced many adventurers to join his standard.
Thus, during the three following years, he founded
the settlements of Baeza, Maspa, Avila, Archidona,
and Tena, in the dense forests through which the
feeders of the river Napo flow, to join the Amazons.
Finally he retired to Rio-bamba, near Quito, where,
in the time of Velasco, his numerous posterity still
resided. In the year 1599, however, the wild Indians
of the tribe of Jibaros rose in rebellion, and destroyed
all these flourishing settlements, Archidona alone
remaining.[1]

Early in the seventeenth century the territory
along the shores of the Upper Marañon, and its tributary the Santiago, was explored, and the government
of Maynas formed.[2] A small fort had long been es-

[1] Jaen, in 1549, had been founded by Don Diego Paloma, on
whom the government of the district, near the river Chinchipe, had
been conferred by La Gasca.

[2] The course of the Marañon, as far as the *pongo* or rapid of

tablished on the river Santiago, near the Pongo de Manseriche, to check the incursions of the fierce Jeberos Indians. In 1616 some Spanish soldiers, prompted by curiosity and the love of adventure, started from this fort in a canoe, and reached a settlement of Indians of the Mayna nation, who received them hospitably. They finally succeeded in reaching Lima, where they reported their discovery to the Viceroy Prince of Esquilache, a nobleman of the family of Borgia.

The Prince of Esquilache conceived a strong desire to conquer the territory on the Upper Marañon; and he chose an officer named Don Diego de Vaca y Vega, who had defended Panama against the English, and had served as commandant of the port of Callao, to perform this service, appointing him governour of all the countries he might conquer, in the year 1618.

In 1619 Don Diego occupied Maynas with his soldiers, and founded a settlement, which he named San Francisco de Borja, in honour of the Viceroy, soon afterwards resigning the government into the hands of his son Don Pedro. A considerable number of Spaniards settled at the new town of Borja, forcing the Indians to work for them, and treating them with great violence and injustice. At last the Indians rose in rebellion, in the year 1637, and advanced in a tumultuous body, to attack Borja. The Spaniards threw up entrenchments round the church, which were assaulted and carried by the assailants, and they

Manseriche, was explored by Pedro de Mercadillo in 1548, when he was employed in subjugating the province of Yaguarzongo.

d

then retreated into the church itself, where they kept
up a fire from the windows. At this critical moment
the Indians were seized with an unaccountable panic,
and fled in confusion, leaving many of their number
dead or wounded. The Spaniards followed them,
committing a horrible butchery; but the insurgent
Indians rallied on the banks of the river Pastaza,
where they were joined by many other tribes, and
again became formidable to the invaders of their native land.

Don Pedro Vaca, the governor of Maynas, sent a
message to his father, who was living in retirement
at Loxa, saying that he despaired of subjugating the
Indians by force, and that his only hope was, that the
Jesuit missionaries might succeed in tranquillizing
them by persuasion. Accordingly Padre Lucas de la
Cueva, and Padre Cujia, a Sardinian, both Jesuits,
left Quito in the end of the year 1637, and, passing
through the towns of Cuença and Loxa, reached Jaen,
whence, descending the Marañon and passing the
dangerous Pongo de Manseriche,[1] they arrived at the
settlement of Borja.

Meanwhile Don Pedro collected all the Spaniards,
both in Borja, and in the adjacent settlement of Santiago; and also obtained assistance from his generous
ally the chief of the Jeberos Indians. With this
force he defeated and scattered the rebels.[1]

[1] Pongo. A rapid or narrow place in a river, from the Quichua
word *puncu*, a gate or door.

[2] In 1657 Riva Aguero, governor of Caxamarca and Lamas, an
officer named Monroy, and Don Juan Mauricio Vaca de Vega,

Things were in this state when, on the 6th of February 1638, fathers Cujia and Cueva arrived on the spot ; and thus the famous Jesuit missions of the Upper Marañon were commenced.

There was a boundless field for the labour of the good fathers ; and when father Cueva asked the chief of the Jeberos how many nations there were in those forests, the chief took up a handful of sand and, scattering it in the air, exclaimed " Countless as the grains of sand are the nations in this land ; for there is neither lake nor river, hill nor valley, plain nor forest, which is not full of inhabitants." The chief of the Jeberos conducted father Cueva down the river Marañon in his canoe, visiting all the villages of his tribe, which were built on the banks. Thus the Indians of the tribe of Jeberos, whom Velasco describes as " a noble, amiable, and excellent people," were the first-fruits of the Jesuit missions.

Father Acuña, in the narrative of his voyage, mentions the labours of these missionaries, and says that he had received many letters from them, describing the grandeur and vast extent of the country which they were engaged in exploring.[1]

While the rivers Santiago, Pastaza, and Upper Marañon were thus explored by the followers of

son of Don Pedro, contended for the appointment of governor of Maynas. The viceroy, Count Alba de Liste, decided in favour of Don Juan Mauricio, who, in 1653, succeeded his father in the government of Maynas. The evidence of Father Cueva, who was in Lima at the time, was the cause of Don Juan Mauricio's success.—*Manuel Rodriguez.*

[1] Acuña, No. 47, p. 91, of this volume.

Vaca, and the Jesuit fathers who came to his assistance, attempts were also made in Peru, by solitary priests, to penetrate into the regions watered by
the great rivers Huallaga and Ucayali ; a land where
ancient legends placed the Peruvian El Dorado, and
the city of Manoa.

In the year 1631, the Franciscan father Felipe de
Lugando left the ancient city of Huanuco, and, travelling through the ravine of Chinchao, and across
the mountains, to the district of Cuchero, eventually
reached the banks of the rivers Monzon and Tulumayu. In a short time he succeeded in forming six
villages of converted Indians, of the Cholones, Jibitos,
Lamistas tribes, on the banks of the Huallaga and
the Monzon.[1] In 1636 another Franciscan, named
Jeronimo Ximenes, departed from Tarma, and, descended by difficult and dangerous roads to the Cerro
de la Sal,[2] where he built a chapel. From this station
he descended the river Perene, in company with Fray
Cristoval de Larios, and both were massacred by the
Antis Indians in the year 1637. When their untimely
fate became known at Tarma, two other fearless
priests, named José de Santa Maria and Cristoval
Mesa, set out to succeed them, and in 1640 they had
founded seven villages on the banks of the Chanchamayu. A year later father Matias de Yllescas, with
two lay-brothers, explored the river Perene, and even
reached the banks of the Ucayali, but they were all

[1] Castelnau, iv, cap. liii, p. 416; Poeppig, *Reise in Peru, und
auf dem Amazonenstrome,* ii, p. 246.
[2] Mentioned by Acuña, p. 120 of this volume.

three murdered by the Setebos Indians. At about the same time other Franciscans began to follow the footsteps of Lugando down the Huallaga valley. In 1641 two missionaries, named Gaspar de Vera and Juan Calazas, were preaching to the Indians at Cuchero; and in 1644 Ignacio de Irraga, Jeronimo Ximenes, and Francisco Suarez, left Tulumayu, and made a journey of twenty-four leagues into the forests, founding four Missions amongst the Payansos Indians.

Such were the energetic enterprizes of the Franciscan Missionaries, in the valleys of the Huallaga and Ucayali; and they continued during another century and a half to send devoted men into the forests, who preached fearlessly, explored vast tracts of previously unknown land, and usually ended their days by being murdered by the very savages whom they had come to humanize.

The discoveries of the Portuguese on and near the mouth of the great river of Amazons, during the same period, were conducted on very different principles. In the year 1580 Portugal had been united with Spain, so that the expeditions conducted by the Portuguese from that time to the year 1640, when they regained their independence, were undertaken by orders from the Spanish government.

In 1613 Gaspar de Souza was appointed governor of Maranham, with orders to prosecute discovery and conquest in the direction of the river of Amazons. Accordingly, in 1615, an officer named Caldeira, with three vessels, and two hundred men, was sent to conquer Gram Parà ; and he founded the city of Santa Maria de Belem de Gram Parà, in 1616, on a low elbow of land, at the junction of the river Guamà with the Parà, and about eighty miles from the sea. In 1618, Francisco de Caldeira was superseded by Jeronimo Fragoso de Albuquerque ; while a miscreant named Benito Maciel was sent to take the command against the Tupinambas Indians, and he commenced a career of devastation and murder in the district of Parà. On the death of Albuquerque, Pedro de Texeira became governor of Parà, and he was succeeded in 1622 by the brutal Maciel ; but the cruelty of the latter became so intolerable that another officer named Manoel de Sousa was sent to supersede him in 1626. In 1630 Francisco Coelho was governor of Parà, and he was followed, on his death in 1633, by Jacome Raymundo de Noronha.

The enterprizes of these successive governors were chiefly confined to murdering and rooting out Dutch settlers ; varied by occasional inroads into the interior to burn the villages, and carry off the unfortunate Indians, to be sold into slavery.

The principal expeditions, undertaken to explore the vast valley of the Amazons, from the days of Gonzalo Pizarro to the year 1635, have thus been briefly reviewed ; and we now come to those events which led to the voyage of Acuña.

In 1635 some Franciscans left Quito, and entered the province of Sucumbios, where they were received by Juan de Palacios, who commanded at a small fort called San Miguel. They embarked, with Palacios and ninety soldiers, on the river Aguarico, which they descended until they came to the country of a tribe of Indians, whom Ferrer had formerly named "Los Endabellados," from their long hair. Here Palacios, delighted with the rich and abundant soil, established a settlement called Ante,[1] a little above the junction of the Aguarico with the Napo ; but he was attacked and killed by the Encabellados, while most of the Franciscans and soldiers escaped back to Quito. Two monks named Diego de Brieba, and Andres Toledo, with six soldiers, fortunately happened to be in the forests, a little below the spot where the murder of Palacios took place. On hearing of it they got into a canoe, and began the descent of the Napo, in the month of June 1637. The adventurers finally reached Parà, at the mouth of the Amazons; and were thus the first Europeans who had navigated the whole length of this mighty river, since the days of Aguirre. On their arrival, Noronha, the governor of Parà, determined to send an expedition commanded by Pedro de Texeira, up the river ; which arrived at Quito in 1638.

Acuña, who was rector of the college at Cuença, accompanied Texeira in his returning expedition from Quito, down the Napo and Amazons to Parà ; with orders to observe everything on the way ; to note down the names of all Indian tribes, their manners and customs; the names of the rivers flowing into the Amazons ; the natural productions of the country ; and to send in a full report to the council of the

Or " Anete."—Acuña, p. 92.

Indies, on his return to Spain. These instructions were ably carried into execution by the good father, and the results of his observations were published in Madrid, in the year 1641. Acuña's voyage was perfectly successful; the people were well supplied with provisions; there appears to have been scarcely any sickness, no accident of any importance occurred, and they floated down pleasantly, with the current of the river. The good father was an intelligent traveller, and was indefatigable in collecting information of every kind. He describes the manners and customs of the Indians, their modes of fishing and hunting, and their arms. He enumerates the productions of the forests and the rivers, and points out the infinite capabilities of the magnificent country through which he passed. Indeed he seems to have been fully alive to the extraordinary advantages which would be reaped by any country whose merchants could succeed in establishing a trade with the settlers in the Amazonian valley, and in navigating the broad deep rivers up to the very feet of the Andes.

Acuña's work, entitled *El Nuevo Descubrimiento del gran rio de las Amazonas*, was published at Madrid in the year 1641; but before it had issued from the press, the Portuguese had shaken off the yoke of Spain, and again become an independent state. The wretched government of Philip IV, terrified lest the Portuguese should take advantage of any information contained in Acuña's book, and forgetting that Texeira and all his officers knew quite as much about the Amazons as the Spanish priest, ordered

every copy of the work to be immediately and effect-
tually destroyed. It has consequently become exceedingly scarce. The French translator (in 1682) said
that Philip IV, fearing that the narrative would serve
to guide his enemies into the heart of Peru, caused all
the copies to be suppressed except one only, which
is in the library of the Vatican. He adds,—" On
auroit de la peine d'en trouver un autre, ny dans le
vieux, ny dans le nouveau monde, que celui sur lequel
cette traduction a estè faite."

There are, however, certainly three other copies in
existence. One in the King's library at the British
Museum, from which I have made this translation :
another which was bought at Colonel Stanley's sale ;
and a third, formerly in the possession of Lord Stuart
de Rothsay.

A French translation was published by M. de
Gomberville in 1682,[1] which, however, wants the
address to the reader, the certificate of Texeira, the
instructions from the Audience of Quito, and the
memorial at the end.[2] An English translation, from
the French, was published in London, in 1698. It
is full of omissions, mistakes, and long interpolations
in the text.

When Portugal became independent, Acuña submitted a number of suggestions, in the form of a

---

[1] Two vols., 12mo., Paris, 1682 ; "par M. de Gomberville de
l'Academie Françoise, avec une dissertation sur la rivière des Ama-
zones pour servir de preface."

[2] Manuel Rodriguez gives Texeira's certificate, and Acuña's
memorial.

memorial, to the council of the Indies, proposing measures, with a view to preserving all the benefits of the late discoveries, to Spain ; but the sleepy government of Philip IV never took any steps to secure these advantages. The good father eventually returned to South America, and died in the city of Lima.[1]

The narrative of Acuña is the earliest published account of the river of the Amazons in existence ; and another century passed away before a second educated European navigated the mighty stream, and gave the results of his observations to the world. Meanwhile, during the latter half of the seventeenth century, many expeditions continued to be made into the valley of the Amazons, generally conducted by intrepid Jesuits and Franciscans. It will not, I think, be out of place to conclude this introduction by giving a brief summary of the most important of these enterprizes, subsequent to the voyage of Acuña.

Four distinct objects have given rise to the various enterprizes undertaken to explore the valley of the Amazons, since the days of Acuña. The first and most effective was the conversion of the Indians ; the second was the search for the fabulous golden Empire of Enim, Paytiti, or El Dorado; the third was the pursuit of commercial advantages ; and the last has been the advancement of science and geographical knowledge.

Rapid and extensive discoveries were made through the zeal and energy of the Jesuit missionaries of

[1] His companion, Artieda, returned to Quito, by way of Carthagena, in 1643 ; where he advocated the establishment of missions on the Marañon.—Manuel Rodriguez, lib. ii, cap. xv, p. 151.

Maynas, a territory including the shores of the Upper Marañon, Santiago, Pastaza, Huallaga, and Ucayali.[1] The Jesuit fathers, who had arrived at Borja in 1638, found that none of the Indians of the Marañon lived in permanent settlements; but Father Cueva succeeded in collecting some of the Jeberos, and induced them to live in a village on the river Apena, which he named "Concepcion de Nuestra Señora de Jeberos," in 1640.[2] In the same year two more missionaries, named Bartolomé Perez, of Talavera, in Spain, and Francisco de Figueroa, of Popayan, arrived at Borja, and established schools for the Mayna children.

In 1644 Cujia and Perez made an expedition into the country of the fierce Cocomas Indians, on the Huallaga, and in the following year they visited the Omaguas. Thus these indefatigable men laboured for many years ; and, by the year 1650, they had established several villages amongst the Cocomas and Cocomillas Indians.

[1] "The echoes of their sermons resounded through those desert wilds."—M. Rodriguez, lib. iii, cap. ii, p. 162.

[2] *Jeberos*, in the time of Spanish power, was the most important town of Amazonas. The most distinguished men of Spain came out to fill the post of "Intendente General" of Jeberos, and the natives still remember the name of Señor Calvo, so remarkable for his firmness and integrity. At that time the population of Jeberos was fifteen thousand. Even to this day there exist the remains of its former grandeur, and the ruins of a college and a government house are pointed out. At present it scarcely counts seventeen hundred inhabitants. The city is situated in an extensive plain, watered by numerous streams which flow into the river Apena.— *Heraldo de Lima*, September 13th, 1855.

xxviii   INTRODUCTION.

As a geographical discoverer, the most distinguished worthy of the first missionary epoch of the Marañon, was Father Raymundo de Santa Cruz. He was born at San Miguel de Ibarra, twenty leagues from Quito, of noble parents, his father being descended from the Aragonese family of Santa Cruz, and his mother, Catalina, being a daughter of the house of Calderon. He was educated at the college of San Luis at Quito, and, after having been ordained, he joined the Marañon missions. The scene of his most important labours was amongst the Cocomas Indians, on the banks of the Huallaga; where, in the midst of incredible difficulties and hardships, he acquired a knowledge of their language, gained their affections, and preached to them with some success, for several years. In 1654 he first turned his attention to the discovery of more easy routes from Quito to the missions; and determined, in the first place, to explore the route by which Acuña had descended the Napo, with Texeira's expedition, fifteen years before. He collected eighty Indians, and began his voyage in canoes, from the mission village which he had established on the Huallaga. The brave explorer descended the Marañon until he reached the mouth of the Napo, and, ascending that river, arrived at Archidona after a voyage of fifty-one days. During this long and perilous undertaking, he suffered much from the plagues of mosquitoes and other insects; from hunger; and from the anxiety and perplexity caused by the difficulty in finding the way; as there are several rivers, such as the Coca and Curaray, which, though tributaries, are of equal volume with the Napo ; so that in ascending the latter river, there was constant danger of choosing the wrong stream.

Leaving half the Indians in charge of the canoes, Father Raymundo set out with the rest for the city of Quito, travelling through the dense forests, and over the mountains, on foot.

Great excitement was caused at Quito, by the arrival of the father, after succeeding in performing this journey. He was received outside the city by a procession of ecclesiastics, with banners and images ; and he entered in the midst of his Indians, who were dressed in cotton shirts, with a headdress of feathers, bows in their hands, and quivers of arrows hanging from their shoulders. Thus they marched through the streets to the sound of music, amidst a vast crowd of spectators, until they reached the great square, where the members of the Royal Audience, the bishop, and the dean received them.[1] After remaining about a month in Quito, Father Raymundo returned to Archidona with his Indians, and three fresh missionaries. They descended the Napo in eight days, and arrived safely at the mission of the Cocomas, on the Huallaga.

In 1656 Father Raymundo was employed to accompany General Don Martin de la Riva Aguero in an expedition to subdue the Jeberos Indians ; but it proved unsuccessful, owing to the mismanagement

---

[1] M. Rodriguez, p. 197. He says : "This was one of the most memorable days, which the city of Quito has ever seen."

and greedy avarice of the Spanish commander, who was governor of Caxamarca. The good missionary, however, still thirsted after the discovery of new territory, and of better routes between Quito and the missions of the Marañon. He explored several rivers, and finally, in 1662, ascended the Pastaza, with a few Spaniards and Indians, in light canoes. On the third day, the canoe in which Father Raymundo was embarked, entered a rapid near the confluence of the Bombonaza, and was overset. The good man, giving one last look at the overhanging forest, sank beneath the waves, which became his grave.[1]

This indefatigable explorer, and zealous missionary, led a life of constant self-denial. His usual dress consisted of an old battered hat, a coarse cotton shirt, and a pair of sandals; and his mode of life was more simple than that of the Indians who surrounded him. Thus for many years he laboured to increase the temporal and spiritual welfare of these wild hunters of the Huallaga, seeking out medicines, and administering them with his own hands; as well as teaching them the Christian religion. His was truly a noble and well spent life; but it should be remembered that there were many other intrepid and devoted men on the banks of these rivers, at the same time, who were equally zealous in preaching to the Indians, and in exploring the vast forests, and unknown rivers, and who, generally, like Father Raymundo de Santa Cruz, met with a violent death, as the welcome reward of their exertions.

[1] M. Rodriguez, p. 270.

In 1658 Father Cueva extended the labours of the missionaries to the banks of the Napo, and became himself the permanent priest at Archidona. Thus, through the untiring zeal of these Jesuits, the missions attained great prosperity, and in 1663 Father Figueroa stated that there were fifty-six thousand baptized Indians scattered through the missions which had been established on the Upper Marañon, Pastaza, Huallaga, Lower Marañon, and Ucayali; and between 1640 and 1682 no less than thirty-three villages were established by the missionaries. This period is known as the first missionary epoch.[1]

[1] A history of the first missionary epoch on the river Marañon (1640 to 1682), was written by Father Manuel Rodriguez, and published at Madrid in 1684, with the following title, "El Marañon y Amazonas. Historia de los descubrimientos, entradas, y reduccion de naciones, por el Padre Manuel Rodriguez, de la Compañia de Jesus, Procurador General de las Provincias de India en la corte de Madrid." He divides his work into six books, three being devoted to temporal conquests and information, and three to spiritual triumphs, and the deaths of missionaries.

The names of the principal missionaries during this period deserve to be recorded here, in memory of their extensive geographical discoveries, in the valley of the Amazons. They were as follows:—

Padre Cueva.
  ,, Cujia (a Sardinian).
  ,, Perez, of Talavera.
  ,, Figueroa, of Popayan.
  ,, Santa Cruz, the first who learnt the Cocoma language.
  ,, Majano, of Guayaquil.
and thirteen others.

Padre Camacho, of Spain.
  ,, Lucero, of Pasto.
  ,, Suarez, of Carthagena.
  ,, Navarro, a Spaniard.
  ,, Hurtado, of Panama.
  ,, Durango, of Naples.
  ,, De Cases,

The second missionary epoch extended from 1683
to 1727. During this period Father Juan de
Lucero converted the Panos, and collected them in
a village on the Huallaga, called Santiago de la
Laguna. Forty-three missionaries entered upon the
work in Maynas, amongst whom were two distinguished Germans, named Henry Ricter and Samuel
Fritz.

Henry Ricter was born at Czaslau, in Bohemia, in
the year 1653, and entered a Jesuit college in his
tenth year. He was seized, when very young, with
a longing to go to the Indies, to convert the heathens,
and finally to obtain the crown of martyrdom. After
much opposition, he was at length permitted to go,
and departed from his native land in the year 1684.
Soon after his arrival at Borja, he was sent on a
mission to the Indians of the river Ucayali, where he
laboured for many years to effect their conversion.
The most heroic devotion could alone have enabled
him to face the difficulties which surrounded him.
During twelve years he performed forty difficult
journeys, through dense forests, or in canoes on
rapid and dangerous rivers. He never took any
provisions with him, but wandered bare-footed and
half naked through the tangled underwood, trusting
wholly to Providence for support, and feeding on
herbs and roots. His efforts were rewarded with
success, and, having learnt some of the Indian languages, he at last surrounded himself with a number of converts.

In 1695 he was sent on a mission, with a few

Indian guides, to the fierce tribes of the Conibos and Pirros,[1] who treacherously murdered him.[2]

Samuel Fritz was also a native of Bohemia, and commenced his labors amongst the Indians of the Marañon in 1687. He is generally known as the "Apostle of the Omaguas," as he established forty villages amongst them, and also preached to the Yurimaguas and Ticunas. His numerous journeys and voyages embraced the whole course of the river of Amazons, and many of its tributaries. He descended to the city of Para at its mouth, and ascended it again to Quito. He went up the Huallaga to Huanuco, and thence to Lima, returning by way of Jaen, to the missions of the Marañon. These numerous expeditions gave him an extensive knowledge of the geography of those vast regions; and he is well known as having published a map of the valley of the Amazons at Quito, in the year 1707.[3] He was well fitted for the wild life he was forced to lead, for, besides being a good priest and an intrepid explorer, he was

[1] In the German they are called *Schibaren*; but, I suppose, from the resemblance in the name, that the tribe of Jeberos must be meant.

[2] Stochlein's *Reise-Beschreibungen*. A collection of letters from Jesuit missionaries from all parts of the world, from 1642 to 1726, published at Augsburg in 1726. No. iii, p. 60.

[3] It is published in the *Reise-Beschreibungen*, and Stochlein says:—"Samuel Fritz made the first map of this river, from his own observations and experience: by which the former maps of the lovers of geography, for the measurement of the world, may be corrected. The places where any of the missionaries suffered martyrdom are marked, in the map, by a small cross." He makes the lake of Lauricocha to be the source of the Amazons.

f

a physician, a painter, a carpenter, and a joiner.
Many of the rude mission churches, in those forests,
were ornamented by the paintings of Samuel Fritz.
He died in 1730, at the good old age of eighty years,
in a mission village of the Jeberos Indians, attended
by a priest named Wilhelm de Tres, and surrounded
by his sorrowing flock, who loved and revered their
kind old friend.[1]

During this period the missionaries, in addition to
the natural difficulties of their position, had to contend against the triple scourge of Portuguese invasion,
rebellion, and pestilence. The Portuguese made continual incursions up the river, burning the villages,
and carrying away the Indians for slaves. In 1660
the Cocomas Indians, eleven thousand strong, after
sixteen years of peace, rose in rebellion and killed
their Missionary, Father Thomas Majano. The insurrection continued until 1669, during which time
Father Figueroa and forty-four neophytes were murdered. The Cocomas were joined by the Maparinas
and Chepeos, and the Avigiras rose in 1667, and
slaughtered Father Suarez; while Fathers Ricter and
Herrera were killed by the Indians of the Ucayali
in 1695. The missions on that river were entirely
destroyed, and the superior, Francisco Viva, who
attempted to regain them with the aid of the Spanish
troops, was disgracefully defeated. In 1707 the Gaes
rose, and massacred Father Durango, and seven thousand catechumens; and in 1753 all the tribes on the

---

[1] Letter from Wilhelm de Tres, dated Cuença, June 1st, 1731.
Reise-Beschreibungen, vol. iv, No. 561; xiv, p. 61.

Napo were in rebellion. To these calamities pestilence was added. The small-pox first appeared at Borja in 1660, and forty-four thousand Indians died. In 1669 upwards of twenty thousand more were swept away; and in the years 1680, 1749, 1756, and 1762 the disease committed such frightful ravages, that the surviving Indians deserted the mission villages, and fled into the woods.

The third missionary epoch of Maynas comprised a period of forty-one years, from 1727 to 1768, during which time eighty-six missionaries[1] entered the field, and forty-five mission villages were founded.

After the great pestilence of 1756, Borja was refounded on a new site, by order of the Royal Audience of Quito, between the mouths of the Morona and Pastaza, on the banks of the Marañon. At the end of the last century it was a wretched little village, composed of the relics of the Mestizos and Indians, left by the insurrections, and the small-pox, about four hundred in number.[2] The capital of the missions, where the superior resided, was removed to Santiago de la Laguna, in 1756, a village which had been founded by Father Lucero in 1670, on the east bank of a beautiful lake formed by the river Huallaga. The government of the Upper Marañon missions was

---

[1] Among these there were six Germans : Father Henry Francen, who worked for forty years, and died in 1767; Francis Rhen; Carl Bretan; Adam Widman, who died in 1769, aged 70; Adam Scheffen; and Leonard Deubler, who died 1770, aged 80.

[2] Though some remains of its former prosperity are still left, Borja is now no more than a cemetery of desolation, covered with trees and underwood.—*Heraldo de Lima*, 1854.

placed under the Bishop of Quito ; and, at the commencement of the present century they were fourteen in number.[1] The vice-superior of the missions
resided at a village on the Marañon called San Joaquim de Omaguas, composed of the small remnant
of the once flourishing missions, left by the Portuguese and the small-pox. The same causes reduced
the missions on the Napo to five missionaries, and
ten villages. The expulsion of the Jesuits still further tended to reduce these once flourishing missions.

[1] In 1808 the whole of the missions on the Marañon, including
the mouths of the rivers Napo, Pastaza, etc., were placed under the
jurisdiction of the Viceroyalty of Peru, by a law or *Real Cedula,*
the original of which is still extant. This fact will be of some
importance in deciding the dispute concerning the boundary between the Republics of Peru and Ecuador, which has lately led to
the blockade of Guayaquil. Among the South American Republics,
by a tacit agreement, which, however, is recognized and respected
on all occasions, the principle of the right of territorial jurisdiction has been fixed by the *uti possidetis* of the year 1810,
when the viceroyalties began to shake off the yoke of Spain. On
this principle the lower part of the courses of the Pastaza and
Napo, as well as both banks of the Marañon, certainly belong
to Peru.—*Memorandum* by Don Manuel Tirado, Oct. 30th, 1855.

Moreover, the present bishop of Chachapoyas, in Peru, is in
possession of documents which will prove that his predecessor,
Bishop Rangel (during the Spanish times) exercised ecclesiastical
jurisdiction in the province of Quijos, now claimed and occupied
by the authorities of Ecuador.—Letter from the Bishop, in the
Heraldo de Lima, September 14th, 1855.

Dr. Villavicencio, who was governor of Canelos for many years,
not only denies the Peruvian claim, but also claims several districts
in Peru, to the south of the Amazons, for Ecuador. He proposes,
as the best mode of settling the dispute, to adopt the Amazons as
the boundary line.—*Villavicencio's Pamphlet,* 1859.

The enterprizes of the Franciscans on the upper waters of the Huallaga and Ucayali were, though partially successful at first, almost entirely paralyzed towards the end of the last century. In 1651 Father Alonzo Caballero reached the banks of the Ucayali, and resided for some years amongst the Callisecas and Setebos, but he was eventually murdered; and the same fate befell numerous other intrepid priests who, during the latter half of the seventeenth century, attempted to establish missions on the Ucayali, and its tributary streams. Thus, at the commencement of the eighteenth century, nearly all the missions in the vast plains between the Huallaga and Ucayali, known as the Pampa del Sacramento, were abandoned. It was at this time, when the prospects of forming any establishments in the valley of the Ucayali seemed so hopeless, that Father Francisco de San José[1] founded the college of Ocopa, in a valley of the Peruvian Andes, between the towns of Tarma and Guamanga, with a view to the education of missionaries. Father San José himself penetrated into the forests, and formed the mission of Pozuzu in 1712. The exertions of this brave Franciscan gave a new stimulus to missionary zeal : in 1730 ten new villages had been established on the Chanchamayu,

---

[1] A native of the city of Mondejar, in Spain. In 1712 he arrived at Huanuco, whence he proceeded to Pozuzu, a village which still exists. He also caused a hospital to be built at a place called Chaglla. Between 1726 and 1755 the Franciscans penetrated, eight times, from Pozuzu to the port on the river Mayru, but without any permanent results.—*Letter from Father Sobreviela*, Guardian of the College of Ocopa in 1792.

and in 1732 Father Simon Zara discovered the vast
territory which was named "Pampa del Sacramento,"[1] because he entered it on the festival of
Corpus Christi.

Exertions continued to be made throughout the
last century, to establish missions in the valley of the
Ucayali. The missionaries were sometimes successful; but more frequently they met with terrible
disasters; and the labours of the century were concluded by the most interesting expeditions of Father
Girbal, on the Ucayali.[2] In 1670, missions were

---

[1] The "Pampa del Sacramento" is bounded on the east by the
Ucayali, on the west by the Huallaga, on the north by the Marañon, and on the south by the Aguatya. "The two continents of
America," says Smyth, "do not contain another country so favour-
ably situated, and so fertile." It is three hundred miles long, by
forty to one hundred broad; and numerous streams, navigable for
canoes, rise in its interior, and flow off on either side, to the Huall-
laga or Ucayali. The soil is a red clay, thickly covered with vegetation, its forests are filled with an almost endless variety of beautiful
birds, and its rivers furnish an inexhaustible supply of fishes,
turtles, and manatees. Coffee, sugar, balsam, sarsaparilla, cotton,
indian rubber, resins, gums, dyes, wax, indigo, vanille, tapioca, a
great variety of fruits and herbs, are amongst its vegetable products; and the climate is agreeable and healthy. It is inhabited
by several wandering tribes of Indians, who pass their time in
hunting and fishing.

[2] The letters of Father Girbal were published in a Peruvian
periodical called the *Mercurio Peruano*, in 1791-92. His accounts
of the countries which he explored, of the manners and customs of
the Indians, and of his own adventures, are most interesting. In
No. 150 of the *Mercurio Peruano*, the instructions of Father
Sobreviela, the guardian of the College of Ocopa, to Father Girbal,
are published. They contain very judicious rules for the establishment of mission villages amongst the Indians. In No. 194, there

established on some of the tributaries of the Huallaga ; the Cholones, Lamistas, and Jibitos Indians
were collected into villages ; and have ever since been
retained in a semi-civilized condition. Poeppig has
given us a minute account of these Indians of the
Huallaga.[1]

The extensive territory on the banks of the river
Mamoré, which stretches far away to the eastward of
that grand chain of the Andes, where Sorata and
Illimani rear their snowy heads above all the mountain peaks of America, was first visited by a missionary
in 1674.

In that year Cypriano Baraza, a jesuit of Lima,
embarked, in a canoe, on the Rio Grande ; and, after
a voyage of twelve days, arrived in the territory of
the Moxos Indians, who inhabit the banks of the
Mamoré.[2] He spent four years amongst them, learn-
ing their language, and gaining their good will ; at
the end of which time, exhausted by ague, he was
obliged to retire to Santa Cruz de la Sierra, to recruit
his health. After passing five years amongst the
savage Chiriguanas, he returned to his beloved Moxos,
and collected many of them into mission villages.
He dressed their wounds, administered medicine to

is a letter from Fray Juan Dueñas, giving an account of his journey across the Pampa del Sacramento, from the Ucayali to the
Huallaga.

Girbal was succeeded, in the Ucayali mission, by Father Plaza,
who laboured for fifty years, and died about twelve years ago.
There are now four mission villages on the Ucayali.

[1] See the list, at the end of the volume.
[2] *Reise Beschreibungen*, No. 112, p. 62.

their sick, taught them weaving, carpentry, and agriculture, introduced cattle into their country, and gained their good will and respect. The first mission village established by Baraza was called Loreto,[1] the second was Trinidad, where he built a handsome brick church. Every family had its portion of land, which it was required to cultivate for its own use; and there were public lands and herds of cattle, for the support of the church and hospital. Maize, mandioc, rice, cotton, and cacao were cultivated with success; while vanille, cinnamon, wax, and copaiba balsam, were collected in the forests.

With the untiring energy of a minister of Christ, Baraza voluntarily combined an amount of bodily suffering, far exceeding in severity the useless penances of St. Simeon Stylites. He lived on roots, sometimes, though rarely indulging in a small piece of smoked monkey, which the Indians gave him out of compassion. He never slept more than four hours, his bed being the steps of the church when at the missions, and the bare ground when on a journey,

[1] Loreto, and Trinadad de los Moxos, were visited by Lieutenant Gibbon, U.S.N., in 1852. The former is in a ruinous condition. The latter is twelve leagues north-north-west of Loreto, separated by a marshy plain, covered with long grass, and frequented by cattle, deer, peccaries, tapirs, and jaguars. Trinidad, on the banks of the Mamoré, now the capital of the Bolivian Department of Beni, with about two thousand inhabitants, was laid out by Baraza, in wide streets built at right angles. The houses are of one story, and are roofed with tiles, which extend over the side walks, and are supported by a line of posts, thus forming a piazza. The plaza is in the centre of the town, and contains the cathedral, and the government house.

without shelter from rain or cold. Other priests, when travelling on the rivers in canoes, used umbrellas to protect their heads from the burning rays of the sun, but Baraza would never use one; nor would he take the least precaution to protect himself from the tormenting bites of mosquitoes and sandflies. With his own hand Baraza baptised forty thousand heathens. He found the Moxos an ignorant people, more savage and cruel than the wild beasts; and he left them a civilized community, established in villages, and converted to Christianity.[1]

In 1702, Baraza visited the Baures, a tribe living in the country to the eastward of the Moxos, near the banks of the rivers Itenez and Blanco. The good man was murdered by these Indians on the 16th of September, 1702, in the sixtieth year of his age, after having labored amongst the Moxos for upwards of twenty-seven years. Few people have studied the history of the Jesuit missions more attentively than Mr. Southey, and he says of Baraza, (in his History of Brazil,) " He was, perhaps, the most enlightened Jesuit that ever laboured in South America."[1]

The Moxos missions continued to flourish, after the

[1] " Account of the Life and Death of Father Cyprian Baraza, the first Apostle of Christ to the Moxos Indians." Printed in Spanish, at Lima, by command of the Bishop of La Paz, and translated into French, in the tenth selection of the *Lettres Edifiantes*, Paris, 1713. Also translated into German in the *Reise-Beschreibungen*, No. 112; with a map of the Moxos Missions, and of the courses of the Beni and Mamoré rivers, copied from one which was drawn by the Jesuits of Peru. It is headed " Mission bei den Moschen durch die Jesuiter von Peru."

murder of their benefactor. The churches in their villages were large, well built, and richly ornamented; as the Spaniards of Peru sent them costly presents, and the Indians themselves soon became expert in carving and painting. In 1737 the Portuguese secured the territory now called Matto Grosso, on the borders of Moxos, and built a fort, called Beira, on the Itenez, which river, by the treaty of 1777, became the boundary between the Spanish and Portuguese dominions. When the Jesuits were expelled, other priests were sent to take charge of the Moxos Indians; and, at the end of the last century, they were a thriving, industrious people ; famous as carpenters, weavers, and agriculturists. In the list of tribes at the end of this volume, I have added a few further particulars respecting the Moxos Indians.

While the good and faithful priests were thus sacrificing all their hopes in this world, and usually meeting with a violent death in the valley of the Amazons, many restless spirits, in the Viceroyalty of Peru, still dreamed of the stories of El Dorado. It was remembered that a great flight of Inca Indians had taken place soon after the conquest, and it was generally believed that they had established a rich Empire, called Paytiti, in the forests many leagues to the eastward of Cuzco; while the Empire of Enim was said to exist somewhere in the valley of the Ucayali.

These fables were very generally credited during the seventeenth century, and were the exciting cause of many strange adventures. In 1659, a crazy Spanish soldier, named Pedro Bohorques, who had served in

Chili, introduced himself amongst the Colchaquies, an Indian tribe of Tucuman, and declared himself to be an Inca. It seems that he had heard the legend respecting the rich and powerful city of Pay-titi, or Yurac-huasi, (white-house) which he believed to be near the mouth of the Huallaga; and he adopted this means of inducing the Indians to submit to him, as their chief.

Several Colchaquies, whom he created nobles of his court, followed him in a long expedition in search of Paytiti. He descended the Huallaga, and lived amongst the Pelados Indians until 1665; but was eventually captured by the Spanish authorities, and executed at Lima in 1667.

In spite of the failure of Bohorques, many people continued to believe that a great nation existed some-where in the valley of the Amazons, and that their capital was Paytiti. In 1670, a number of Spaniards in Lima, led by Don Benito de Rivera, a very rich cavalier, started on an expedition to search for this fabulous city, and penetrated into the plains of Moxos, from Chuquisaca; but they returned, after enduring many hardships, without having seen anything, save vast forests and wild Indians. A Jesuit who accompanied the expedition, says that " the soldiers, instead of finding gold, found only hardships, sickness, and death; while the people, who accompanied us from Chuquisaca, attributed our not finding the court of Paytiti, to the sorcery of the Indians."[1]

It seems, however, not wholly impossible that the

[1] M. Rodriguez, lib. vi, cap. iv, p. 384.

legend of Paytiti may have been founded on facts ; and Velasco expressly says that the Inca Indians who fled with Tupac Amaru into the forests, founded the nation of Chunchus. In 1681 Father Lucero reported that, at a distance of thirty days navigation from Laguna, on the Huallaga, he had ascended a large river which comes from the vicinity of Cuzco, and had communicated with five small Indian tribes, called Manamabobos, Campas, Pirros, Remos, and Unibueses, who numbered about ten thousand souls. The Pirros told him that they had intercourse with a great nation, called *Curiveos*, which had a descendant of the Incas for its king. Lucero added that he himself had seen plates, half-moons, and ear-rings of gold, which were brought from that nation.[1]

Still more authentic news, respecting Paytiti, was obtained by the good father Baraza, the missionary of Moxos, when he visited the Baures Indians in 1702. These people lived on the banks of the river Itenez, in villages built on hills, and fortified by pallisades, with loopholes for their archers. The largest building in the village, called *Manacicas*, was their temple and banqueting house. They used shields of plaited cane, covered with feathers, their women were decently clad, and they were governed by hereditary rulers called Aramas. A neighbouring tribe, called Cayubabas, resembled the Baures in every respect, except that their supreme chief was also high priest, and his title was Paytiti.[2]

---

[1] *M. Rodriguez*, lib. vi, cap. iv, p. 387.

[2] *History of Brazil*, vol. iii, from *Hervas*, and the *Almanaque de*

The testimony of Baraza and Lucero, added to the voice of universal tradition from the time of the conquest to the present day, unite to strengthen the probability that the Incas actually did succeed in prolonging their civilization, apart from Spanish contamination, in the vast plains to the eastward of the Andes, for one or two centuries after the time of Pizarro. The same story was told to me, when I was on the shores of the Purus in 1853, and my informant[1] pointed to the forests which stretched away to the horizon, at the same time describing a lake, on the banks of which Ynti (the Peruvian Deity) still found adorers. It is a pleasant reflection that this story may possibly be true.

The empire of Paytiti was, at all events, fully believed in, during the year 1740, when a native of Guamanga, named Juan Santos, descended into the forests near Tarma, declared himself to be an Inca, adopted the name of Atahualpa, induced the Chunchos Indians to join him, and commenced a war of extermination against the Spaniards. He received a supply of arms from the Portuguese, who had advanced as far as the mouth of the Yavari, destroyed many of

Lima. Mr. Southey adds : " Here then is the great Paytiti, whom the early conquerors supposed to have succeeded to the Inca's treasures, and to have founded a rich empire in the centre of the continent. Their more improved customs were, in reality, the wreck of Peruvian civilization." This will, perhaps, be considered a hasty conclusion ; but it is certain that the Incas extended their conquests eastward, as far as the Itenez.

[1] Don Ramon Ordoñez, proprietor of the farm of La Cueva, in the " montaña" of Paucartambo.

the missions, and frequently defeated the Spaniards who were sent against him. Thus the empire of Paytiti, in the valley of the Amazons, became a terrible reality to the Spanish government.

In 1745 the Count of Superunda, Viceroy of Peru, was reduced to sending an envoy to the Chunchos to sue for peace, for which service a Jesuit named Carlos Pastoriza was chosen. He was well received at the court of the Chuncho chief, and reported that the insurgent army was full of Europeans and Negroes. The pretended Inca declared his reverence for the Pope, and his enmity to Spain, agreeing, however, to make peace; and Pastoriza was dismissed, with a firm belief that all the forces of Peru would not suffice to reduce the Chunchos. They became less formidable after the death of Juan Santos; but there can be no doubt that this disastrous insurrection assisted in raising the power of the Portuguese, on the ruins of the mission of the Marañon.

The third motive for exploring the valley of the Amazons has been the pursuit of commercial advantages; but, in this field, the Portuguese have far outstripped the Spaniards, both in energy and in the success of their undertakings.

In 1640, when Portugal became independent, the Portuguese claimed the whole course of the Amazons, up to the mouth of the Napo, on the ground that Texeira had ascended the river up to that point: ignoring the facts that Texeira was then a Spanish subject, and that Orellana, Aguirre, and the two Franciscan monks had previously discovered the whole course of

the Amazons. The Portuguese commenced hostilities
by attacking the Omaguas, and other peaceful Indians,
burning their villages, and carrying their women and
children away, to sell as slaves. Thousands of unfortunate people were thus treated, and for a century
the Portuguese continued to perpetrate similar atrocities. Meanwhile, even at this early period, petty
traders of that nation pushed their way up many of
the Amazonian tributaries, exchanging manufactured
goods with the Indians, for sarsaparilla, copaiba,
gums, resins, wax, and other articles.

The treaty of San Ildefonso, signed between Spain
and Portugal in 1777, established the following boundary between their possessions in South America.

" From the mouth of the Igurey the line shall follow that river up to its source. Thence a straight
line shall be drawn to the nearest river which falls
into the Paraguay on its eastern side, which will probably be the Corrientes. The line shall follow that
river to the Paraguay, and ascend the latter river to
the swamps which form its source, crossing these
swamps in a straight line to the mouth of the Jaurú.
From the mouth of the Jaurú, the line shall go in a
straight line to the eastern banks of the Itenez. It
shall then descend the Itenez and Madeira to a point
equally distant from the junction of the Mamoré and
Beni, and the mouth of the Madeira. Thence in a
straight line to the river Yavari, descending that
stream to the Marañon. The line shall then descend
the Marañon to the mouth of the Japura."[1]

[1] It was agreed, by the contracting parties, that commissioners

The Portuguese thus secured to themselves the lion's share of the valley of the Amazons; and the Spaniards never attempted, with any degree of energy, to improve the commercial advantages of that rich and fertile portion which they retained.

They formed small farms on the eastern slopes of the Cordilleras, for the cultivation of sugar, cocoa, coca leaves, and fruits, which, however, never extended far into the plains; they established gold washings on some of the smaller tributaries; and they employed Indians to collect bark and sarsaparilla in the forests; but beyond this, they never attempted to turn the boundless capabilities of the Amazonian valley to any profitable account, nor to establish commercial intercourse on its enormous navigable rivers. Yet the natives of Peru and Quito were fully alive to the advantages which would be gained by the navigation of the Amazons; and the brilliant anticipations of old Father Acuña were repeated, in 1791, by the authors of the *Mercurio Peruano*[1], in the following words:—

" Who can calculate the advantages which would result to the state, if, together with religion, com-

should be sent out to arrange the position of this boundary line. The Spanish commissioner, Don Antonia Alvarez Sotomayor, accordingly arrived at Santa Cruz de la Sierra, and waited long for his Portuguese colleague. Indeed, he waited so long that he actually died of extreme old age in 1835, and the other commissioner never arrived. The Portuguese never sent one, thus showing their disposition to evade the treaty.—Dalence, *Bosquejo estadistico de Bolivia.*

[1] *Mercurio Peruano*, No. 77, p. 85 (September 29th, 1791).

merce and navigation might be introduced into those rivers ? The discovery of America caused a general revolution in the system of the arts, and even of the sciences. The civilization of El Dorado, of Enim, and of Paytiti, would enhance the colours which embellished the picture of South America."

" San Joaquim de Omaguas, at the confluence of the Ucayali[1] and Marañon, would then become a

[1] The *Ucayali* is the longest, and one of the most important of the affluents of the Amazons. It flows through a country of inexhaustible fertility, and is navigable for a distance of one thousand and forty miles from its mouth, three thousand three hundred and sixty miles from the mouth of the Amazons. It is formed by three great tributaries, the *Vilcamayu*, *Apurimac*, and *Pachitea*. The river first takes the name of *Ucayali*, at the junction of the two former of these tributaries. Only three men of scientific attainments, namely, Smyth, Castelnau, and Herndon, have as yet navigated the *Ucayali*. In 1835 General Miller examined the valley of Santa Anna, through which the *Vilcamayu* flows, with a view to the establishment of a military colony. In 1846 Castelnau left Echarate, in the valley of Santa Anna, (one hundred and twenty miles from Cuzco), and reached Sarayacu, on the Ucayali, in forty-four days, after suffering innumerable hardships. From Echarate, for one hundred and eighty miles, the *Vilcamayu* is obstructed by many cascades and rapids, where it is necessary to unload the canoes, and drag them through the forests ; but, after that distance, the river is free from obstructions of this nature. Yet there are still several rapids where the river only has a depth of three feet; but two hundred and seventy miles lower down, the strait known as the *Vuelta del Diablo* is reached, a dangerous passage, blocked up by heavy trunks of trees, against which the current dashes with great violence. The Vuelta is seven hundred and seventy miles from the mouth of the Ucayali, and for this distance the river is navigable for steamers. It averages a breadth of half a mile, a depth of three fathoms and a half, with a current running three

h

mart like ancient Tyre, at whose ports arrived the ships and productions of the whole world. By the river of the Amazons would enter the vessels of North America, Europe, Asia, and Africa. By the Pastaza and Marañon, the city of Quito would send her cloths and statues. By the Huallaga[1] and Mayru,[2] Lima would contribute her delicious oils, taken from the shady olives which beautify the coasts of the Pacific ocean. By the Apurimac would be conveyed the paintings and sugars of Cuzco, and the gold of Caravaya. By the Beni would come the productions of Moxos, and all the riches of Paytiti. Rendered opulent by her commerce, Omagua, formerly regarded as the capital of the Empire of El Dorado, would

knots an hour; while the wind is constantly blowing up the course of the stream. The fall of the river is about 0.8 of a foot per mile. The mission village of Sarayacu is four hundred and ninety-five miles from the Vuelta del Diablo, and two hundred and seventy-five miles from the mouth of the Ucayali. The town of Nauta is situated at the confluence of the Marañon and Ucayali, where the former river is at least three-quarters of a mile across.

[1] The *Huallaga* rises in the mountains above Huanuco. The canoe navigation commences at Tingo Maria, eighty miles from the city of Huanuco. Thence to Chasuta is a distance of three hundred and twenty-five miles, taking seventy-four working hours to descend it, and falling $4\frac{27}{100}$ feet per mile. From Chasuta to its mouth the river is navigable for vessels drawing five feet, at the lowest stage, a distance of two hundred and eighty-five miles; the descent taking sixty-eight hours, and falling $1\frac{25}{100}$ per mile. The difference between the times of ascent and descent is about three to one. Laguna is twenty-five miles from the mouth of the Huallaga. The mouth is three hundred and fifty yards wide; the Amazons, at the junction, five hundred.—*Herndon*, p. 179.

[2] The Mayru is an affluent of the Pachitea, which falls into the Ucayali.

cease to belie the ideas of her splendour, which were
then entertained.

" The city of Huanuco, situated between the points
of embarkation on the Huallaga and the Mayru,
might enjoy the same advantages.

" The revolution which this new commerce will
cause in the system of navigation, will be followed by
an equal revolution in the sciences. The philosopher
will have to contemplate the channels opened by the
hands of nature, in the midst of the formidable Cordilleras of the Andes. With admiration history will
relate that, in Ferrol, vessels were constructed which
had to navigate on the summits of the Andes, passing
over a plain, to an elevation of two thousand fathoms
above the surface of the ocean. All will appear . . . .
the idea is enchanting ;--the reality will be the work
of time."

The reality has indeed been the work of time!

Yet from the time when the above words were
written to the present day, there has been a slowly yet
constantly increasing traffic on the Amazons, and its
affluents. When the yoke of Spain was thrown off
in Peru, the event was hailed as the harbinger of a
great era in the progress of the Amazonian provinces.
Vain hope! So dreamed the enthusiastic Acuña two
hundred years ago. When lieutenants Maw and
Smyth passed down the Amazons, the former thirty
years since, there were, however, evident symptoms
of the first early pulsations of life and commerce
through the extensive regions, covering more than
two millions, three hundred thousand square miles,

which form the basin of the Amazons. Petty traders,
the pioneers of a stirring future, were then busy, each
in his little traffic. One man came from a village
forty days journey up the Rio Negro, bringing a
cargo of grass hammocks to Barra, another came to the
same place, with a cargo of hats which he had conveyed from Quito down the Napo and Marañon;
while numbers of canoes were passing down the various tributaries into the Amazons, laden with sarsaparilla, and other valuable products; and returning
with European and American manufactured goods.[1]

But since that date an immense stride in advance
has been taken. In 1857 there were eight steamers
plying on the bosom of the Amazons, carrying pas-
sengers, and bearing up and down a ceaseless ebb and
flow of commerce.[2]

---

[1] Wallace says that about a thousand pounds' worth of European goods enter the Uaupés, a tributary of the Rio Negro, every
year: consisting chiefly of axes, cutlasses, knives, fish hooks,
arrow heads, mirrors, beads, and cotton cloths: which are exchanged for sarsaparilla, pitch, string, hammocks, Indian stools,
baskets, feather ornaments, etc.—*Wallace*, p. 502; *Edwards*, p.
140-2.

[2] A treaty respecting the navigation of the Amazons, was signed
between Brazil and Peru, on the 23rd of October, 1851. The
Yavari was fixed as the boundary between the two nations. All
merchandize crossing the frontier was exempted from duty. The
two governments agreed to grant aid to a steam navigation company. In August 1852, the Brazilian government gave the exclu-
sive privilege of navigation for thirty years, to Ireneo de Souza, a
Brazilian. Don Manuel Tirado, the Peruvian minister, also obtained a grant of two hundred thousand dollars from Congress in
1853, towards the exploration by steamboats of the Peruvian tribu-

The fourth and last object which has attracted adventurous travellers to the valley of the Amazons, has been a desire to advance the interests of science, and geographical discovery. The first expedition of this kind was that which left Paris in 1735, to measure the arc of a degree near Quito, and so discover the true shape of the earth. It consisted of M.M. De la Condamine,

taries. In April 1853 the Peruvian government decreed that the vessels of all nations, having treaties with Peru, might ascend the Amazons as far as Nauta, at the mouth of the Ucayali; but the Brazilians refused to allow this. The Peruvian decree of April 1853 conceded the power to hold land, and other advantages, to all emigrants.—*Memorandum* by Don Manuel Tirado, dated October 30th, 1855 : sent to me by Don Felipe Barreda, of Lima.

In 1857 the Brazilian Company had eight steamers on the river Amazons, and two new boats were expected. The names of those actually running were the *Tapajoz, Rio Negro, Marajo, Monarca, Cameta, Tabatinga, Solimoes, City Bay.*

There is a weekly packet from Para to Barra, on the Rio Negro. The *Marajo* runs every two months from Barra to Nauta; the *Monarca* runs from Barra, up the Rio Negro, to the mouth of the Branco. The *Solimoes* is for the river Tapajos, the *Cameta* makes monthly trips from Para to Cameta, on the Tocantins. All these steamers have more business than they can do, they pay well, and are very good boats.

The Peruvians bought two steamers at New York, named the *Tirado* (one hundred and ten feet long) and *Huallaga* (ninety feet long), which arrived safely at Nauta. The *Huallaga* has never moved from Nauta since, and is rotting. The *Tirado* has made a few trips up the river, and, on one occasion, Mr. Nesbitt, the American engineer, took her up the Huallaga, as far as Chasuta, three thousand five hundred miles from the sea. In 1857 the American engineers went home; and, I believe, both the steamers are now rotting at Nauta.

Godin, Bouguer, and Jussieu ; and when their work
was completed, in 1739, De la Condamine started from
Jaen, and navigated the whole course of the river of
Amazons, to its mouth at Para.[1]

Since the time of Condamine, many scientific men
of various European nations, have visited the valley
of the Amazons. In 1787 the editors of the " Flora
Peruviana," Ruiz and Pavon,[2] visited the valley of

[1] M. Godin, the colleague of Condamine, being ordered to
Cayenne in 1745, was obliged to leave his wife at Quito. After
waiting many years, and his letters having failed to reach her,
Madame Godin heard a rumour that a party had been sent to meet
her on the Upper Marañon. She, therefore, determined to undertake the voyage down the Amazons, with two children, three ser-
vant girls, and her brother. They passed over the Cordilleras,
and descended the river Pastaza without much difficulty ; but, at
the village where they expected to find the party which was believed to have come to meet them, all the inhabitants had died of
small-pox, but two. Madame Godin had no canoe-men, nor guides,
and her canoe was full of water. Finally, the canoe sank, and
they attempted to make their way on foot, without map or compass. They all died of fatigue, except Madame Godin herself,
who, unable to bury her eight dead companions, took her brother's
boots and pushed bravely on, during nine days of wretchedness
and nights of horror. On the ninth day she was taken into a
canoe by a party of Indians. They conveyed her to one of the
mission villages on the Marañon, whence, after a long delay, she
was at length taken down the river of Amazons to Para ; and
joined her husband at Cayenne, after a separation of nineteen
years.

[2] In 1778 Don José Pavon, Don Hipolito Ruiz, and M. Dombey
were sent on a botanical expedition to Peru, by Charles III, and
their labours produced that most valuable work the *Flora Peruviana*. Ruiz is often called the Linnæus of Peru. Poeppig tells
us that from the time of Ruiz and Pavon to the date of his own

the Huallaga : in 1799 Thadeus Häenke explored the valleys of the Beni and Mamorè : in 1827 lieutenant Maw, R.N. descended the Huallaga, and Amazons, to Para: in 1832 Poëppig performed the same journey: in 1835 Lieutenant Smyth, R.N. descended the Huallaga, crossed over the Pampa del Sacramento, and sailed down the Ucayali and Amazons: in 1847 Count Castelnau left Cuzco, and descended the whole course of the Ucayali and Amazons : in 1852 Lieutenant Herndon, U.S.N., followed in the footsteps of Smyth, while his colleague, Lieutenant Gibbon, U.S.N. penetrated to the sources of the Purus, and descended the rivers Mamorè and Madeira : and, finally, Dr. Villavicencio published the results of his exploring journeys, along the banks of the Napo, in 1858. From Para Dr. Von Martius, in 1820, examined part of the courses of the Amazons, and Japura ; and Von Spix ascended the Amazons, as far as Tabatinga, in the same year. Prince Adalbert of Prussia ascended the Xingu ; and Edwards and Wallace the Rio Negro. Numbers of botanists and zoologists, French, German, and English, have also traversed these extensive regions, and several are at this moment engaged in exploring the forests of the Amazonian valley.

The energy and talent of these dauntless men of science has added immensely to our stock of knowledge. Yet much remains to be done. There is still a broad field for geographical discovery in the basin

travels in 1829-30, no botanist had visited the valley of Huanuco, and the banks of the Upper Huallaga.

of the Amazons. The courses of the Jurua, Jutay, Teffè, Coari, and Yavari,—rivers which in Europe would be considered of the first magnitude,—are entirely unknown to geographers : and the great Purus, one of the largest secondary rivers in the world, remains quite unexplored, save for a short distance from its mouth, by Brazilian traders.

There is, there must be, a bright future for this great country, which Providence has blessed so wonderfully, but which man has so wilfully neglected. The mind is almost bewildered in the endeavour to grasp within its compass, a due conception of the stupendous proportions of that grand river which flows so majestically through the most fertile of soils, and receives tributaries whose sources are thousands of miles distant from each other, on either side :[1] and one naturally flies from the tension of intellect, consequent on the study of its physical features, to dwell with pleasure on the picture of the great future which must be in store for the broad basin of the Amazons, when many nations will people its banks, and a constant flow of commerce will add fresh interest to its ceaseless tide.

[1] Every stream and river in South America, east of the Andes, from 4° north to 20° south, falls into the Amazons. The area drained by the Amazons, and its affluents (without counting the valley of the Tocantins, which is as large as that of the Ohio), is two millions three hundred thousand square miles; and the mighty queen of rivers sends five hundred and fifty thousand cubic feet of water per second, through the narrows of Obidos. The Amazons, and its tributaries, include forty-five thousand miles of navigable water communication. Such are the stupendous proportions of this gigantic river system.

Nothing can be more likely to conduce to this, than the thorough examination of those splendid navigable rivers which form its chief affluents, and some of the most important of which are still so little known to geographers. In no other part of the world is there a grander field for geographical discovery and research, and in no other part would the labours of the explorer be more richly repaid.

But while we are engaged in contemplating the unlimited commercial advantages, and the vast fields for scientific research, which are offered by the valley of the Amazons; it should not be forgotten that the most interesting, and by far the most important portion of the subject is undoubtedly the former history, present condition, and future prospects of those aboriginal tribes, who wander through its trackless forests.

This is not the place to enter fully upon an enquiry of such magnitude; but a few remarks respecting the tribes of the Amazonian valley will serve to illustrate an alphabetical list of all those that are mentioned in this volume, with brief accounts of many of them, which I have prepared, and placed at the end of Acuña's voyage, in the hope that it may prove useful for purposes of reference.

The most striking facts connected with this portion of the American race are the immense number of tribes and sections of tribes into which they are divided, and the extraordinary number of dialects which have sprung from these innumerable divisions. Von Martius has enumerated more than two hundred

and fifty distinct tribes in Brazil alone ; Acuña learnt
the names of one hundred and fifty in his voyage
down the great river ; and in the whole Amazonian
valley there are probably not less than seven hundred ;
while Mariano Rivero tells us that these tribes speak
more than two hundred and eighty different languages.[1] Yet it appears probable that all these languages, and consequently all the tribes in which they
are spoken, may be traced up to two, or at most to
three original sources. This would lead us to the
conclusion that at some very remote period two or
three united and powerful nations occupied the country which is now tenanted by their descendants, split
up into isolated tribes.

The causes which led to this disintegration of nations, and confusion of tongues, can never be known
to us ; but it would seem that they must have been
in operation for many ages, before so complete and
deplorable a disruption of all the bonds of society
could have taken place. Inexplicable as this pheno-
menon must appear, it certainly points to one inevitable result, namely the entire disappearance of the
whole race, at no very distant period, unless prompt

---

[1] Dobrizhoffer says : " The multitude and variety of tongues,
spoken in Paraguay alone, exceeds alike belief and calculation.
Nor should you imagine that they vary only in dialect. Most of
them are radically different. Truly admirable is their varied struc-
ture ; and I have often affirmed that the variety and artful construction of languages should be reckoned amongst the other
arguments, to prove the existence of an eternal God."—*Abipores*, ii,
p. 157.

and vigorous steps are taken to prevent it. I will presently shew that even now there are noble hearts in South America, which warm towards these children of the forests.

The innumerable Amazonian tribes may all, apparently, be traced up to three parent stems,—the Tupi or Guarani, the Omagua, and the Pano; to which must be added the tribes descended from Inca Indians, to whom the name of Quichua may be applied.

The Tupi races extend from the borders of Guiana to the Rio de la Plata, and from the mouth of the Amazons to beyond the Rio Negro; but they are split up into countless petty tribes, which wander through the forests and navigate the rivers in search of food, holding little communication with each other, without religion, and without hope. " They have skins of a copper or brown colour of various shades, jet black straight hair, black eyes, and little or no beard. In many of both sexes the most perfect regularity of features exists, and there are numbers who in colour alone differ from a good-looking European. Their figures are generally superb, and the developement of the chest is splendid."[1] The Omaguas, remarkable for their strange custom of flattening the head, were formerly considered to be the most civilized and intellectual of all the Amazonian Indians; and it seems probable that they originally sprung from the Tupis. The Pano race includes all the tribes on the Ucayali, Huallaga, and Upper

[1] *Wallace*, p. 478.

Marañon: the Conibos, Sencis, Remos, Cashibos,
Setebos, and other tribes, all speaking a dialect of
the Pano language. The Antis, Chunchos, and some
others, are said to be descended from Inca Indians
who fled from the tyranny of the Spanish conquerors.[1]

Though the numerous tribes may be thus traced up to
two, or at most to three original sources; yet many
of them are now radically different, not only in language, but in habits, and in physical appearance.
The Mayorunas, Cashibos, and Remos of the Ucayali
are fierce and untameable, wandering in the forests,
and attacking all strangers. The Panos, Conibos,
Cocomas, and Omaguas, on the contrary, willingly
settle in the mission villages, and are fond of navigating the rivers, and trading with their neighbours.
The Remos[2] have round faces and narrow eyes like
the Chinese; while the Cholones[3] of the Huallaga
resemble the North American Indians in their high
cheek bones, and fine aquiline noses.

It would be vain to attempt to account for these
differences; as it is clear that all the tribes derive
their origin from one or two parent stocks, and that
the varieties of disposition, and even of physical appearance, have arisen from local or accidental causes
acting during a course of ages. The history of this
section of the human race is very melancholy; and
previous efforts, to civilize and humanize these Indian tribes (not even excepting the admirable and

[1] These tribes, however, speak a totally different language from
the Quichua of the Incas.
[2] *Smyth.*   [3] *Poeppig.*

persevering labours of the Jesuits and Franciscans), have proved fruitless, so far, at least, as any permanent result is concerned.

Yet the wild hunters and fishers of the Amazons possess many fine and even noble qualities. Is it absolutely certain that they must perish from the earth! Must we inevitably behold the enactment of the well known wicked theory, that " they must be improved off the face of creation!" It is to be hoped that efforts may yet be made to try how far the Amazonian Indians are capable of improvement. The land belongs to them, and the first thought should be for their benefit. If they could be collected in villages on the banks of the rivers, as has already been done at Sarayacu, Santa Catalina, and Tierra Blanca on the Ucayali; and at several points along the courses of the Huallaga, Napo, and Marañon, without being led into drunken habits, hopes might still be entertained of preserving the race from annihilation.[1] If, too, such men as the late Father Plaza, the apostle of the Ucayali, or as Bovo Revello, the true-hearted and devoted missionary of the Purus, could be found to superintend these villages, then the future of the aboriginal race would be full of promise.

Men of this stamp are still to be found in Peru, whose hearts are full of love for their Amazonian fellow-countrymen; and at the head of them may be placed Don Pedro Ruiz, the excellent bishop of Cha-

[1] The Cashibos, on the Pachitea, even in their wild state, are said to be increasing in numbers.—*Herndon's Voyage.*

chapoyas, whose diocese extends over all the wide region which is watered by the Marañon, and its Peruvian tributaries. He thus concludes an eloquent appeal to the government at Lima, for assistance in his diocese:—[1]

" If, on account of my insignificance, you will not listen to me; hear me for the sake of the nation's honour, in the name of justice to the Indians, to whom you owe so much; who carry your burdens, who conduct you in canoes on the rivers, who live buried in mines for you, who fight your battles, and who contribute to your revenue. I consider myself the born defender and advocate of Amazonas; and in the name of twenty-three thousand Christians on the banks of the Marañon, the Huallaga, and the Ucayali; in the name also of those wild and naked savages who people the vast forests, I persist in my just agitation to obtain money for the priests, and funds for the missions." This conviction of the rights of the aboriginal races is not confined to the priests. Colonel Espinosa, an officer in the Peruvian army, expresses himself in still stronger terms. " Unjust men !" he exclaims, addressing his countrymen, " now that you have lost so great a part of your Indian brethren, treat with some consideration those who are left;"[2] and he goes on to advocate their cause with great eloquence.

While such feelings exist amongst educated men

[1] *Commercio,* September 1855.

[2] *Diccionario Republicano,* pp. 609-21; alluding to a recent epidemic, which had carried off great numbers of Indians.

in Peru, need we despair of the preservation of the Amazonian Indians from destruction?

While men who have it in their power to effect great and lasting good, are actually bestirring themselves in the right direction, despair for the destiny of the Indian tribes is not justified by the circumstances. It is yet possible that the fierce and naked hunters, now fast diminishing in numbers, may become thriving and happy agriculturists, increasing, peopling the fertile districts which are now uninhabited, and humanizing each other by the influence of social and domestic ties.

Yet the other side of the picture is that which gains most credit amongst the philosophers of Europe, and it has thus been depicted by the learned German traveller Von Martius:—

" The present and future condition of this race of men is a monstrous and tragical drama, such as no fiction of the poet ever yet presented to our contemplation. A whole race of men is wasting away before the eyes of its commiserating contemporaries; no power of philosophy or christianity can arrest its proudly gloomy progress towards a certain and utter destruction. From its ruins there arises, in the most motley combination, a new and reckless generation, anxious to estrange their newly acquired country from its former masters. The east brings blood and blessings; social union and order; industry, science, and religion; but with selfish views, only for itself; for itself it erects a new world; while the race of men, which was once here the master, is fleeting away like a phantom, from the circle of existence."

On the conquerors must rest the whole responsibility of the destruction of the Red race. If the leading men of South America, of the present day, adopt the example of Acuña, instead of that of Gonzalo Pizarro, the dark picture thus sketched out by Von Martius may never become a reality. Let them, by all means, give every encouragement to commerce, and geographical discovery. Let them invite steamers to navigate their splendid fluvial highways. Let them promote the establishment of profitable estates along the banks of their rivers. Let them use every means to develope the inexhaustible resources of their magnificent country. But, at the same time, let them not forget their duties to the ancient owners of the soil : and let the rights and interests of the Indians receive a due share of attention at their hands.

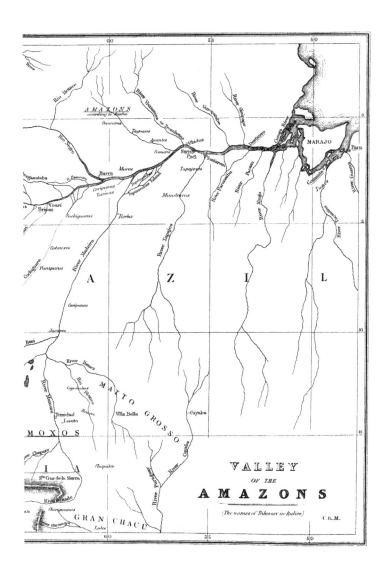

VALLEY
OF THE
AMAZONS

(The names of Tribes are in Italics)

C.R.M.

THE EXPEDITION

OF

GONZALO PIZARRO

TO

THE LAND OF CINNAMON,

A.D. 1539-42.

BY

GARCILASSO INCA DE LA VEGA.

FROM THE SECOND PART OF HIS ROYAL COMMENTARIES,

BOOK III.

THE

EXPEDITION OF GONZALO PIZARRO.

I.

Gonzalo Pizarro sets out to conquer the land of Cinnamon.

In the year 1539 the Marquis Don Francisco Pizarro, being in the city of Cuzco, received tidings that beyond the city of Quito, and beyond the limits of the empire formerly ruled by the Incas, there was a wide region where cinnamon grew;[1] and he determined to send his brother, Gonzalo Pizarro, that he might conquer such another land as the Marquis himself had found, and become governor of it.

Having consulted with those in whom he could confide, the marquis therefore handed over the government of Quito to his brother, in order that the people of that city might supply him with all things that he might require, for from thence he would have to make his entrance into the land of Cinnamon, which is east of the city of Quito.

With this object in view he sent for his brother, who was then in Charcas, arranging the affairs of that territory.

Gonzalo Pizarro soon arrived in Cuzco, and having arranged the projected conquest of the land of Cinnamon with his brother, the Marquis Don Francisco, he set out; thus accepting the adventure with a stout heart, regarding it as an opportunity of proving his valour, by deeds worthy of his former fame.

[1] *Canelos*, or the land of Cinnamon, was first discovered by Captain Gonzalez Diaz de Pineda in the year 1536.

He levied more than two hundred soldiers in Cuzco, one hundred cavalry, and the rest infantry, at a cost of sixty thousand ducats ; and marched to Quito, a distance of five hundred leagues, where Pedro de Puelles was governor. On the road he had encounters with the Indians, and was so hard pressed at Huanuco that his brother, the marquis, sent him assistance under Francisco de Chaves.

Freed from this danger, and from others of less importance, Gonzalo Pizarro reached Quito ;[1] and having shewn his commission from the marquis to Pedro de Puelles, the latter at once resigned the government. Gonzalo then made all the necessary preparations for the expedition, and added one hundred soldiers to his force, making a total of three hundred and forty; one hundred and fifty cavalry, and the rest infantry.[2] He also took with him more than four thousand Indians, laden with arms, supplies, and all things requisite for the service, such as iron, hatchets, knives, ropes, hempen cords, and large nails ; likewise nearly four thousand head of swine, and a flock of llamas, the latter carrying part of the baggage.

Gonzalo Pizarro left Pedro de Puelles in Quito as his deputy,[3] and after having put the affairs of that city in order, he set out on Christmas day, 1539. He marched with perfect success, and well supplied with provisions by the Indians, until he reached the limits of the ancient empire of the Incas. He then entered a province called Quijos.

As Francisco Lopez de Gomara and Agustin de Zarate

[1] On his road, he passed through Piura and Guayaquil.—Herrera.

[2] He appointed Don Antonio de Ribera to be master of the camp, and Don Juan de Acosta to be " Alferez General." Ribera led the vanguard. —Herrera.

[3] Gonzalo also ordered Don Francisco de Orellana to take charge of the Port of Guayaquil, and he accordingly assumed the government of that new settlement ; but, soon afterwards, Gonzalo sent for Orellana to accompany his expedition.—Herrera, *Hist. Gen.*; Velasco, *Hist. de Quito.*

agree well together, describing the occurrences nearly in
the same words, and as I have heard many of those who
were with Gonzalo Pizarro relate their adventures, I will
describe the facts, sometimes making use of one authority,
and sometimes of the other.[1]

In this province of Quijos, which is north of Quito, many
warlike Indians sallied forth against Gonzalo; but when
they beheld the multitude of Spaniards and horses, they
quickly retired, and were seen no more. A few days afterwards there was such an earthquake, that many houses, in
the village where Gonzalo's party were resting, were thrown
down.[2] The earth opened in many places; there was
lightning and thunder, insomuch that the Spaniards were
much astonished: at the same time such torrents of rain
fell, that they were surprised at the difference between that
land and Peru. After suffering these inconveniences for forty
or fifty days, they commenced the passage of the snowy
cordillera, where the snow fell in such quantities, and
it was so cold, that many Indians were frozen to death,
because they were so lightly clad. The Spaniards, to es-

[1] Garcilasso might well have rested his authority on his own information, obtained from the companions of Gonzalo; for Gomara, who wrote
a history of the Indies, never visited the New World, and was notoriously
careless in collecting his materials, as Garcilasso himself has told us;
and Zarate, during his brief residence in Lima as a financial commissioner, could not have had the same opportunities of obtaining information as were possessed by Garcilasso.

Cieza de Leon has also written an account of the expedition of Gonzalo Pizarro, in his *Cronica del Peru*, and his authority is more valuable
than either of the preceding historians, as he actually accompanied
La Gasca in his campaign against Gonzalo, and commenced the compilation of his narrative during his stay in Peru, 1540-50.

I have compared the accounts of Gomara, Zarate, and Cieza de Leon,
with that of Garcilasso de la Vega, without finding any further information respecting this expedition; but Herrera, in his *General History of
the Indies*, gives several additional particulars, which I have added in
notes.

[2] Zarate says five hundred. Velasco adds that this place was at the
foot of the volcano of Pichincha.

cape from the cold and snow of that inclement region, left the swine and provisions behind them, intending to seek some Indian village. But things turned out contrary to their hopes, for, having passed the cordillera, they were much in want of provisions, as the land they came to was uninhabited. They made haste to pass through it, and arrived at a province and village called Sumaco, on the skirts of a volcano, where they obtained food.[1] But, during two months, it did not cease to rain for a single day; so that the Spaniards received great injury, and much of their clothing became rotten.

In this province, called Sumaco, which is on the equinoctial line, or very near it, the trees, which they call cinnamon, grow, and of which the Spaniards were in search. They are very tall, with large leaves, like a laurel; and the fruit grows in clusters, and resembles an acorn. Many of these trees grow wild in the forests, and yield fruits; but they are not so good as those which the Indians get from the trees, which they plant and cultivate for their own use, and for that of their neighbours, but not for the people of Peru. The latter never wish for any other condiment than their *uchu*, which the Spaniards call *aji*, and in Europe pepper.[2]

[1] Herrera calls it the valley of *Zumaque*, thirty leagues from Quito ; and says that Orellana here joined the expedition, and was appointed lieutenant-general by Gonzalo.

Gonzalo Pizarro, unfortunately for himself and his men, chose the most difficult route into the forests of Quijos ; a route by which Texeira, a century later, also reached Quito from the river Napo, by way of Paya-mino and Baeza. Dr. Jameson, in 1857, and other modern travellers, have usually chosen another road to the Napo, by Archidona, which is shorter and less difficult. Dr. Jameson left Quito on January 18th, 1857, and reached the port of Napo, sixteen miles from Archidona, on the 13th of February. The voyage from the fort to the river Amazons takes fifteen days, the return voyage three months. Dr. Jameson left Archidona on the 1st of May, and reached Quito on the 14th of the same month.

[2] Herrera describes the cinnamon trees to be like olives, with large pods.

II.

*The hardships which Gonzalo Pizarro and his followers suffered; and
how they made a bridge of wood, and a brigantine to pass to the
great river.*

In Sumaco, and its neighbourhood, the Spaniards found
that the Indians went naked, without any clothes ; the
women having a little cloth in front for the sake of modesty.
They go naked because the country is so hot, and it rains
so much that clothes would become rotten, as we have before
said.

In Sumaco, Gonzalo Pizarro left behind the greater part
of his men ; and taking with him the most active, he went in
search of a road, if any could be found, to pass onwards ;
because all the country they had as yet traversed, which was
nearly one hundred leagues, was dense forest, where in many
parts they had to open a road by main force, and with the
blows of hatchets. The Indians, whom they took as guides,
deceived them, and led them through uninhabited wilds,
where they suffered from hunger, and were obliged to feed
on herbs, roots, and wild fruits.[1]

Suffering these hardships, and others which can be more
easily imagined than described, they arrived at a province
called Cuca, where they found supplies. The chief received
them well, and gave them food.[2] Near this place a great

The cinnamon tree attains a height of about thirty feet. It belongs
to the natural order Lauraceæ.

[1] When Gonzalo Pizarro did not receive the answers he wished respecting the country in his front, he ordered the Indians to be tortured ;
burning some alive, and causing others to be torn to pieces by his dogs.
The misfortunes which finally overtook this cruel though fearless savage
were a just retribution for his manifold atrocities.

[2] Herrera says that the cacique of Coca told lies, and said all that the
Spaniards could wish respecting the country in their front, for fear of
being treated in the same way as the people of Sumaco.

river passes, which is supposed to be the largest of those
streams, which unite to form that river which some call the
Orellana, and others the Marañon.[1]

Here they waited nearly two months for the Spaniards
who were left at Sumaco. Having been joined by them,
and recovered from their fatigue, they all proceeded together along the banks of that great river; but for more than
fifty leagues they found neither ford nor bridge by which
they might pass over, for the river was so broad as not to
admit either the one or the other.

At the end of this long journey, they came to a place
where the river precipitates itself over a rock, more than
two hundred feet high; and makes so great a noise, that the
Spaniards heard it at a distance of six leagues before they
arrived at it. They were astonished to see a thing so great
and so strange; but much more did they wonder, forty or
fifty leagues lower down, when they saw that the immense
volume of water, contained in this river, was collected into a
channel made by another enormous rock.

The channel is so narrow, that there are not more than
twenty feet from one bank to the other; and the rock is so
high, that from the top (where these Spaniards presently
passed over) to the water was another two hundred feet, the
same height as the fall. Certainly it is a marvellous thing
that in that land should be found things so great and wonderful as those two rapids, and many others.

Gonzalo Pizarro and his captains, thinking that they might
not find so easy a way of crossing the river again, to see
what was on the other side, because all they had yet seen
was a sterile and unprofitable land, bethought themselves
of making a bridge over the chasm; but the Indians

---

[1] This is the river Coca, which rises in the Cordillera, forms a great
curve, and falls into the Napo. It is nearly equal to the Napo in size.
"The Indians navigate the Coca for eight days, when further progress
is prevented by a great cascade."—*Report of Don Manuel Villavicencio.*

on the other side, though few in number, defended the pass bravely. The Spaniards were thus obliged to fight with them, a thing which they had not yet done with any Indians of that region. They fired their arquebusses, and killed a few, and the rest retired about two hundred paces, astonished at so strange a sight. They were terrified at the bravery and ferocity of that race, which they said brought lightning, rain, and thunder, to kill those who did not obey them. The Spaniards, seeing the passage clear, made a bridge of wood ; and it must be considered what an undertaking it was to place the first beam across a chasm, at such a height above the water, that even to look down was an act of rashness. And so it proved to a Spaniard, who, wishing to look at the furious rush of water from the top of the rock, became giddy and fell in. On beholding the misfortune which had befallen their companion, the others were more careful ; and with much labour and difficulty placed the first beam, and with help of it, as many more as were necessary. Thus they made a bridge, by which men and horses safely passed over. They left it as it was, in case it should be necessary to return by it. They journeyed down the course of the river, through such dense forests, that it was necessary in many places to cut a road with hatchets.

Suffering these hardships, they reached a land called Guema, as poor and inhospitable as the most sterile of those they had passed ; and they met few Indians, while even those, on seeing the Spaniards, entered the forests, and were seen no more.

The Spaniards, and their Indian followers, supported themselves on herbs and roots. Owing to hunger, and fatigue, and the heavy rains, many Spaniards and Indians fell sick and died ; but, in spite of these disasters, they advanced many leagues, and arrived at another land, where they found Indians, a little more civilized than those they had seen before ; who fed on maize bread, and dressed in cotton clothes. Gonzalo Pizarro then sent people in all directions, to see if they could find any open road, but all returned in a short time with the same story, that the land was covered with dense forest, full of lagoons and swamps, which could not be forded. On this account they determined to build a brigantine, in which they might pass from one side of the river to the other, the river being nearly two leagues broad.   They accordingly set up a forge for making nails, and burnt charcoal with great trouble, because the heavy rains prevented the tinder from taking fire. They also made roofed huts to burn the wood in, and defend it from the rain.   Some of the nails were made from the shoes of horses, which had been killed as food for the sick, and the rest of the iron they had brought with them.   They now found it more valuable than gold.

Gonzalo Pizarro, as became so valiant a soldier, was the first to cut the wood, forge the iron, burn the charcoal, and employ himself in any other office, so as to give an example to the rest, that no one might have any excuse for not doing the same.   For tar, for the brigantine, they used resin from the trees ; for oakum, they had blankets and old shirts ; and all were ready to give up their clothes, because they believed that the remedy for all their misfortunes would be the brigantine. Thus they completed and launched her, believing that on that day all their troubles would come to an end.   But in a few days their hopes were destroyed, as we shall presently see.

III.

Francisco de Orellana deserts with the brigantine, and proceeds to Spain to obtain a grant of his discovery. His death.

THEY put all their gold on board the brigantine, amounting to more than one hundred thousand dollars, with many fine emeralds, also the iron, the forge, and everything else of value. They also sent the sick on board, who were unable to travel by land. Thus they started from this place, having journeyed already nearly two hundred leagues; and began the descent of the river, some by land, others on board the brigantine, never being far from each other, and every night they slept close together. They all advanced with much difficulty; for those on shore had to open the road in many places, by cutting with axes; while those on board had to labour hard to resist the current, so as not to get far from their comrades. When they could not make a road on one side of the river, owing to the dense nature of the forest, they passed to the other side in the brigantine, and four canoes. Having gone on in this way for more than two months, they met some Indians who told them by signs, and by means of some words understood by their own Indians, that ten days journey from the place where they then were, they would find an inhabited land; well supplied with provisions, and rich in gold, and in all other things which they wanted. They also told them, by signs, that that land was on the banks of another great river which joined the one down which they were now travelling.[1] The Spaniards rejoiced at this news. Gonzalo Pizarro

---

[1] This was the junction of the rivers Coca and Napo. The Napo rises near the volcano of Cotopaxi, in the canton of Latacunga. It flows for one hundred and ninety miles from west to east, and then changes its course, flowing north-west to south-east. In front of the port of Napo it is thirty yards across, in front of Santa Rosa it is three hundred yards broad. Its windings and islands present the most lovely views. The voyage from

selected, as captain of the brigantine, his lieutenant, Don Francisco de Orellana, with fifty soldiers ; and ordered him to proceed to the place indicated by the Indians, (which would be distant about eighty leagues) ; and, having arrived at the point where the two rivers meet, to load the brigantine with provisions, and return up the river, to relieve the people, who were so afflicted with hunger, that each day there died several men, Spaniards as well as Indians. Of four thousand who started in this expedition, two thousand were already dead.

Francisco de Orellana continued his voyage, and in three days, without oar or sail, he navigated the eighty leagues, but did not find the supplies which had been promised ; and he considered that if he should return with this news to Pizarro, he would not reach him within a year, on account of the strong current, though he had descended in three days ; and that if he remained where he was, he would be of no use either to the one, or to the other. Not knowing how long Gonzalo Pizarro would take to reach the place, without consulting with any one, he set sail, and prosecuted his voyage onwards, intending to ignore Gonzalo, to reach Spain, and obtain that government for himself.

Many of his crew objected to this, suspecting his evil intentions ; and they declared that it was not right to go beyond the orders of his captain general, nor to desert him in his great necessity. A monk named Fray Gaspar de Carbajal, and a young cavalier named Hernan Sanchez de Vargas, a native of Badajos, whom the malcontents took for their chief, also dissented. Francisco de Orellana, however, appeased them for the time with fair speeches ; though afterwards, when he had reduced them to obedience, he broke his word, and told the good monk that if he would

the port of Napo to the Amazons is made in small undecked canoes ; and the dangers consist of trees fallen into the stream, and shoals at the points of the islands.—*Report of Villavicencio; Journey of Dr. Jameson.*

not follow him, he would leave him behind, like Hernan
Sanchez de Vargas. That he might suffer a more cruel
death, he did not kill Hernan Sanchez, but left him in that
dreary place, surrounded on one side by the dense forest,
on the other by a mighty river, so that he could neither
escape by water nor land, and thus he would perish of
hunger.

Francisco de Orellana continued his journey; and soon, to
render his intention more clear, he renounced his obedience
to Gonzalo Pizarro, and elected himself a captain of His
Majesty, independent of any one else. A foul deed (what
else can such treason be called?) such as has been done by
other worthies in the conquest of the New World; as
captain Gonzales Hernandez de Oviedo y Valdes, Chronicler
to his Catholic Majesty the Emperor Charles V, says in
book 17, cap. 20, of his *General History of the Indies ;*
" those who did these things, were paid in the same coin."

Francisco de Orellana, in descending the river, had some
skirmishes with the Indians inhabiting that shore, who
were very fierce, and in some parts the women came
out to fight, with their husbands. On this account, and to
make his voyage the more wonderful, he said that it
was a land of Amazons, and besought His Majesty for a
commission to conquer them. Further down the river, they
found more civilized Indians, who were friendly, and were
astonished to see the brigantine, and such strange men.
They made friends with them, and gave them food, as much
as they wished. The Spaniards stayed with them some
days; and then they sailed down to the sea, two hundred
leagues to the Isle of Trinidad, having suffered the hardships that have been described, and many great dangers on
the river. In that island Orellana bought a ship, with
which he went to Spain, and besought His Majesty to
give him a commission to conquer that country, magnify-
ing his discovery, by saying it was a land of gold and

silver, and precious stones, and demonstrating his assertions by the fine show of these things, which he brought with him. His Majesty gave him power to conquer the land, and to govern it. Orellana then collected more than five hundred soldiers, many of them distinguished and noble cavaliers, with whom he embarked at San Lucar, and died at sea, his people dispersing in different directions. Thus this expedition met an end, in conformity with its evil beginning.

From it we will return to Gonzalo Pizarro, whom we left in great distress. He, having dispatched Orellana with the brigantine, made ten or twelve canoes, and as many balsas, so as to be able to pass from one side of the river to the other, when they were impeded on land by dense forest, as they had been before.[1] They journeyed on with the hope that their brigantine would soon succour them with food, to preserve them from the hunger which they suffered, for they had no other enemy in all their journey.

They arrived, at the end of two months, at the junction of the two great rivers, where they expected to find the brigantine, which they thought would be waiting for them with provisions, and which might not have been able to reach them before, on account of the strong current of the river. They found themselves deceived ; and the hope of escaping from that hell, for such a land might be called by that name, was lost ; (where they had passed through so many hardships and miseries, without remedy, or hope of escape.) They found, at the junction of the two great rivers, the good Hernan Sanchez de Vargas, who, with the constancy of a

---

[1] Gonzalo sent Captain Mercadillo down the river in search of Orellana, with some canoes, but he returned in eight days without any news. Gonzalo Diaz de Pineda was then sent in search, who, after navigating for a few days, found that the river entered another much larger one, where he saw traces of Orellana's people. He found some roots of the yuca plant (jatropha manihot), with which he returned. A Spaniard named Villarejo went mad, and many others fell sick and died from eating these roots.—*Herrera.*

true gentleman had insisted on being left behind, suffering hunger, and other hardships, to give Gonzalo Pizarro a complete account of what Francisco de Orellana had done against his captain general, and against Hernan Sanchez himself, for having opposed his wicked intentions. The captains and soldiers were so grieved at being thus deceived of their hopes, and deprived of all relief, that they were ready to give way to despair.

Their general, although he felt the same grief as the rest, consoled and cheered them, saying that they should take heart, to bear like Spaniards these and even greater hardships, if greater there could be ; that they had succeeded in being the conquerors of that empire, and should, therefore, behave like men chosen by Divine Providence for so great an enterprise. With this speech they were all refreshed, seeing the steadfastness of their captain general. They continued their journey, still along the banks of the great river, sometimes on one side, and sometimes on the other, as they were forced to pass from one side to the other. The work they had was incredible, to take the horses across on balsas, as they still had more than eighty, out of one hundred and fifty that they took from Quito. They also had nearly one thousand Indians, out of the four thousand they took from Peru; who served like sons to their masters, in these hardships and privations, searching for herbs and roots and wild fruits, frogs and serpents, and other wretched food.

IV.

Gonzalo Pizarro attempts to return to Quito.

SUFFERING these miseries, they travelled down the river another hundred leagues, without finding any better land, nor any hope in advancing further ; for, from day to day they were worse off, without any chance of better times. These things having been considered by the general and his captains, they agreed to return to Quito (if it were possible), whence they had marched more than four hundred leagues.[1]

But, as it was impossible to navigate up the river, on account of the strong current, they determined to take another road, and to return by the north of the river, because they had received notice that in that direction there were fewer lagoons and morasses. They plunged into the forest, opening a road with axes and bills.

V.

Gonzalo Pizarro, having passed through incredible hardships, departs from the land of Cinnamon.

GONZALO PIZARRO, and his party, struggled with many obstacles in the shape of mighty rivers, and morasses which

[1] Gonzalo was doubtful as to what road he should take to return. He consulted with Don Antonio de Ribera, Sancho de Carbajal, Villegas, Funis, and Juan de Acosta ; and they determined to send Gonzalo Diaz de Pineda up the river to reconnoitre. He met fifteen canoes, with eight armed men in each. Gonzalo Diaz took the only arquebuss they had, and his lieutenant, Diego de Bustamante, the only crossbow. With the arquebuss one Indian was killed, and another was wounded in the arm with a crossbow. The Indians, with loud shouts, threw their darts; but the Spaniards killed two more, and then fell upon them with their swords. The Indians then jumped out of their canoes, and swam away. The Spaniards found some food in the canoes, for which they gave thanks to God. Diaz de Pineda and Bustamante made crosses on the trees, as marks for Pizarro, when he should arrive at the place. Next day they came in sight of hills, which they believed to be the Cordilleras of Quito, and they found stones in the bed of a torrent. They then returned to seek for Pizarro, whom they found by the noise made by his people in cutting a road. He was in great misery, and only had two dogs left out of nine hundred, one belonging to himself, the other to Ribera.—*Herrera.*

they could not wade through. The forests were full of dense
thorny foliage ; and the trees were of great size. Gomara,
in the end of his eighty-sixth chapter, describing the
discovery made of that land by Vincente Yanez Pinçon,
after narrating what happened to the discoverer, finally
speaks of the wonderful things which he saw, in these
words:—"The discoverers brought the bark of certain trees,
which seemed to be cinnamon, and a skin of that animal
which puts its young into its bosom ; and they related, as a
wonderful thing, that they saw a tree which sixteen men
could not span round."

Besides these difficulties, Gonzalo Pizarro and his followers had to contend against hunger, a cruel enemy both of
men and beasts, which had destroyed so many of them in
that uninhabitable land.

Gonzalo Pizarro intended to return to Peru, by leaving
the river, and journeying by dense forests, no better than
what he had passed before, where the road was formed by
dint of strength of arms ; feeding on herbs, roots, and wild
fruits, and it was very little even of such food that they
found, considering themselves lucky travellers to get any.
Through the lagoons, morasses and marshes, the worn
out and sick people were carried on the backs of their
comrades ; and those who laboured most among them, were
Gonzalo Pizarro himself, and his captains, who thus gave
fresh vigour to their followers to emulate their examples.
Thus they went on for more than three hundred leagues,
without escaping from the difficulties which have been
mentioned, or lessening the labour which they had to
endure : by which any one can imagine how great were the
hardships they endured in the four hundred leagues in going,
and three hundred in returning ; when their hunger was so
great, that they were obliged to kill their horses: and
previously they had eaten the greyhounds and mastiffs they
had with them : and, as Gomara says in chap. 144, they

3

even eat the Spaniards who died, according to the evil
custom of the savages of those forests.

Many Indians perished from hunger, and Spaniards also,
though the flesh of the horses was equally divided.

One of the greatest miseries which they suffered was the
absence of salt, which in more than two hundred leagues,
as Zarate says (Lib. iv. cap. v.) they did not find, and for
want of which they were attacked by scurvy. On account
of the constant waters from above and below, they were
always wet; and their clothes rotted, so that they had to go
naked.   Shame obliged them to cover themselves with the
leaves of trees, of which they made girdles to wind round
their bodies.   The excessive heat of the region made their
nakedness bearable ; but the thorns and matted underwood
of those dense forests (which they had to cut by blows of
their axes), cruelly tore them, and made them look as if they
had been flayed.

The labour and want of food that Gonzalo Pizarro and his
people suffered, was so great that four thousand Indians
died of hunger, and among them was an Indian beloved by
Gonzalo, whose death Gonzalo mourned as if he had been
his own brother; two hundred and ten Spaniards also died,
out of the three hundred and forty who started, without
counting the fifty who followed Orellana. The eighty
survivors, having passed the three hundred leagues of forest,
reached a land more open, and less covered with water ;
where they found some game of different kinds, among
which were deer. They killed what they could with slings,
and with the arquebusses and the powder they had preserved.
Of their skins they made short little coats, to cover their
nakedness: thus on foot, without shoes, worn out and thin,
so that they scarcely knew each other ; they reached the
borders of Quito.

They kissed the earth, giving thanks to God, who had
delivered them from such great perils and hardships.   Some

began to eat with such will that it was necessary to stop
them. Others were of a different constitution, and could
not eat what they wished, because their stomachs, used to
fasting and abstinence, would not receive what was given
to them.

The city of Quito, which (on account of the wars of Don
Diego de Almagro) was half depopulated, received notice
of their condition, and those who remained sent clothes to
Gonzalo Pizarro and his party.

They collected six suits of clothes, each man assisting
with what he had, a cloak, a cap, a shirt, shoes, or a hat;
and thus they dressed Gonzalo and five others, it being impossible to clothe the rest.

A dozen horses were sent out, they had no more, as they
had all been taken away, when the people went to serve his
Majesty against Don Diego de Almagro. With the horses
they sent much food; they would willingly have sent all the
presents in the world; because Pizarro was the best beloved
of any man in Peru, and had, by his own most noble qualities, endeared himself as much to strangers as to his own
friends.

They chose a dozen of the principal people of the city to
bring these gifts. These men went, and found Gonzalo
Pizarro more than thirty leagues from the city; where they
were met with much joy, and many tears, so that they
could not determine of which of those two things there was
most abundance. Gonzalo Pizarro and his party received
the people from Quito with great joy; because, in their
former misery, they had never hoped to reach this place.
The citizens wept for grief to behold those who came, and
to know that the missing had died of hunger. They consoled each other in thinking that there was no remedy for
the past, and that tears availed little.

VI.

Gonzalo Pizarro enters Quito.

GONZALO PIZARRO, his captains and soldiers, received the
gifts with joy ; but seeing that there were only clothes and
horses for the captains, they would neither dress nor mount, so
that they might be on equal terms with their good soldiers :
and thus they entered the city of Quito one morning, going
to the church to hear mass, and to give thanks to God, for
delivering them from such evils.

What follows, I heard from persons who were present.
The twelve citizens who brought the presents to Gonzalo
Pizarro, seeing that neither he nor his captains had either
dressed themselves, or mounted the horses; and that they
were determined to enter the city naked and barefooted;
bethought themselves also of entering in the same plight, so
as to share the honour, fame, and glory, that was merited by
those who had passed through so many and such great hardships. Thus they entered all alike. Having heard mass, the
citizens received Pizarro with all the welcome possible. This
entrance took place in the beginning of June, 1542, they
having spent two years in the expedition.

THE VOYAGE

OF

FRANCISCO DE ORELLANA

DOWN

THE RIVER OF THE AMAZONS,

A.D. 1540-41.

BY

ANTONIO DE HERRERA.

———————

FROM THE SIXTH DECADE OF HIS "GENERAL HISTORY OF THE
WESTERN INDIES." BOOK IX.

THE

VOYAGE OF FRANCISCO DE ORELLANA.

I.

Of the voyage which Captain Orellana commenced, on the river which
they call San Juan de las Amazonas.

Some say that Orellana and his companions deserted Pizarro
without his knowledge, and others that they continued the
voyage with their commander's permission, in a barque which
they had built, and some canoes. Voyaging, as they say,
with the design of returning to Gonzalo Pizarro, with provisions, they found themselves, after going over two hundred
leagues, unable to return, and, therefore, continued to sail
on until they came out into the ocean.

The second day, after they parted from Gonzalo Pizarro,
they expected to have been lost in the midst of the river,
as the barque struck upon a floating tree, and stove in a
plank; but being near the land, they ran her on shore,
repaired her, and continued the voyage. They made twenty
or twenty-five leagues a-day, assisted by the current. Passing the mouths of many rivers on the south side, they continued their course for three days, without seeing any
habitation. Finding that the provisions they brought with
them were exhausted, and that they were so distant from
Gonzalo Pizarro, they thought it best to pass on with the current, commending themselves to God by means of a mass,
which was performed by a Dominican monk named Carbajal.
Their difficulties were now so great, that they had nothing

to eat but the skins which formed their girdles, and the leather of their shoes, boiled with a few herbs.

On the 8th of January, 1541, when they were all expecting their deaths, Orellana heard the drums of Indians, at which they rejoiced, as it now seemed that they would not die of hunger. After going on for two leagues, they came upon four canoes of Indians, who presently retired, and Orellana came to a village, with a great number of Indians ready to defend it. The captain ordered all his people to land in good order, and to take care not to straggle. At the sight of the village these afflicted soldiers plucked up such courage that, attacking the Indians with valour, the latter fled, leaving their provisions behind them, with which the Spaniards satisfied their excessive hunger. Two hours after noon the Indians returned in their canoes, to see what was going on. The captain spoke to them in the Indian language, and, although they did not understand all he said to them, yet when he gave them a few Spanish trifles, they remained content, and offered to give him all he required. He only asked them for food, and they at once brought abundance of turkeys, partridges, fish, and other things. On the following day thirteen chiefs arrived, with plumes of feathers, and gold ornaments. Orellana spoke to them with great courtesy, requested them to be obedient to the crown of Castille, and took possession of the country in the king's name.

As he knew the good feeling of the Indians, and his people being rested; knowing also the danger of sailing in the barque and canoes, if they reached the sea; he proposed to build another brigantine. One of the chiefs, according to the account of friar Gaspar de Carbajal, gave information respecting the Amazons, and of a rich and powerful chief in the interior. Having commenced building the brigantine, they found no difficulty except in getting nails, but it pleased God that two men should make that which they had

never been taught to make, whilst another took charge of
burning the charcoal.   They made bellows of their leathern
buskins, and worked hard at everything else; some carrying,
some cutting, and others doing various things, the captain
himself being the first to put his hand to the work.   They
manufactured more than two thousand nails in twenty days,
a delay which was prejudicial, because the provisions were
consumed which had previously been collected.

Up to this point they had made two hundred leagues in
nine days, having lost seven companions, who had died of
hunger during their former sufferings.   They now determined (in order not to exhaust the Indians) to depart
on the feast of Candlemas.[1]   Twenty leagues further on, a
stream flowed into the river on the right hand, which
was so swollen, that at the point of junction with the larger
stream, the waters struggled with such violence that the
Spaniards expected to have been lost.   Escaped from this
danger, for the next two hundred leagues that they traversed,
they met with no habitations, and suffered much from toil
and dangers, until they arrived at some villages where the
Indians seemed to be quite off their guard.   In order not
to disturb them, the captain ordered twenty soldiers to land
and ask them for food.   The Indians were delighted to see
the Spaniards, and gave them plenty of provisions, turtles
and parrots.   Orellana then went to a village, at another
part of the river, where he met with no resistance.   The
natives gave him provisions; and, continuing the voyage
in sight of villages, on another day some Indians in
four canoes came to the vessel, and offered the captain
some turtles, good partridges, and fish; they were much
pleased, and invited Orellana to come and see their chief,

---

[1] It would appear that Orellana intended to have built his brigantine
at this spot, but that, after making the necessary preparations, he
changed his mind, deferring the execution of his project until he reached
the territory of the chief Aparia.

who was named Aparia, and who now approached with
more canoes. The Indians and Christians landed, and
the chief Aparia came, and was well received by captain
Orellana, who treated him to a discourse on the law of God,
and the grandeur of the King of Castille; all which the
Indians listened to with much attention. Aparia inquired
if he had seen the Amazons, whom in his language they call
Coniapuyara, meaning Great Lord. He added that his people
were few, while the Amazons were numerous. Continuing
the conversation, the captain begged the chief to name all
the lords in the country. Having enumerated twenty, he
ended saying, that all were children of the sun, and that as
such, he ought to hold them as friends. They were rejoiced,
and supplied plenty of provisions of good quality; and the
captain took possession of the land, placing a cross on a high
place, at which the Indians expressed wonder and satis-
faction.

II.

Of what happened to Captain Orellana in his voyage, and in his
discovery of this river of the Amazons.

WHEN captain Orellana found that he met with a cordial re-
ception, he determined to build the brigantine at this place;
and it pleased God that there should be an engraver in his
company, who, though ship building was not his business,
proved of great use. The timber having been cut and
prepared with great labour, which the men endured with
much willingness, in thirty-five days she was launched,
caulked with cotton, and the seams payed with pitch which
was given them by the Indians.

At this time four tall Indians came to the captain, dressed
and adorned with ornaments, and with hair reaching from
the head to the waist. With much humility they placed

food before the captain, and said that a great chief had sent them to inquire who these strangers were, and whence they came. Orellana gave them some articles of barter, which they valued very much, and he spoke to them in the same way as he had done to the others, and so they departed. The Spaniards passed all Lent at this place, and all the Christians confessed to the two priests who were in the company, and the priests preached to them, and urged them to endure the hardships they would have to encounter with constancy, until there should be an end of them.

The new brigantine being completed, and fit to navigate the sea, they set sail on the fourth of April from the residence of Aparia, and voyaged for eighty leagues without encountering a single warlike Indian. The river passed through an uninhabited country, flowing from forest to forest, and they found no place where they could either sleep or fish. Thus with herbs and a little toasted maize for food, they went on until the 6th of May, when they reached an elevated place which appeared to have been inhabited. Here they stopped to fish, and it happened that the engraver, who had been so useful in building the vessel, killed a guana with his cross bow. The creature was in a tree near the river, and fell into the water. A soldier named Contreras also caught a large fish with a hook, and, as the hook was small and the fish was large, it was necessary to take hold of it with his hand; and when it was opened, the nut of the cross bow was found in its stomach.

On the twelfth of May they arrived at the province of Machiparo,[1] which is thickly peopled, and ruled by another chief named Aomagua.[2] One morning they discovered a number of canoes, full of warlike Indians, with

[1] Also mentioned in Aguirre's voyage, as the place where Ursua was murdered ; it is probably on the Putumayu river, near its junction with the Amazons.

[2] Evidently the *Omaguas*. Orellana mistook the name of the tribe for the name of the chief.

large shields made of the skins of lizards and dantas,[1] beating
drums, and shouting, with threats that they would eat the
Christians. The latter collected their vessels together, but
met with a great misfortune in finding that their powder
had become damp, and that they were thus unable to load
their arquebusses. The Indians approached with their
bows, and the cross-bows did them some damage ; and thus,
while reinforcements continued to arrive, a gallant conflict
was maintained. In this way they descended the river,
engaged in a running fight until they reached a place where
there was a great crowd in the ravines. Half the Spaniards
then landed, and followed the Indians to their village ; and as
it appeared large, and the people were numerous, the ensign
returned to make his report to Orellana, who was defending
the vessels against the Indians, who were attacking him from
their canoes.

Understanding that there was a quantity of provisions in
the village, the captain ordered a soldier, named Cristoval
de Segovia, to take it. He started with twelve companions,
who loaded themselves with supplies, but were attacked by
more than two thousand Indians, whom they resisted with
such vigour, that they forced them to retreat, and retained the
food, with only two Spaniards wounded. But the Indians
returned with reinforcements, and pressing on the Spaniards,
wounded four. Cristoval de Segovia, though he wished to
retire to the ships, said that he would not leave the Indians
with the victory, nor place his retreat in such peril, and,
making a gallant resistance, he succeeded in retiring in safety.
In the meanwhile another body of Indians attacked the
vessels from two sides, and, having fought for more than two
hours, it pleased the Lord to assist the Spaniards, and some,
of whom little was expected, performed wonderful deeds
of valour. Such were the acts of Cristoval de Aguilar, Blas
de Medina, and Pedro de Ampudia.

---

[1] The *tapir*, also called by the Spaniards " Gran bestia."

The Indians having retired, the wounded, who amounted
to eighteen, were ordered to be attended to.   All recovered
except Ampudia, a native of Ciudad Rodrigo, who died of
his wounds in eight days.   In this encounter the value of
the commander's example was shown ; for Orellana did not,
because he commanded, cease to fight like any common
soldier ; while his good disposition, his form, his promptitude,
and forethought animated the soldiers.

As it appeared to Orellana that it was useless, and could
serve no purpose to fight with the Indians, he determined
to continue his voyage.   He embarked a great part of the
provisions, and got under weigh; while the Indians on shore,
amounting to nearly ten thousand, gave loud shouts, and
those in canoes continued to assault the Spaniards with much
audacity.   In this way the whole night was passed until
dawn, when they saw many villages.   The Spaniards,
fatigued by so bad a night, determined to go and take
refreshments on an uninhabited island ; on which, however,
they were unable to get any rest, from the crowds of Indians
who landed and attacked them.

On this the captain determined to proceed.   He was
continually followed by one hundred and thirty canoes
containing eight thousand Indians, and accompanied by four
or five sorcerers, while the noise of their drums, cornets, and
shouting was a thing frightful to hear.   If the Spaniards
had not had arquebusses and cross-bows, they must have
been destroyed, for the Indians advanced with the determination of grappling with and boarding the vessels.   Orellana
sent forward an arquebusier named Cales, who shot the
Indian general, and the other Indians crowded round to
assist him.   The ships then set out down the river, followed
by the canoes, without resting for two days and nights, and
in this way they departed from the settlements of the great
chief who was named Machiparo.[1]

[1] Ribeiro, in 1775, mentioned that a chief of a tribe of Juris, on the

Having left the canoes behind, the Spaniards came to a
village defended by several Indians. Orellana thought it
would be well to rest here for four days, after the former
toil, and having brought the vessels to, he landed his men
with arquebusses and cross-bows. The Indians fled, and he
took possession of the village.

III.

*Captain Orellana continues the discovery of the river, which is also
called by his name.*

THEY remained at this village for three days, eating plenti-
fully. The captain calculated that they had sailed down the
river for three hundred leagues from Aparia, two hundred of
which were through uninhabited regions. Having embarked
a good supply of the biscuit which the Indians make from
maize, yucas, and fruit, they set sail on the Sunday after Ascen-
sion ; and a league further on, Orellana found that another
great stream entered the river, with three islands at its mouth,
for which reason he called it the river of the Trinity. The
land appeared to be well peopled and fertile, and many
canoes came out into the river.

On another day they discovered a small village in a very
beautiful spot, and, though the Indians resisted, they
entered it and found plenty of provisions. There was a
country house containing very good jars of earthenware,
vases, and goblets of glass enamelled with many bright
colors, resembling drawings and paintings. The Indians
at this place said that these things came from the interior,
together with much gold and silver. They also found idols
worked from palm wood in a very curious fashion, of

Putumayu, was named Machiparo.—*Southey's Brazil.* (See *Juris,* in
the list of Indian tribes at the end of the volume.)

gigantic stature, with wheels in the fleshy part of the arms. The Spaniards found in this village, gold and silver ; but as they only thought of discovery and of saving their lives, they did not care for anything else.

From this village two highroads branched off, and the captain walked about half a league along them, but finding that they did not end, he returned and ordered his people to embark and continue the voyage, because in a country so well peopled, it was not advisable to remain on shore during the night.

Having sailed for one hundred leagues through this inhabited country, always in the middle of the river, to keep clear of the Indians ; they reached the territory of another chief named Paguana, where the people were friendly, and gave the Spaniards what they required. These Indians had sheep of Peru, the land was productive, and yielded very good fruit.

On Whit-sunday they passed in sight of a great village with many suburbs, and large crowds of people at each suburb. When they saw the vessels pass, the Indians got into their canoes, but returned, owing to the damage they received from the arquebusses and cross-bows of the Spaniards. On another day they reached a village which ended the dominion of Paguana. They then entered the territory of another chief of a warlike people, whose name they did not know ; and on the eve of Trinity Sunday they came to off a village where the Indians defended themselves with large shields ; but the Spaniards entered their village, and supplied themselves with food. Soon afterwards they discovered a river, on the left hand, with water as black as ink, the force of which was so great that, for more than twenty leagues, its waters flowed separately, without mingling with the Amazons river.[1] They saw many small villages, and entered one where they found quantities of fish,

[1] This was the Rio Negro.

though it was necessary to force open a door in a wooden wall which surrounded the village.

Continuing the voyage, they passed through a populous country, well supplied with provisions ; and when they were on one side of the river, it was so broad that they could not see the other bank.

They came to a place where they captured an Indian who told them that the territory belonged to the Amazons ; and they found a house containing many dresses made of different coloured feathers, which the Indians wear, when celebrating their festivals and dances. Afterwards they passed by many other villages, where the Indians were shouting and calling, on the banks ; and on the 7th of June they landed at a village without meeting any resistance, because there was no one in it, but women. They loaded themselves with fish, and, owing to the importunities of the soldiers because it was the eve of the festival of Corpus Christi, Orellana consented to stay there. At sunset the Indians returned from the fields, and finding such guests, they seized their arms; but the Spaniards resisted and discomfited them. Nevertheless the captain embarked his people, and, continued his voyage, always through an inhabited country, until they came among Indians with gentle dispositions. Passing onwards they discovered a large village, in which they saw seven gibbets with men's heads nailed on them, on which account they named this land "the Province of the gibbets." Paved roads issued from this village, with fruit trees planted on each side. On another day they came to a village, where they were obliged to land for provisions. On seeing this, the Indians concealed themselves, and when the Spaniards landed they attacked them, led on by their chief; but a cross-bow man aimed at and killed him, on which the Indians fled; and the Spaniards found a supply of maize, turtles, turkeys, and parrots.

With this large supply of provisions they went to rest on

an island ; and they learned from an Indian woman of intelligence whom they captured, that in the interior there were many men like the Spaniards, and two white women, with a chief, who had brought them down the river. The Spaniards supposed them to be of the party of Diego de Ordas, or Alonzo de Herrera.

Passing by villages, without touching at any of them, because they were supplied with provisions ; at the end of some days they came to another large village, where the Indian woman said they would find Christians, but, as there was no sign of any, they passed on.

Two Indians came out in a canoe, and looked at the brigantine, but although the Spaniards called them, they would not come on board. After four days, they came to a village which the Indians did not defend. They found maize, and Castillian oats, of which the Indians made a liquor like beer ; and the Spaniards discovered a store house of this liquor, also good cotton cloths, and a temple with warlike arms stored up, and two mitres like those of bishops, woven with various colors.

According to their custom, the Spaniards went to pass the night on the other side of the river, where many Indians came in canoes to disturb them.

On the twenty-second of June, they discovered many villages on the left bank, but they could not get at them on account of the strength of the current. The following Wednesday they came to a village, with a large square, through the midst of which flowed a stream. Here they obtained supplies, and they continually passed the habitations of fishermen. In doubling a point of the river, they came upon some very large villages. The Indians were prepared for the Spaniards, and came out to attack them on the water. Orellana called to them, and offered them articles for barter ; but they mocked at him, and a great multitude of people advanced against him in different troops. The

5

captain ordered the ships to retire to the place where his
people were searching for food; but the flights of arrows
which the Indians discharged were such that, having wounded five persons, and among others the Father Fray Gaspar
de Carbajal, Orellana made great haste to bring the vessel
to, and land his people; where the Indians fought bravely
and obstinately, without taking account of the number of
killed and wounded.   Father Carbajal affirms that these
Indians defended themselves so resolutely, because they were
tributaries of the Amazons, and that he and the other
Spaniards saw ten or twelve Amazons, who were fighting in
front of the Indians, as if they commanded them, with such
vigour that the Indians did not dare to turn their backs; and
those who fled before the Spaniards were killed with sticks.

These women appeared to be very tall, robust, fair, with
long hair twisted over their heads, skins round their loins,
and bows and arrows in their hands, with which they killed
seven or eight Spaniards.   This account of the Amazons I
repeat as I found it in the memorials of this expedition,
leaving the credibility of it to the judgment of others; for
the name of Amazons is that which these Spaniards chose to
give them.[1]

As reinforcements were coming up from other villages,
the Spaniards embarked and retired; calculating that up to
that day they had gone over one thousand four hundred
leagues, without knowing how far it might be to the sea.
Here they captured an Indian trumpeter, aged thirty years,
who told them many things respecting the interior; but some
of the Spaniards were of opinion that Captain Orellana
should not have given the name of Amazons to these
women who fought, because in the Indies it was no new
thing for the women to fight, and to use bows and arrows;
as has been seen on some islands of Barlovento, and at Carthagena, where they displayed as much courage as the men.

[1] This encounter with the Amazons appears to have taken place near
the mouth of the river *Trombretas*.

IV.

End of the discovery of the river of Orellana.

HAVING reached the centre of the river, at a short distance they discovered a large village, and, yielding to the importunities of the soldiers, the captain went to it to get provisions, though he said that if Indians were not to be seen, it was because they were concealed, which proved to be true. On reaching the banks, they discovered a great number, who discharged a flight of arrows, and, as the Spaniards had not put up the defensive cloths, which were made after they left the country of Machiparo, they received much damage. Father Gaspar de Carbajal was so badly wounded by an arrow in the eye, that he lost the use of it; an accident which caused much sorrow to every one, because this father, besides being very religious, assisted them in their difficulties by his cheerfulness and sagacity.

The multitude of people, and the number of villages, which were not half a league distant from each other, as well on the south side of the river, as in the interior, showed Captain Orellana the dangers which he must encounter, and induced him to keep his people well together, and advance cautiously. Here they took particular care to notice the qualities of the country, which appeared genial and fertile. The forest consisted of ever-green oaks, and cork trees, and contained plenty of game of all kinds. Orellana named this country " the Province of St. John," extending more than one hundred and fifty leagues. From the time that they entered it, they sailed in the middle of the river, until they came to a number of islands which they believed to be uninhabited; but the natives, on seeing the vessels, came out in two hundred piraguas, each one containing thirty or forty persons, decked out in warlike dresses, with many drums, trumpets, an instrument played with the mouth, and another with three strings. They attacked the brigantine with loud shouts ;

but the arquebusses and cross-bows stopped their onslaught ; and on shore there were a vast number of people with the same instruments. The islands appeared, high, fertile, and very beautiful, the largest being fifty leagues long. The brigantines went on, always followed by the piraguas, and they were unable to get any provisions.

Having left this province of St. John, and the piraguas having desisted from following them, they determined to rest in a forest. Captain Orellana, by means of a vocabulary which he had made, asked many questions of a captured Indian, from whom he learned that that land was subject to women, who lived in the same way as Amazons, and were very rich, possessing much gold and silver. They had five houses of the sun plated with gold, their own houses were of stone, and their cities defended by walls ; and he related other details, which I can neither believe nor affirm, owing to the difficulty in discovering the truth. The tales of Indians are always doubtful, and Orellana confessed that he did not understand those Indians, so that it seems that he could scarcely have made, in such a few days, so correct and copious a vocabulary as to be able to understand the minute details given by this Indian : but each reader may believe just as much as he likes.

Having rested themselves in this wood, they continued their voyage, not expecting to find more people ; but on the left side of the river they discovered, on an eminence, some large and beautiful villages, and the captain did not wish to approach them so close as to aggravate the Indians. But many of them came out into the water up to their middles, looking at the brigantines, as if they were terrified. The captive Indian said that this territory extended for more than one hundred leagues, under a chief named Caripuna,[1]

---

[1] Acuña mentions a tribe of Indians called *Caripunas*, on the river Madeira. They were seen, in 1852, by Lieutenant Gibbon, U.S.N., near the falls of that river.—*Acuña ; Gibbon*, p. 295.

who had great quantities of silver. Finding a small village, the Spaniards landed to obtain provisions. The Indians, in defending it, killed Antonio de Carrança, a native of Burgos; and here they found that the Indians used poisoned arrows. At this place also the Spaniards first noticed signs of the ebb of the tide. The captain, continuing the voyage, desired to rest his men, and halted in a forest. Here they surrounded the brigantines with bulwarks, as a protection from poisoned arrows. Although they desired to remain here for two or three days, canoes soon began to arrive, and also people by land. Father Carbajal affirms that a bird followed them for more than a thousand leagues, and often cried *huy, huy*; at other times, when they approached villages, it cried *huis*, which means *houses*. He also relates other marvellous things.

At this place the bird left them, and they never saw it again. After going on for a whole day, they arrived at some other peopled islands, where, with great delight, they became aware of the presence of the tide; and a little further on they came to a small arm of the sea, whence two squadrons of piraguas came out, and furiously attacked the brigantines with loud shouts. The bulwarks were here of great service; and when the Indians saw the effect of the arquebusses and cross-bows, they retired, but not without doing the Spaniards some harm. They killed Garcia de Soria, a native of Logroño, with a wound from an arrow, which did not enter more than half a finger deep, but, being poisoned, he died in twenty-four hours. This land was well peopled, and belonged to a chief named Chipayo. Once more the crowds of piraguas attacked the brigantines, which were under weigh; and Alferez, with a shot from his arquebuss, killed two Indians, and, frightened by the report, many others fell into the water. A soldier named Perucho, a Biscayan, struck one of their chiefs, on which the piraguas retired, and left the brigantines.

V.

*Concludes the discovery of the river of Orellana, and the captain enters
the sea, and reaches the island of Cubagua.*

On account of the many villages on the right hand, they
kept on the left side of the river, which had none, though
they could see that the interior was well peopled. After
resting for three days on the banks, the captain sent some
soldiers to go at least a league inland, and reconnoitre.
They soon returned, saying that the land was good and
fertile, and that they had seen many people who seemed to
be going to hunt. From this place the land was low, and
there were many inhabited islands, to which they went to
obtain food. Never more were they able to return to the
main land on either side, till they reached the sea; and it
appeared that they sailed amongst these islands for about
two hundred leagues, to which distance the tide rose with
much force. Continuing their voyage, with great scarcity
of food, they saw a village, and the larger brigantine came
to in front of it; the other struck on a snag, and, breaking a
plank, it filled.

They landed to get supplies, and so great a multitude of
Indians attacked them, that the Christians were obliged to
retreat to their vessels; of which one had sunk, and the
other was left high and dry by the tide. In this great
danger and difficulty, Captain Orellana ordered that half his
company should fight, and that the other half should get the
large vessel afloat, and stop up the hole in the smaller one.
It pleased God that this was done with great diligence; and,
at the end of three hours labour, the Indians left off fighting,
and all the Spaniards embarked with some food, and slept
on board in mid channel.

Another time they came to, near a forest, to repair the
vessels, which delayed them eighteen days, as it was neces-

sary to make nails. They suffered much from hunger, but
God succoured them with a tapir, as big as a mule, that came
to the river, and on it they fed four or five days.

Having arrived near the sea, they made their rigging and
ropes of grass, and their sails of the blankets in which they
slept. Here they remained fourteen days, eating nothing
but the shell fish that each man could pick up, and thus ill
provided they started on the eighth of August 1541. They
went under sail, taking advantage of the tides, which often
when it turned, carried the vessels back; but it pleased
God to deliver them from these perils, because as they went
by lands which were inhabited, the Indians gave them
maize and roots, and treated them well. They got water on
board in pitchers and jars, toasted maize and roots; and
thus they got ready for sea, to go where fortune might
choose to take them, without either pilot, compass, or anything useful for navigation; nor did they know what direction they should take.

The two fathers of the expedition declare that in this
voyage they found all the people to be both intelligent and
ingenious, which was shown by the works which they performed in sculpture, and painting in bright colours.

They left the mouth of the river, between two islands
four leagues apart, judging that the mouth of the river
extended fifty leagues, and that the fresh water extended
into the sea for more than twenty leagues. They sailed out
on the twenty-sixth of August 1541, at such a good season
that neither in the river nor in the sea did they experience
rains. They continued in sight of land by day and night, and
saw many rivers which entered the sea; and the small
barque, having separated from the large one in the night,
she was never seen again during the passage. At the end of
nine days they reached the gulf of Paria, and though they
struggled for seven days, they could not get on, while their
food only consisted of fruit like prunes, which they call *hogos*.

God led them through the mouth of the Dragon,[1] and at the end of two days after getting out of that prison,[2] without knowing where they were, or where they were going, they reached the island of Cubagua on the eleventh of September, two days after the smaller brigantine had arrived.

They were very well received in Cubagua, and from thence captain Orellana determined to go and give an account of his great discovery to the king, certifying that it was not the river Marañon, as the people of Cubagua declared, and many called it El Dorado. According to Father Carbajal they sailed for one thousand eight hundred leagues, including the windings of the river.

[1] The strait at the north end of the gulf of Paria, separating the island of Trinidad from the main land.

[2] Namely, the gulf of Paria ; which is entirely surrounded by land excepting at the two straits, one called "the mouth of the Dragon," the other, "the mouth of the Serpent."

A NEW DISCOVERY

Of the great river

OF THE AMAZONS,

By FATHER CRISTOVAL DE ACUÑA,
a Priest of the Company of Jesus, and
Censor of the Supreme General Inquisition.

*Which was made by order of
His Majesty in the year*
1 6 3 9,

from the Province of *Quito*, in the kingdom of *Peru*.

Dedicated

*to the most excellent Lord the
Count Duke of Olivarez.*

I.H.S.

By Permission. In Madrid, *in the Royal Press,
in the year* 1641.

TO THE READER.

HERE *are born, oh curious reader, in affairs of great moment, two brothers—namely, Novelty and Unbelief, which appear to be the twins of one birth : and while admiration is excited by what is new, at the same time credit is endangered. Though it is true that natural curiosity inclines us to desire the knowledge of new things ; uncertainty respecting their accuracy deprives them of that higher degree of pleasure which they would undoubtedly afford, if, persuaded of their truth, all the perplexity caused by doubt could be dispelled. Desirous, then, to bring before the view of all, the new discovery of the great river of the Amazons (which I undertook by order of his Majesty, as you will presently see) ; and wishing that, though my story is novel, it should also be relished ; while I do not cease to suffer from my fears in respect to accuracy, I hope to assure myself both of the one and the other :* the first, *by the promise of a new world, new nations, new countries, new occupations, new modes of life, and, to say all in one word, a river of sweet water navigated for more than one thousand three hundred leagues, all, from its sources to its mouth, full of new things :* the second, *by placing before your eyes the obligations of my position, as a priest of the company of Jesus, as a deputy of his Majesty, and in other capacities, which it neither signifies to you to know, nor to me to repeat ; and if, with all this, I can persuade you that I have succeeded in what I laboured for with some care, I shall be rewarded. Now hear what sworn testimony gives credit to my narrative.*

CERTIFICATE OF PEDRO TEXEIRA, THE COMMANDER OF THIS EXPEDITION.

I, PEDRO TEXEIRA, Capitan Mayor in this Captaincy of Gran Para, and formerly head of the expedition which went to the discovery of the river of the Amazons, as far as the city of San Francisco de Quito, in the kingdom of Peru:—certify, on oath by the holy Evangelists, that it is true that, by order of His Majesty, and dispatched by particular provisions of the Royal Audience of Quito, the Reverend father Cristoval de Acuña, a priest of the company of Jesus, came with me from the said city of Para, and also his companion the Reverend father Andres de Artieda:—that in this voyage they both served His Majesty, as regards the objects on which they were sent, like his good and faithful subjects, noting down everything that was necessary to give a full and complete account of the said discovery; to which entire credit should be given, before any other:—that as regards the obligations due to their profession, and to the service of God, they complied with what is required by their religion, preaching, confessing, and teaching the whole army, satisfying their doubts, reconciling their quarrels, animating them at their work, like true fathers in everything:—that they endured the same hardships and labour as the meanest soldiers, both as regards food, and all other things:—that not only did these said fathers make this voyage at their own expense, without His Majesty giving them any help, but also that all they had with them, as well food as medicines, was common to all who required it, to whom they gave assistance with great love and kindness :—and as attestation of all that is here written, I give this certificate, signed with my hand, and sealed with the seal of my arms, in this city of Para, the 3rd of March, 1640.

(Signed)   PEDRO TEXEIRA,

(Capitan Mayor.)

CLAUSE OF THE ROYAL PROVISION

WHICH THE ROYAL AUDIENCE OF QUITO ISSUED, IN THE NAME OF HIS MAJESTY, AS AUTHORITY FOR THIS DISCOVERY.

IN conformity with that which was done by the said President and Judges, I order that this my letter and royal order be given to you, and each one of you ; and I hold it good that you, the said fathers Cristoval de Acuña, and Andres de Artieda, priests of the said company of Jesus, shall take all that you require for the better completion of your mission and voyage ; and that the useful results which I anticipate may be attained, I order that no impediment be, on any account or reason, placed in your way. I charge you, the said father Cristoval de Acuña, that, in compliance with the wishes of the said President and Judges, and in conformity with the nomination of your Prelate, and with the offer of your services which was presented, having received this my letter from my Fiscal, to read what it contains, and to comply with and execute its orders ; for which objects you shall depart from my court at Quito, with the said companion, for the said province of Para, in company with the commander Pedro de Texeira, and the rest of the troops under him ; and you shall take particular care to describe, with clearness, the distance in leagues, the provinces, tribes of Indians, rivers, and districts which exist from the first embarkation, to the said city and port of Para ; informing yourself, with all possible precision, of all things, that you may report upon them, as an eye witness, to the Royal Council of the Indies; and that you shall perform this duty in the said provinces, as I order you, appearing personally, with this my letter on the part of the said audience of Quito, before my president and judges of the said Royal Council, and presenting a narrative of all this before my royal person, according to the directions of the Audience of Quito; and, in your default, I confide the discharge of this duty to the said father Andres de Artieda, expecting him to perform it with the care and punctuality with which those of your religion are accustomed to serve me:—and in an undertaking of such importance for the service of God our Lord, and of our own, in the conversion of so many souls as are reported to be in the said newly discovered provinces, I shall hold your services to be valuable to religion. Given at Quito, this 24th day of January, 1639.

(Signed)

        The Licentiate Don Alonzo de Salazar ;
        Doctor Don Antonio de San Isidro y Manrique ;
        The Licentiate Don Alonzo de Mesa y Ayala ;
        The Licentiate Don Juan de Valdez y Llano ;
        The Licentiate Don Geronimo Orton Zapata ;
            Don Juan Cornejo *(Secretary)*.

NEW DISCOVERY

OF THE

GREAT RIVER OF THE AMAZONS.

I.

Remarks on this great river.

ALMOST on the first discovery of that part of America, which now bears the name of Peru, vehement desires arose in Spain, though the information was still defective, for the discovery of that great river of the Amazons, called, by a vulgar error among those little versed in geography, the river of Marañon.[1] These desires did not arise on account of the abundant riches which that river was always supposed to possess, nor on account of the multitudes of people who dwelt on its banks, nor on account of the fertility of the lands, and the pleasant climate; but chiefly because it was believed with reason to be the only channel, and as it were a great highway, which flowing from Peru, was fed by all the tributaries which descend from the lofty Cordilleras.

2.

Francisco de Orellana discovers this river.

These desires tempted the heart of Francisco de Orellana; who, in the year 1540, in a frail vessel, with a few compan-

---

[1] Velasco (*Historia de Quito*) says that this river of Marañon derives its name from the circumstance of a soldier, who was sent by Francisco Pizarro to discover the sources of the Piura river, having beheld the mighty stream from the neighbourhood of Jaen, and, astonished at

ions, descended the current of this great river (which from that time also received the name of Orellana), and passing on to Spain, His Imperial Majesty the Emperor Charles V, on account of the relation he gave of its riches, ordered three ships to be prepared for him, with men and all things necessary, that he might return and people the land in his royal name. He set out in 1549, but met with such ill fortune, that, half his soldiers dying at the Canaries and Cape de Verds and the rest daily diminishing in number, he at last reached the mouth of this great river with so few men, that he was forced to abandon two ships, which up to that time he had preserved. Not having a sufficient force to man more vessels, he prosecuted his design, with all his people, on board two launches which he built. Entering the river, after a few leagues, he was convinced that the expedition would be fruitless, and so, putting all on board one single vessel, they retired along the coast of Caraccas, until they reached Margarita, where the enterprise came to an end; and, with it, the hopes that His Majesty would come into possession of that which he desired, and which Orellana had promised.

3.

The tyrant Lope de Aguirre enters this river.

Twenty years afterwards, in 1560, these hopes were re-vived by the expedition which was undertaken to this river under the General Pedro de Ursua, by order of the viceroy of Peru; who descended with a large army to its waters, to be an eye-witness of its grandeur, which had only reached him by report. But he met with ill success. He was killed through the treason of the tyrant Lope de Aguirre; who, raising

beholding a sea of fresh water, having asked " Hac mare an non ?" The historian of Quito adds, that the name of Solimoens is given to this great river by the Portuguese, out of contradiction, and in opposition to the whole world.

himself not only to the rank of general, but to that of king, continued the voyage. God did not permit that he should discover the principal mouth by which this great river empties itself into the ocean (thus depriving loyal Spaniards of the discovery of a thing of such importance to our Lord and King) ; but he came out on the coast opposite the island of Trinidad, where, by order of His Majesty, he was put to death, and his houses sown with salt ; the place being still shown in that island.

4.

Others attempt this discovery.

These same aspirations to discover this river, induced the Sargente Mayor Vincente de los Reyes Villalobos, Governor and Captain General of Quixos, in the jurisdiction of the Province of Quito, to offer to commence it from those parts.[1] In consequence of this, a *cedula* was dispatched by the catholic person of our great king Philip IV, who now lives, and may he live many years! to the royal audience and chancellery of San Francisco in Quito in 1621, that they should arrange the conditions which might be necessary for the discovery. But, as this governor had retired from office in the interval, they did not take effect. In like manner, the ardent desires of his successor, Alonzo de Miranda, were checked by death : which also attacked General José de

---

[1] In 1551 the Marquis of Cañete, viceroy of Peru, sent Don Egidio Ramirez Davalos as governor of Quijos, who founded the town of that name in 1552, on the river Quijos.

In 1558 his brother, Gil Ramirez Davalos, who had subdued the Cañaris and founded Cuença, succeeded him. He established the settlements of *Baeza* (between the Maspa and Vermejo) 1558 ; *Maspa* (on the Maspa) 1558 ; *Avila* (on the Suna) 1560 ; *Archidona* (near the Misagualli) 1560 ; *Tena* (on the Tena) 1566.

Don Gil retired to Riobamba, where his numerous posterity still reside. The Jibaros Indians rebelled in 1599, and entirely destroyed these settlements. Archidona alone remained.—*Velasco*, iii, p. 147.

7

Villamayor Maldonado, governor of Quijos before either of
the above, and put a stop to his ardent zeal to subject to God
and the king, the multitude of nations on this river.

5.

Benito Maciel attempts the discovery.

The same desires not only animated the minds of the Spaniards in Peru, but also extended to the Portuguese on the
coast of Brazil. They desired to seek the origin, and bring to
light the riches of this river, commencing from its mouth ;
and they were led on by that zeal which they always exhibit
to augment the power of their crown. Benito Maciel,[1] who
was then Capitan Mayor of Para, and is now Governor of
the Marañon, offered himself for that service. In accordance
with his wishes, a *real Cedula* was dispatched in 1626,
authorizing him to carry his intentions into effect; but they
were indefinitely postponed, as His Majesty required his
services in the war of Pernambuco.

6.

Francisco Coello is sent on this enterprise.

It does not seem that the heart of our king could be
satisfied until he had seen an affair which he so much desired,
carried into execution. Though all the ways and means which

---

[1] In 1618 Benito Maciel was appointed to command a force to operate
against the Tupinambas Indians. He commenced a career of devastation and murder, amongst the Indians round Para. For several years
he continued his vile trade of hunting down Indians, and selling them
as slaves. In 1622 he was appointed governor of Para; and in 1623 he
assumed the title of " First discoverer of the rivers of Amazons and
Curupa ;" though the islands and channels near Para had been explored by a Portuguese pilot, named Meirinho, half a century before.—
Southey's Brazil.

Of all the savages, who were employed in the Portuguese conquests,
Benito Maciel was the most notorious for his atrocious cruelties.

human prudence could suggest had failed, not for this reason
did he desist from persevering in the chief enterprize. With
this view, he dispatched a *real Cedula,* in 1633-4, to Francisco
de Coello de Caravallo, who was then Governor of Marañon
and Para, with an express order that he should presently
make this discovery; and if he had no one to send, that he
should set out in person to put it in execution. Much as His
Majesty wished that this should be effected, which had been
tried in all directions, and never successfully; yet on this
occasion his desires were again disappointed. The Governor
did not consider that he could prudently divide his forces, at a
time when the Dutch were daily infesting the coast, and when
he had scarcely power enough to resist their attacks. But
there was no need to despair, because human endeavours
failed; when Providence had prepared a way almost miraculous, by which this grand discovery should be made, as will
be presently related.

7.

Two monks of the order of San Francisco navigate this river.

The city of San Francisco de Quito, which is one of the
most celebrated in all America, is built on a mountain, in
that lofty Cordillera which traverses the whole of the New
World. Situated only half a degree south of the equator, it
is the capital of a province—the most fertile, abundant, and
gifted, and of the most pleasant climate of any in Peru; and
which, in the multitude of inhabitants, civilization, in-
struction, and Christianity, has the advantage of all. From
this city, in the years 1635, 1636, and the beginning of
1637, several Franciscan monks set out,[1] by order of their

[1] In 1635 they entered the province of Sucumbios, and were received
by the captain of the Presidio of San Miguel, Juan de Palacios, with
whom, and ninety soldiers, they embarked on the river Aguarico, till they
reached a tribe which Ferrer had called Los Encabellados, from their

Superiors, in company with Captain Juan Palacios and other soldiers, to work, the former in their spiritual, the latter in their temporal calling, for the discovery of this river. It was thirty years since the fathers of the company of Jesus had commenced the same labours, among the *Cofanes,* where the natives cruelly murdered father Rafael Ferrer, in reward for the doctrine which he had taught them.[1] The Franciscan monks arrived in the country of the Encabellados, a very numerous tribe, but well prepared for the burning zeal with which these servants of God, as is always their wont, endeavoured to reduce them to the yoke of the church. The fathers laboured

long hair. Here Palacios, enamoured of the rich and abundant land, made a settlement called *Ante,* a little above the junction with the Napo: but he was attacked and killed by the Indians, and a few only of the Franciscans escaped back to Quito.—*Velasco.*

[1] In 1602 the Jesuit Padre Rafael Ferrer set out from Quito *alone.* He was a native of Valencia, pious and learned, and earnestly seeking for martyrdom amongst the heathen.

The country of the *Cofanes* is sixty leagues east of Quito, on the eastern slope of the Grand Cordillera. It is covered with steep mountains and thick forests, where many great rivers take their rise. The Cofanes Indians are divided into twenty tribes, each governed by a *curaca* or chief.

Ferrer had no other arms than a little crucifix in his breast, a breviary, and writing materials. The Indians abhorred the Spaniards, and knew that he was one ; but, seeing him alone, unarmed, seeking their friendship, and bearing in his countenance an amiable sweetness, they received him kindly. He soon obtained great influence over them ; he collected many of them into a village, where a church was built in June, 1603, and the place was called San Pedro de Cofanes.

Ferrer learned that a vast multitude of infidels dwelt in the immense regions to the eastward, and in 1605 he set out *alone,* to preach to them. He journeyed on from the Cofanes, down the Napo to the Marañon, returning to the Cofanes in 1608. In 1611 some traitors followed him in one of his journeys, watched him while he was crossing a torrent on a frail plank, and toppled him over into the abyss.

When he fell, instead of being carried away like an arrow by the water, he stood up in the midst of it like a block of marble, and, with outstretched arms, preached to them for a long time on their wickedness, and then disappeared. The Cofanes returned to their former barbarism.—*Velasco,* vol. iii, lib. iv, 3°., p. 136.

amongst the natives for several months, when some returned to their convent at Quito, and others remained with the few soldiers who chose to stay by the side of their captain. But in a few days they saw him, with their own eyes, murdered by those to whom they had come to do so much good. They were thus obliged to evacuate the country, and return to Quito. Two monks, however, named Domingo de Brieba, and Andres de Toledo, with six soldiers, descended the current of the river in a small canoe, with no other intention than, influenced by a Divine impulse, to make the discovery of this river, in their frail vessel.

8.

The two monks reach the Marañon.

God favoured the enterprize of these two monks, and after many days of navigation, in which they experienced the providence of God, they arrived at the city of Para, a Portuguese settlement which is situated forty leagues from the place where the river empties itself into the ocean, within the jurisdiction of the Government of Marañon. They had passed, without any hindrance, through immense provinces of savages, many of them Caribs, who eat human flesh; receiving from them the necessary supplies, to enable them to complete the enterprise they had commenced. They went on to the city of San Luis de Marañon, where the Governor was Jacome Reymundo de Noroña, chosen, I believe, more through divine Providence, than through the voice of the people; for no other man could have surmounted so many difficulties, or faced so many misfortunes, who had not the zeal and determination which were prominent in his character, to serve disinterestedly in this discovery, for the service of his God and his king. The two monks gave him an account of their voyage, which was like that of persons who were each day in the hands of death; and the most remarkable thing was that they declared themselves ready to return by the way they had come, if there should be any who were ready to follow this route.[1]

9.

Pedro Texeira is named to undertake the conquest.

Our discovery would have remained in this state, if the Governor had not undertaken to clear up these shadows, and, against the opinion of all, to send an expedition up the river to the city of Quito, which, with more attention and less risk, might note down that which they found worthy of remark. He named Pedro Texeira[2] for this expedition, as head, and captain of those discoveries for His Majesty. Texeira was a person whom Heaven had undoubtedly chosen on this occasion, on account of his prudence ; and the work he performed in the service of the king, in this enterprize, was the cause of not only loss to himself, but also of much injury to his health. If this is nothing new in one who, for so many years, had served His Majesty; at least he has never been ambitious of anything, but to give an honorable account of all that has been put under his charge, which has been much, and under circumstances of no small importance.

---

[1] The monks returned to Quito with Texeira, where the Franciscans were astonished at seeing their lost brethren still alive.— *Velasco.*

[2] Alferez (Ensign) Pedro Texeira accompanied Caldeira, in 1615, when he founded Para ; and he was sent by land to Maranham, to announce the success of his commander's expedition. In 1618 Texeira became governor of Para ; but was superseded, in 1622, by Benito Maciel. In 1625 the Dutch, who had entered the Curupa, were routed by Texeira, and in 1626 he ascended the Amazons, and the Tapajos, to obtain slaves. In 1629 he was sent to destroy an Irish settlement, under one James Purcell, on the island of Tocuyos, who capitulated after a gallant defence. Texeira had thus seen a great deal of service before he was sent on this memorable expedition.

10.

Pedro Texeira commences his voyage.[1]

This excellent leader set out from Para on the twenty-eighth of October, 1637, with forty-seven canoes (vessels of which I shall speak hereafter), containing seventy Portuguese soldiers, and one thousand two hundred Indians, who, with their women and boys, brought the total number up to two thousand persons. The voyage lasted more than a year, both on account of the force of the current, and the time which it was necessary to spend in collecting supplies for so large a force, and in exploring the ways, that they might discover the shortest and most direct course, by which they ought to follow their road. On account of this being so difficult, and of the hardships they had to endure, the friendly Indians began to exhibit little relish for continuing the voyage, and some returned to their own country. The commander, being anxious that the rest should not do the same, and thus make the prosecution of the voyage impossible, used every means to retain those who were wavering. Though they were not half way, he gave out that they were near their destination, and, choosing eight canoes well supplied with provisions and soldiers, he sent them on ahead of the main body, as if to announce their approach, but really to discover the best road, of which he was very uncertain.

11.

Colonel Benito Rodriguez is sent ahead.

Pedro Texeira, named Colonel Benito Rodriguez of Oliveira, a native of Brazil, as head of this detachment, who,

---

[1] Pedro Texeira had under him Pedro de Acosta, and Pedro Payon. The expedition embarked under these three Peters in forty-seven great canoes.— *Velasco*, iii, p. 185.

having been brought up all his life among the natives, could divine their thoughts, and understand what was in their hearts. He was known and respected by all the Indians, and, in the present discovery, his presence was of no small importance, to assist in bringing the enterprize to a happy termination. After having overcome many difficulties, the Colonel and his squadron arrived at the port of Payamino, on St. John's day, the twenty-fourth of June, 1638. This is the first settlement of the Spaniards in those parts, subject to the province of Quijos, in the jurisdiction of Quito, and near the banks of the river Quijos. If they had chosen the Napo (a river of which I shall speak presently), the fleet would have met with better ports, more provisions, and fewer losses not only of Indians, but also of goods.

I2.

The captain leaves the army among the Encabellados.

The captain always guided his course by the advices which the colonel left at the sleeping places, and each day the people thought that the following would be the last of their voyage. Sustained by these hopes they reached a river, which flows from the province of the Encabellados, who were formerly friendly Indians, but now inimical, on account of the murder of captain Palacios. This place seemed adapted for a station where the whole of the troops might remain. The captain, therefore, named as commander of them, Pedro de Acosta Favela, who was to remain stationary, until he received further orders. Texeira also left behind captain Pedro Bayon. Both these officers displayed on that occasion the valour which they had exercised for so many years; and the fidelity, with which they obeyed the orders of their superiors, was most praiseworthy. They remained waiting for eleven months, without food, except such as they obtained with their arms; and that so scanty, that it seemed scarcely

sufficient to sustain life. But the captain was well satisfied
that those whom he left in this position would only be
prevented from complying with his orders by death.

13.

The captain arrives at Quito.

With this confidence, and a few companions, Pedro Texeira
set out in the footsteps of the colonel, who had previously
reached the city of Quito, where he was well received,
both by the laity and clergy, all showing their joy at seeing
the famous river of Amazons, not only discovered, but
also navigated, from its mouth to its source, by vassals of
His Majesty. The monks of that city, who were numerous and influential, took no small share in these rejoic-
ings, each one offering himself as a faithful labourer, ready
to enter on the work in that great and uncultivated vineyard of innumerable heathens, of which news had been received from the recent discoverers.

14.

Resolution of the viceroy of Peru.

Having received news which was sufficient to convince
them of the importance of this grave business to both
Majesties—divine and human, the President and Auditors
of the Royal Audience decided on doing nothing, without
first reporting all to the Viceroy of Peru, who at that time
was the Count of Chinchon.[1] He, having first consulted

---

[1] Velasco says that the Viceroy in question was Marquis of Mancera (fif-
teenth viceroy); but he was mistaken. The Count of Chinchon, whose wife
was cured of fever by the Peruvian bark, and who introduced it into
Europe, was the Viceroy who sent these orders to Quito, though he resigned his government the same year. His wife, the Countess of Chinchon, was ill of a tertian fever ; and the corregidor of Loxa, Don Juan
Lopez de Cannizares, sent some powder procured from the bark, to her

with the most eminent persons in the city of Lima,—the court of the New World,—sent orders in a letter to the President of Quito (then the licentiate Don Alonzo Perez de Salazar), dated the tenth of November 1638, that the captain Pedro Texeira, with all his people, should presently return by the same road by which they had come, to the city of Para; ordering them to be supplied with all things necessary for the voyage. Their return was ordered, because so many good officers and soldiers would be wanted on a frontier which was usually infested by the hostile Dutch. He likewise directed that, if it were possible, two persons should accompany them, who might give an account to the court of Castille, of all that had been discovered, and all that might be discovered on the return voyage.

15.

General Don Juan de Acuña volunteers for the service.

The execution of this last order of the Viceroy put every one into confusion, on account of the many inconveniences which presented themselves at the first glance. However, there were not wanting officers zealous in the service of the country, who desired, each one, to be of the number of those who should be chosen for an enterprize of such importance. But he who, above all, displayed most ardent zeal in seeking new occasions of prosecuting the service of his King, which he had now done for thirty years, and his ancestors before him, was Don Juan Vazquez de Acuña, a knight of Calatrava, lieutenant of the captain general of the Viceroy of Peru, and actual Corregidor for His Majesty, over the Spaniards and natives, in the same city of Quito, and its district. He not only offered his own personal services, but also, at his own expense, to raise troops, pay them, buy provisions, and

physician, Don Juan de Vega. In memory of the cure effected on this occasion, Linnæus afterwards named the plant *Cinchona*.

provide for all the necessary expenses of the expedition ; with thè sole motive, which always influenced him, of further- ing the service of his King and Lord. His desire did not take effect, because, as inconvenience would arise from his vacating. the office which he actually held, permission was denied him. However, God did not permit that such honor- able desires should be wholly frustrated, so disposing things that, though he did not go, his brother, Padre Cristoval de Acuña, a priest of the company of Jesus, went in his place.

16.

The Royal Audience names Pedro Cristoval de Acuña for this expedition.

The Licentiate Suarez de Poago, Fiscal of the Royal Chancellery of Quito, seeing that the Portuguese expedition was about to depart, considered, like a faithful minister of His Majesty, that it would be of great use, and no harm, if two priests of the company of Jesus should accompany it, noting down with care all that was worthy of remark in this great river ; with which information they might return to Spain, to give a reliable account of all they had observed to the Council of the Indies, and if necessary to the King our Lord, in his royal person. As the Fiscal thought, so he proposed to the Royal Audience,[1] and the proposition seeming good to all, they gave notice of it to the provincial of the company of Jesus, who at that time was father Francisco de Fuentes. He, rightly estimating the honor which might

[1] Quito was a part of the Viceroyalty of Peru until 1718, when it was annexed to New Grenada. Before that time the province of Quito had been governed, under the Peruvian Viceroy, by a Royal Audience established in 1563. It consisted of a President, four *Oidores* or Judges, and a Fiscal, who took cognizance of everything connected with the revenue. The Royal Audience of Quito, abolished in 1718, was re- established in 1739. The President was also governor of the province. —*Ulloa*, i, p. 256 ; *Stevenson*, ii, p. 294.

accrue to his religion, in an affair of such importance, and anxious that, in this way, the gate might be opened by which its sons could enter, to convey the new light of the holy Evangelist to so large a number of souls, who on that great river lie in the shadow of death ; named, in the first place, for this enterprize, father Cristoval de Acuña, a professed priest, and actual rector of the college of the company in the city of Cuença (jurisdiction of Quito) ; and secondly, as his companion, father Andres de Artieda, reader of theology in the college of the city of Quito. The members of the Royal Audience accepted the nomination of the said Jesuits, and caused a royal provision to be given to them, in which they were ordered to set out from the city of Quito, in company with the Capitan Mayor Pedro Texeira, and, having arrived at Para, to go on to Spain, and give an account of all which they may have carefully noted down in the course of the voyage, to the King our Lord, in his royal person.

17.

The fathers set out from Quito.

The said fathers obeyed the orders they had received, and on the 16th February 1639, they commenced their long voyage, which lasted for a space of ten months, when they entered the city of Para, on the 12th of December of the same year. After they had crossed those lofty mountains on foot, which, with the liquor of their veins, feed and sustain that great river ; they voyaged on the waves to where, spread out into eighty-four mouths, it pays its mighty tribute to the sea. They, with particular care, took notes of all that was worthy of remark, measured the heights, noted down all the tributary rivers by their names, became acquainted with the nations who dwell on their banks, beheld their fertility, enjoyed the resources of the great river, experienced its climate, and finally left nothing of which they could not say that they had been eye-witnesses. As such, as persons whom so many considerations oblige to be accurate, I pray to those who read this narrative that they will give me the credit that is just, for I am one of those, and in the name of both I took up my pen to write. I say this because other accounts may be brought to light, which will not be so truthful as this narrative. This will be a true account, and it is an account of things which, with face uncovered, not more than fifty Spaniards and Portuguese can testify to, namely, those who made the same voyage. I affirm that which is certain as certain, and that which is doubtful as such, that in an affair of so much importance, no one may believe more than is stated in this narrative.

18.

The river of Amazons is the largest in the world.

The famous river of Amazons, which traverses the richest, most fertile, and most densely populated regions of Peru, may be, from this day forth, proclaimed as the largest and most celebrated river in the whole world. For if the Ganges irrigates all India, and, with the great volume of its waters, eclipses the sea itself, which loses its very name and is called the Gangetic Gulf (or sometimes the Bay of Bengal): if the Euphrates, the famed river of Syria and Persia, is the joy and delight of those countries : if the Nile irrigates and fertilizes a great part of Africa : the river of Amazons waters more extensive regions, fertilizes more plains, supports more people, and augments by its floods a mightier ocean : it only wants, in order to surpass them in felicity, that its source should be in Paradise ; as is affirmed of those other rivers, by grave authors.

Histories say of the Ganges that thirty great rivers fall into it, and that the sands on its shores are full of gold : but the Amazons also has sands of gold, and irrigates a region which contains infinite riches. The Euphrates, as St. Ambrose observes, is called *lætificando*, because its streams gladden the plains, so that those which it irrigates in one year, are secure of an abundant harvest in the next. But of the river of Amazons it may be affirmed that its banks are a paradise of fertility, and if the natural riches of the soil were assisted by art, the whole would be one delightful garden. The fertility of the land which is bathed by the Nile, is celebrated in those verses of Lucan,[1]

"Terra suis contenta bonis, non indiga mercis
Aut Jovis, in solo, tanta est fiducia Nilo."

The regions bordering on the Amazons require no supplies from foreign lands ; the river is full of fish, the forests of game, the air of birds, the trees are covered with fruit, the plains with corn, the earth is rich in mines, and the natives have much skill and ability, as we shall see in the course of this narrative.

19.

Source of the river of the Amazons.

In assigning a source and origin to this great river of Amazons, which up to this time has remained concealed, each country has striven to make out a title to be the mother of such a daughter ; attributing to their own bowels, the first sustenance which gave it being, and calling it the river Marañon. This latter error is so firmly established, that the city of kings boasts that the Cordilleras of Huanuco,[2] only seventy leagues distant, give it a cradle ; and provide the earliest nourishment for this famous river, in a mountain lake. In truth this is not very far from the truth, because if this is not actually the origin of the river of Amazons, it

[1] Pharsalia, book viii.
[2] The river Huallaga, one of the chief affluents of the Marañon, rises in the mountains of Huanuco ; and the river Marañon itself rises in the Lake of Lauricocha, within a short distance of that ancient city.

is at least that of one of its chief affluents, which supplies it with fresh life, and makes its after career more vigorous.

The kingdom of New Grenada also seeks to augment her credit, by attributing the source of the river to the cascade of Mocoa, which the natives call *El gran Caqueta :* but there is no foundation for this assertion, as the river flowing from Mocoa does not behold the Amazons until after a course of seven hundred leagues, and when they do meet, the *Caqueta*,[1] as if recognizing a superior, turns its course, and comes to do homage to the Amazons.

Peru claims the source of this great river, glorifying her stream as queen of the rest ; but, from this time forth, the city of San Francisco de Quito will not permit the claim ; for at a distance of eight leagues from the site of that city, this treasure is enclosed in the skirts of a Cordillera which divides the jurisdiction of the government of Quijos ; at the foot of two hills, the one called *Guamana*, the other *Pulca*, rather less than two leagues from each other. The former produces a great lake, as mother of the new born stream ; and the latter forms another lake, which, though of smaller dimensions, is of great depth. The stream, flowing from the lakes, pierces a hill, which, envious of the treasure, precipitates it from the summit with the force of an earthquake, as if to destroy it in the beginning, and dash those grand hopes which this little stream had promised to the world. Thus from these two lakes, which are twenty miles south of the equator, the great river of Amazons takes its rise.[2]

20.

Its course, latitude, and longitude.

This river flows from west to east, as a sailor would say ; that, is from the setting to the rising of the sun ; and a few

---

[1] Or Japura.

[2] The error of supposing the Napo to be the true source of the river

degrees to the south of the equator. Its length, from the source to the mouth, is one thousand three hundred and fifty Castillian measured leagues, or according to Orellana, one thousand eight hundred. It flows along, meandering in wide reaches ; and, as absolute lord of all the other rivers which run into it, sends out branches, which are like faithful vassals, with whose aid it goes forth, and, receiving from the smaller streams the lawful tribute of their waters, they become incorporated in the main channel. It is worthy of remark that according to the dignity of the guest, is the harbinger who is sent to receive him ; thus with ordinary arms it receives the more common rivers, increasing them for those of more importance ; and for some which are so great as almost to be able to put shoulder to shoulder, it comes forth in person with its whole current. In breadth it varies very much, for in some parts its breadth is a league, at others two, at others three, and at others many more ; preserving so much narrowness in a course of several leagues, in order that, with greater ease, spread out into eighty-four mouths, it may place itself on an equality with the ocean.

21.

Breadth and depth of the river.

The narrowest part in which the river collects its waters, is little more than a quarter of a league wide. A place, doubt-

Amazons was exposed by the Jesuit Father Samuel Fritz, who, in his chart engraved at Quito in 1707, pointed out the true source to be the Lake of Lauricocha. The Ucayali, also, has had its partizans, and M. Condamine inclines in its favour, but leaves the question doubtful. It is, however, beyond a doubt that the source of the Ucayali is the most distant from the mouth of the Amazons ; but, on the other hand, it is equally certain that the Ucayali is only a tributary of the Amazons, and not the main stream ; the latter river being the largest at the point of junction.

Velasco declares that it is certain and beyond all doubt that the Lake of Lauricocha, pointed out by Fritz, is the true source of the Amazons.

less, which has been provided by divine Providence, where the great sea of fresh water narrows itself, so that a fortress may be built to impede the passage of any hostile armament of what force soever ; in case it should enter by the principal mouth of this mighty river.

The depth of the river is great, and there are parts where no bottom has yet been found. From the mouth to the Rio Negro, a distance of nearly six hundred leagues, there is never less than thirty or forty *brazas*[1] in the main channel ; above the Rio Negro it varies more, from twenty to twelve or eight *brazas*, but up to very near its source there is sufficient depth for any vessel ; and, though the current would impede the ascent, yet there is not wanting usually, every day, three or four hours of a strong breeze, which would assist in overcoming it.

22.

Islands, their fertility and products.

All this river is full of islands, some large, others small, and so numerous that it is impossible to count them, for they are met with at every turn. Some are four or five leagues, others ten, others twenty in circumference, and that which is inhabited by the Tupiñambas (of whom I shall speak hereafter), is more than a hundred leagues round.

There are also many other very small ones, on which the Indians sow their seeds, having their habitations on the larger ones. These islands are flooded by the river every year, and are so fertilized by the mud which it leaves behind, that they can never be called sterile. The ordinary products, which are maize and yuca, or mandioc, the commonest food of all, are in great abundance ; and though it would seem that the Indians are exposed to great loss, on account of the powerful floods ; yet nature, the common mother of us

---

[1] Fathoms.

all, has provided these barbarians with an easy means of preserving their food.   They collect the *yucas,* which are roots
from which they make the *casava,* the ordinary substitute for
bread in all parts of Brazil ; and forming caves or deep holes
in the earth, they bury them, and leave them well covered
up during all the time of the floods.   When the waters
subside, they take them out, and use them for food, without
their having lost any part of their virtue.   If nature teaches
the ant to store up grain in the bowels of the earth, to serve
for food during a whole year : how much more will she
suggest a contrivance to the Indian, how barbarous soever
he may be, to protect him from harm, and to preserve his
food : for is it not certain that Divine Providence will take
more care of men than of dumb animals ?

23.

The kinds of liquor which they use.

This (*yuca ?*) is, as I have said, the daily bread which
always accompanies their other food ; and it not only serves
for food, but also as a drink, to which all the natives are
usually much inclined.   For this purpose they make large thin
cakes, which they place in an oven and bake, so that they will
last for many months : these they keep in the highest part
of their houses, to preserve them from the dampness of the
earth.   When they wish to use them, they melt them in
water, and having boiled the liquor at a fire, they let it stand
as long as is necessary ; and, when cold, it is the usual wine
which they drink.   It is sometimes so strong that it might
be taken for grape wine, and intoxicates the natives, making
them lose their judgment.[1]

---

[1] The roots of the yuca are boiled and set to cool, then chewed by
women, put in a vessel filled with water, and boiled again, being stirred
the whole time.   The contents are poured into great jars half buried in
the floor of the hut, closely stopped up ; and in two days fermentation

With the help of this wine they celebrate their feasts, mourn their dead, receive their visitors, sow and reap their crops; indeed there is no occasion on which they meet, that this liquor is not the mercury which attracts them, and the riband which detains them. They also make, though they are not so common, other kinds of wine, of the wild fruits which abound on the trees; so fond are they of drunkenness. They put the juice into water, and produce a liquor which often exceeds beer in strength, that beverage which is so much used in foreign countries. These wines are kept in large earthen jars, like those used in Spain; also in small pipes made of one piece of the hollowed trunk of a tree; and in large vases woven from herbs, and so smeared with bitumen, that not one drop of the liquor which they contain is ever lost.

24.

The fruits which they have.

The food with which they accompany their bread and wine is of various kinds,—not only fruits, such as plantains, pine apples, and guavas, but very palatable chesnuts, which in Peru they call " almonds of the Sierra," for in truth they more resemble the latter than the former. They name them chesnuts, because they are enclosed in shells which resemble the prickly husk of the real chesnut. The Indians also have palms of different kinds, some of which produce cocoa nuts, others palatable dates which, though wild, are of a very pleasant taste. There are also many other different kinds of fruits, all proper to tropical climates. They have likewise nourishing roots such as the potatoe, the *yuca mansa*,[1] which

takes place. On the drinking day the women kindle fires round the jars, and serve out the warm liquor in half gourds.—*Southey's History of Brazil.*

[1] The yuca, mandioc, or cassava, if eaten raw, or with the juice in it, is deadly poison. When scraped to a fine pulp, ground on a stone, and the juice carefully expressed, it is good food.

the Portuguese call *macachera, garas, criadillas de tierra*,[1] and others which, either roasted or boiled, are not only palatable, but also very nutritious.

25.

The fish of this river, and of the Pegebuey.

After all, that which supplies them with most food, and, as they say, fills up their dish, is the extensive fishery. Every day they procure an incredible abundance from this river, with full hands.

But above all, the fish, that like a king lords it over all the others, and which inhabits this river from its sources to its mouth, is the *pegebuey*,[2] a fish which, when tasted, only can retain the name, for no one could distinguish it from well-seasoned meat. It is as large as a calf a year and a half old, but on its head it has neither ears nor horns. It has hair all over its body, not very long, like soft bristles, and the animal moves in the water with short fins, which in the form of paddles, serve as propellers. Under them the females have their dugs, with which they give sustenance to their young. The Indians make shields of their skin, which is very thick. When well cured these shields are so strong that a ball from an arquebuss would not pass through them. This fish supports itself solely on the herbage on which it browses, as if it was in reality a bullock; and from this circumstance the flesh derives so

---

[1] A kind of truffle.

[2] This is the *manatee* or *vaca marina*, a kind of porpoise, frequently eight feet long, which abounds in the Amazons, and its affluents. "*Pege*" or "*pexe*," a fish, and "*buey*," an ox. "Like the cetaceous family to which it belongs, it suckles its young, and also feeds among the grass on the banks of the rivers."—*Dr. A. Smith's Peru as It Is.*

Smyth caught one which was seven feet eight inches long. It took the united strength of at least forty men to drag it out of the water by means of ropes.—*Smyth*, p. 197.

good a flavour, and is so nutritious, that a small quantity leaves a person better satisfied and more vigorous than if he had eaten double the amount of mutton. It cannot keep its breath long under water; and thus, as it goes along, it rises up every now and then to obtain more air, when it meets with total destruction, the moment it comes in sight of its enemy.

As soon as the Indians see it, they follow in small canoes, and kill it with harpoons which they make of shells. They cut it into moderate sized slices, which, having been toasted on a wooden gridiron, remain good for more than a month.

They preserve them throughout the year with ashes (which are of great value), as they have not salt in any quantity; and that which they use to season their food is made from the ashes of a certain kind of palm, which is more like salt-petre than salt.

26.

The turtles of the river, and how they keep them.

But although they cannot preserve their food for a very long time, they are not wanting in industry to procure fresh meat throughout the winter, which, though it is not so palatable as the above, is more wholesome. For this purpose they make large inclosures surrounded by poles, and completed inside so as to form lakes of little depth, which always retain the rain water.

Having finished these at the time when the turtles go out to lay their eggs on the beach, the Indians also leave their houses and, hiding themselves near the places most fre-quented by the turtles, wait until the creatures come forth, and begin to occupy themselves in constructing a cave in which to deposit eggs.

Then the Indians come out, and station themselves at the part of the beach by which the turtles have to make their retreat to the water, and falling upon them suddenly, in a short time become masters of a great many, with no other trouble than turning them on their backs, thus rendering them unable to move. In this way they keep them until they have pierced holes in all their shells, and strung them together. They then get into their canoes, and tow the turtles without any trouble, until they have deposited them in the inclosures which they had prepared; when they let them loose in that narrow prison; and, feeding them on branches and leaves of trees, keep them alive as long as they think it necessary.

These turtles are as large as good-sized targets, their flesh tastes like tender beef; and the females, when they kill them, have within their stomachs usually more than two hundred eggs each, some even more, and almost as good as hen's eggs, though harder of digestion. They are so fat that from only two a whole jar of grease may be taken, which, seasoned with salt, is as good, more palatable, and much more lasting than that of beef. It is useful for frying fish, and for any other kind of dish, for which purposes this will be found the best and most delicate grease of all.

They collect these turtles in such abundance that there is not an inclosure which does not contain upwards of a hundred. Thus these barbarians never know what hunger is, for one turtle suffices to satisfy the largest family.

27.

Methods of fishing used by the Indians.

With great ease do the inhabitants of this river enjoy all kinds of fish which are contained in it; for never apprehending that they will want anything on the following day, they do not prepare the day before; but that which they collect to-day, sustains them, and they reap another harvest to-morrow.

The mode of fishing is different, according to the variety of seasons, and the rise or fall of the waters. Thus when the waters subside so much that the lakes are dried up, without permitting communication with the river, they use a kind of poisonous branch, which in those parts they call *timbo*, about the size of an arm more or less, and so strong that two or three poles of it being broken to pieces, and the water being beaten with them, scarcely have the fish tasted of its strength, than they all come to the surface, and may be caught with the hand.

But the usual way in which, at all times and on all occasions, the Indians become masters of as many fish as this provision supplying river sustains, is with arrows, which they discharge with one hand from a thin oval board which they hold in it, and the arrows being fixed in the fish, the board serves as a buoy, to shew in what direction the prey has retired, after it has been wounded. They then rush to the place, and grasping the fish, they drag it into the canoe. This mode of fishing is not confined to any particular kind of fish, but extends so generally to all, that neither large nor small are privileged,—all are treated alike.

As these fish are of so many kinds, they are very palatable, and many have very peculiar properties; especially a fish which the Indians call *paraque*, which is like a very large serpent, or, to speak more properly, like a conger eel. It has the peculiarity that, while alive, whoever touches it trembles all over his body, while a closer contact produces a feeling like the cold shiverings of ague; which ceases the moment he withdraws his hand.[1]

28.

Game of the forest, and birds on which they feed.

It may be that these Indians now and then become tired

[1] The electric eel.

of always feeding on fish alone, although so good, and that
they may have a craving for some kind of flesh meat : accordingly nature has indulged their longing by peopling the
land with many kinds of game.

Such are the *dantas*,[1] which are the size of a one year old
mule, and very like one in colour and disposition, while the
taste of their flesh is like that of beef, though a little sweeter.

There are also wild hogs, not like those of Spain, but quite
a different kind, which have humps on their loins ; and they
are numerous all over the Indies. The flesh is very good
and wholesome ; as is also that of another species of these
same animals, which are found in many parts, and are very
like our own domestic pigs.

There are also deer, guinea pigs, cotias, guanas, yagois,
and other animals of the Indies, and of such excellent taste,
that they fall little short of the most dainty dishes of Europe.
There are partridges, in the plains, and the Indians breed
domestic fowls in their houses, which were first brought
from Peru, and have gradually been spread all along the
river. In the many lakes there are an infinite number of
ducks, and other water fowl.

When the Indians desire to provide themselves with any
game, the most wonderful thing is the little trouble which
the chase occasions them, as we experienced in our voyage.
After arriving at the place where we were to sleep for the
night, and after the friendly Indians had employed themselves in making provision for our lodging, which took some
time, they separated,—some on land with dogs in search of
game, and others on the water, with only their bows and
arrows. In a few hours we saw them return, laden with
fish and game sufficient to satisfy the hunger of the whole
party. This did not happen on any particular day, but
during the whole time the voyage lasted. It is a marvel
worthy of admiration, and which can only be attributed to

---

[1] Tapirs, also frequently called the " *gran bestia*."

the paternal care of that Lord, who with only five loaves and
a few fishes fed five thousand men ; remaining with free
arms and full hands, ready for still greater acts of beneficence.

29.

Climate and temperature of the river.

The climate of this river, and of all the adjacent provinces,
is temperate; so that the heat does not molest, and the cold
does not fatigue, neither is there a continual change of weather to annoy. A certain kind of winter may, however,
be distinguished, not caused by the variation of planets
or the course of the sun, (which always rises and sets at the
same hour), but by the rising of the waters, which, by their
damp vapours, impede during some months the seeds and
fruits of the earth. It is by the harvests that we usually
register the difference between winter and summer in those
parts of Peru, which experience various temperatures; so
that the whole time in which the earth produces fruit, we
call summer, and on the contrary we call the time in which
the harvest is impeded by any cause, winter.

These harvests occur twice in the year on this river, not
only as to the maize, one of the principal articles of food, but
also as to all other seeds proper to the country. It is true
that the country more adjacent to the Cordilleras of Quito
enjoys more warmth than any other part of the river,
as there are constant breezes which usually refresh the
land near the sea coast : and this warmth, when greatest, is
equal to that of Guayaquil, Panama, or Carthagena, tempered,
to a great extent, by continual showers almost every day ;
and causing great advantage, in all this land, in preserving
the food uncorrupted for a long time ; as we experienced
in our hosts, with which we said mass. After five months and
a half's absence from Quito, they were as fresh as if they had
only been made a few days, so that at the end of that period,

10

we had not yet found out how long they would last; a thing which astonished those who have endured the different temperatures of the Indies, and who know by experience the rapidity with which even things of more substance than these wafers, become corrupt in hot countries.

In this river there are no dews which do any harm; of which fact I am able to bear witness, for during the whole time that I navigated this river, it was seldom that I did not pass the night in the open air, without ever having a headache, as in other countries; but a small ray of the moon used sometimes to cause an unusual sensation. However it is true that, at first, almost every one who came from a colder country, suffered from quartan ague, but the patient, with as many blood-lettings, became well again.

Neither are there, on this river, any pestilential airs, which with sudden qualities disable those whom they hurt, such as are felt, at the price of health and sometimes of life, in almost all the discovered parts of Peru. If it were not for the plague of mosquitoes which abound in many places, this country might be proclaimed with open mouth to be one vast paradise.

30.

Nature of the land, and of medicinal drugs.

From this mildness of the climate arises without doubt the freshness of all the banks of this river, which, crowned with various beautiful trees, appear to be continually delineating new countries, in which nature brightens, and art is taught. Although for the most part the land is low, it also has tolerably high rising grounds, small plains clear of trees and covered with flowers, valleys which always retain moisture, and, in more distant parts, hills which may properly receive the name of Cordilleras.

In the wild forests the natives have, for their sicknesses,

the best dispensary of medicines ; for they collect the largest
cañafistula, or fruit of the purging cassia, that has ever been
found ; the best sarsaparilla ; healing gums and resins in
great abundance : and honey of wild bees at every step, so
abundant that there is scarcely a place where it is not found,
and it is not only useful medicinally, but also very pleasant
and palatable as food. The wax, though black, is good, and
burns as well as any other.

In these forests too are the oil of *andirova*, trees of price-
less value for curing wounds ; here too is the *copaiba*, which
has no equal as a balsam ; here too are found a thousand
kinds of herbs and trees of very peculiar qualities ; and to
find many others a second Dioscorides or a third Pliny should
come out, to investigate their properties.

31.

Timber and materials for ships.

The woods of this river are innumerable, so tall that they
reach to the clouds, so thick that it causes astonishment. I
measured a cedar with my hands, which was thirty *palmas*
in circumference. They are nearly all of such good wood
that better could not be desired ; there are cedars, cotton
trees, iron wood trees, and many others now made known
in those parts, and proved to be the best in the world for
building vessels. In this river vessels may be built better
and at less cost than in any other country, finished and
launched, without the necessity of sending anything from
Europe, except iron for the nails. Here, as I have said, is
timber ; here are cables made from the bark of a certain tree,
which will hold a ship in the heaviest gale ; here is excellent
pitch and tar ; here is oil, as well vegetable as from fish ;
here they can make excellent oakum which they call *embira*,
for caulking the ships, and also there is nothing better for
the string of an arquebuss ; here is cotton for the sails ; and

here finally is a great multitude of people, so that there is nothing wanting, for building as many vessels as may be placed on the stocks.

32.

Of four valuable products found on the banks of this river.

There are on the banks of the great river of the Amazons four products, which, if cultivated, would undoubtedly be sufficient to enrich not only one, but many kingdoms. The first of these is the timber ; of which, besides there being so many curious kinds, of great value ; there are such quantities fit for building that while as much may be cut as is wanted, there will be the certainty that the supply can never be exhausted.

The second kind is the *cocoa*, of which the banks of this river are so full that in some places the wood of it would suffice, if cut, for lodging a whole army. There is scarcely any difference between this tree, and that which yields this much valued fruit in New Spain ; which, when cultivated, is of such value that the trees, growing a foot apart, are every year worth eight silver rials, after all expenses are paid. It is clear with what little labour these trees may be cultivated on this river, when, without any help from art, nature alone covers them with abundance of fruit.

The third kind is tobacco, of which great quantities are found, in all the country near the banks of this river, and if it were cultivated with the care that this seed requires, it would be the best in the world. In the opinion of those who understand the subject, the soil and climate are all that can be desired to produce prolific harvests.

The product which, in my view, ought to be most cultivated on this river is sugar, which is the fourth kind. It is the most noble, most productive, most certain, and most valuable to the royal crown ; and many farms ought to be established, which in a short time would restore the losses on the Brazilian coast. For this purpose neither much time nor much labour would be necessary, nor, what now-a-days is more dreaded, much outlay, for the land for sugar cane is the most productive in all Brazil, as we can testify who have visited those parts; and the floods, which never last more than a few days, leave it so fertile that it might be thought to be too rich. Nor will it be a new thing to raise sugar cane on the banks of this river; for along its whole vast length, from its first sources, we were always meeting with it: so that it seemed from that time to give signs of its future increase, when mills should be established to work it. These would not be expensive, because all necessary timber is at hand, with water in abundance. Copper is alone wanting, which with great ease might be supplied from Spain, in anticipation of the rich return which would be afterwards received.

33.

Of other valuable products.

Not only may these four products be promised, from this newly discovered land, to supply the whole world; but there are also many others, which, though in less quantities, would not fail to enrich the royal crown. Such, among others, is the cotton which is picked in abundance; the *uruca*,[1] which gives the best dye, and is much valued by foreigners; the fruit of the cassia; the sarsaparilla; the oils which rival the best balsams in curing wounds; the gums and sweet resins; the agave,[2] whence the best cord is obtained, which is plentiful, and many others; which necessity, or the desire of riches, are bringing to light every day.

---

[1] *Achiote*, heart-leaved *bixa* or *anotta*.   [2] The American aloe.

34.

The riches of this river.

I will now treat of the numerous mines of gold and silver of which I heard in the newly discovered land, and which will assuredly be discovered hereafter: these, if my judgment does not deceive me, are richer than all the mines of Peru, although the famed hill of Potosi should be included : nor do I state this without foundation, as an idea arisen solely, as some may think, from a desire to magnify the glories of this river; but my statement is founded on reason and experience. These I have in the gold which we found in possession of some of the Indians of this river, whom we met, and in the information they gave us concerning their mines.

The following argument arose out of what I then saw and heard.

The river of the Amazons receives affluents from all the richest lands of America. On the south side, mighty rivers which descend, some from the neighbourhood of Potosi, others from Huanuco, and the Cordillera near the city of Lima, others from Cuzco, and others from Jebaros, which is the land most famous for gold, all fall into the Amazons. Thus, on this side, vast numbers of rivers, springs, brooks, and little fountains flow towards the ocean, throughout the space of six hundred leagues between Potosi and Quito, and all pay homage to this great river of Amazons.

In like manner all those which descend from New Grenada, not inferior in their yield of gold to the others, are affluents of this great river. If the Amazons then is the chief street, —the principal road by which to ascend to the greater riches of Peru, well may I affirm that she is the chief master of all those riches. If the lake of Dorado contains the gold which common opinion attributes to it ; if, as many affirm,

the Amazons inhabit the richest country in the world; if the
Tocantins are so famous for their gold and precious stones ;
if the Omaguas were so famous for riches that a Viceroy of
Peru dispatched a force under Pedro de Ursua in search
of them ; then all this wealth is now shut up in the great
river of the Amazons. Here is the lake of Dorado, here the
nation of Amazons, here the Tocantins, here the Omaguas,
and here finally is deposited the immense treasure which the
Majesty of God keeps to enrich our great King and Lord,
Philip IV.

35.

The discovered land is four thousand leagues in circumference.

This vast empire, according to good cosmography, is four
thousand leagues in circumference, and I do not think I ex-
aggerate much ; for if in the longitude alone there are one
thousand three hundred and fifty-seven carefully measured
leagues, and according to Orellana, who was the first to navigate the main stream, eighteen hundred ; and if each river
which enters it on one side or the other, according to the best
information from the natives who inhabit their mouths, extends two hundred leagues, and some even four hundred,
without ever reaching a Spanish settlement, and always
passing different Indian nations; we must certainly allow
four hundred leagues of breadth in the narrowest part ;
which, with one thousand three hundred and fifty-six, or
according to Orellana, one thousand eight hundred of longitude, will give for the circumference, according to good
arithmetic, very little less than four thousand leagues, as I
stated.

36.

The multitude of tribes, and of different nations.

All this new world, if we may call it so, is inhabited by

barbarians, in distinct provinces and nations, of which I am
enabled to give an account, naming them and pointing out
their residences, some from my own observations, and others
from information of the Indians.

They exceed one hundred and fifty, all with different
languages. These nations are so near each other, that from
the last villages of one they hear the people of the other at
work. But this proximity does not lead to peace ; on the
contrary, they are engaged in constant wars, in which they
kill and take prisoners great numbers of souls every day.
This is the drain provided for so great a multitude, without
which the whole land would not be large enough to hold
them.

But though, among themselves, they are so warlike, none
of them shewed courage to face Spaniards, as I observed
throughout the voyage, in which the Indians never dared
to use any defence against us, except that of flight. They
navigate in vessels so light that, landing, they carry them on
their shoulders, and, conveying them to one of the numerous
lakes near the river, laugh at any enemy who, with heavier
vessels, is unable to follow the same example.

37.

Arms which the Indians use.

Their arms consist of short spears, and darts made of strong
wood, well sharpened, and which, thrown with dexterity,
easily reach the enemy. Others have *estolicas,* weapons with
which the warriors of the Incas of Peru were very dexterous. These *estolicas* are flattened poles, about a yard long,
and three fingers broad. In the upper end a bone is fixed, to
which an arrow of nine *palmos* is fastened, with the point
also of bone or very strong palm wood, which, worked into
the shape of a harpoon, remains like a javelin hanging from
the person whom it wounds. They hold this in the right

hand, with the *estolica* clutched by the lower part, and fixing the weapon in the upper bone, they hurl it with such tremendous force and with so good an aim, that at fifty paces they never miss. They fight with these arms, with them they hunt, and with them they become masters of any fish that are hidden under the waves. What is more wonderful, with these arrows they transfix the turtles, when, from time to time and for a very few moments, they shew their heads above the water. The arrow is aimed at the neck, which is the only part clear of the shell. They also use shields for their defence, made of strong canes tightly sewn together, which, though very light, are not so strong as those which I mentioned before, made of the skin of the *pegebuey*.

Some of these nations use bows and arrows, a weapon which, among all the others, is respected for the force and rapidity with which it inflicts wounds. Poisonous herbs are plentiful, of which some tribes make a poison so fatal, that an arrow, stained with it, destroys life the moment that it draws blood.

38.

Their means of communication are by water, in canoes.

All those who live on the shores of this great river are collected in large villages, and, like the Venetians and Mexicans, their means of communication are by water, in small vessels which they call canoes. These are usually of cedar wood, which the providence of God abundantly supplies, without the labour of cutting it or carrying it from the forest; sending it down with the current of the river, which, to supply their wants, tears the trees from the most distant Cordilleras of Peru, and places them at the doors of their habitations, where each Indian may choose the piece of timber which suits him best. It is worthy of remark that among such an infinity of Indians, each wanting at least one or two trees for his family, whence to make one or

11

two canoes ; it should cost no further labour than just to go
out to the banks of the river, throw a lasso when the
tree is floating past, and convey it to the threshold ; where
it remains secure until the waters have subsided ; when
each man, applying his industry and labour, manufactures
the vessel which he requires.

39.

The tools which they use.

The tools which they use to make not only their canoes,
but also their houses and anything else they require, are
hatchets and adzes, not forged in the smithies of Biscay, but
manufactured in the forges of their understanding, having,
as in other things, necessity for their master.

By it they are taught to cut from the hardest part of the
shell of the turtle, which covers the breast, a plate about a
palmo long, and a little less in breadth, which, cured in smoke
and sharpened with a stone, they fix into a handle. With
this hatchet, though not with much rapidity, they cut what
they require. Of the same material they make their adzes,
to which the jaw bone of the pegebuey serves as a handle,
which nature formed in a curved shape, adapted for such a
purpose.

With these tools they work as perfectly, not only in the
manufacture of their canoes, but also of their tables, boards,
seats, and other things, as if they were the best instruments
of Spain.

Amongst some of the tribes these hatchets are made of
stone, which, worked by hand, are finer, and run less risk of
breaking than those made of turtle shell, and cut down any
tree however thick it may be. Their chisels, and gouges,
for more delicate work, are made of the teeth of animals fitted
into wooden handles, which do their work as well as those
of fine steel. Nearly all the tribes possess cotton, some

more, some less, but they do not all use it for making clothes. Most of them go about naked,—both men and women, excepting that natural modesty obliges them not to appear as if they were in a state of innocence.

40.

Of their rites, and of the gods they adore.

The rites of all these infidels are almost the same. They worship idols which they make with their own hands; attributing power over the waters to some, and, therefore, place a fish in their hands for distinction; others they choose as lords of the harvests ; and others as gods of their battles. They say that these gods came down from Heaven to be their companions, and to do them good. They do not use any ceremony in worshipping them, and often leave them forgotten in a corner, until the time when they become necessary ; thus when they are going to war, they carry an idol in the bows of their canoes, in which they place their hopes of victory; and when they go out fishing, they take the idol which is charged with dominion over the waters ; but they do not trust in the one or the other so much as not to recognize another mightier God.

I gathered this from what happened with one of these Indians, who having heard something of the power of our God, and seen with his own eyes that our expedition went up the river, and, passing through the midst of so many warlike nations, returned without receiving any damage ; judged that it was through the force and power of the God who guided us. He, therefore, came with much anxiety to beseech the captain and ourselves, that, in return for the hospitality he had shewn us, we would leave him one of our gods, who would protect him and his people in peace and safety, and assist them to procure all necessary provisions. There were not wanting those who wished to console him by leaving in

his village, the standard of the cross, a thing which the
Portuguese were accustomed to do among the infidels, not
with so good a motive as would appear from the action itself.
The sacred wood of the cross served to give colour to the
greatest injustice, such as the continual slavery of the poor
Indians, whom, like meek lambs, they carried in flocks to their
houses, to sell some, and treat the others with cruelty. These
Portuguese raise the cross, and in payment of the kind treat-
ment of the natives when they visit their villages, they fix it
in the most conspicuous place, charging the Indians always
to keep it intact. By some accident, or through the lapse
of time, or purposely because these infidels do not care for
it, the cross falls. Presently the Portuguese pass sentence,
and condemn all the inhabitants of the village to perpetual
slavery, not only for their lives, but for the lives of all their
descendants.

For this reason I did not consent that they should plant
the holy cross; and also that it might not give the Indian,
who had asked us for a god, occasion for idolatry, by attributing to the wood the power of the Deity who redeemed us.

However, I consoled him by assuring him that our God
would always accompany him, that he should pray to him
for what he wanted, and that some day he would be brought
to a true knowledge of him. This Indian was well persuaded
that the gods of his people were not the most powerful on
earth, and he wished for a greater one, to obey.

41.

An Indian would make himself God.

With the same understanding as the above, though with
more malice, another Indian displayed his intellect. As he
could not recognize any power or deity in his idols, he
declared himself to be the god of that land. We had notice
of this man some leagues before we reached his habitation;

and, dispatching news that we brought a true and more power
ful God, we asked him to wait our arrival. He did so, and
our vessels had scarcely arrived at the banks, when, eager
to know the new God, he came out in person to ask for him.
But though it was declared to him who the true God was ;
because he was unable to see him with his eyes, he remained
in his blindness, making himself out to be a child of the
sun, whither he declared he went every night, the better to
arrange for the government of the following day. Such was
the malice and pride of this Indian.

Another shewed a better understanding, when asked why
his companions were retiring into the forests, apprehensive
of the vicinity of the Spaniards, while he alone with a few
relations came out fearlessly to place himself in our power.
He answered that he considered that a people who had once
gone up the river through the midst of so many enemies,
and returned without any hindrance, could not be less than
lords of this great river, who would often return to navigate
and occupy it ; and as this was so, he did not want always
to be attacking them under the shade of night ; but to know
them, and recognize them from that time as friends ; while
others would be forced to receive them. This was a sensible discourse, which, should God permit it, we shall some
day see put into execution.

ǂ2.

Of their sorcerers.

Following the thread of our narrative, and returning to
the rites of these people ; it is worthy of notice that they all
hold their sorcerers in very great estimation, not so much on
account of the love they bear them, as for the dread in which
they always live of the harm they are able to do them.
These sorcerers usually have a house, where they practise
their superstitious rites, and speak to the demon ; and where,

with a certain kind of veneration, the Indians keep all the bones of dead sorcerers, as if they were relics of saints. They suspend these bones in the same hammocks, in which the sorcerers had slept when alive.

These men are their teachers, their preachers, their councillors, and their guides. They assist them in their doubts, and the Indians resort to them in their wars, that they may receive poisonous herbs with which to take vengeance on their enemies.[1]

Their methods of interring their dead differ among the Indian tribes. Some preserve them in their own houses, always retaining the memory of the dead in their minds. Others burn in great fires not only the body, but also all that the deceased possessed when alive. Both the one and the other celebrate the obsequies of their dead, for many days, with constant mourning, interrupted by great drinking bouts.

43.

These Indians are of mild dispositions.

These tribes of infidels have good dispositions, with fine features, and are of a colour not so dark as those of Brazil. They have clear understandings, and rare abilities for any manual dexterity. They are meek and gentle, as was found in those who once met us, conversed with us confidently, and eat and drank with us, without ever suspecting anything. They gave us their houses to live in, while they all lived together in one or two of the largest in the village; and though they suffered much mischief from our friendly Indians, without the possibility of avoiding it, they never returned it by evil acts. All this, together with the slight inclination they display to worship their own gods, gives

---

[1] The sorcerers of the Tupi Indians, at the mouth of the Amazons, were called *payes*. Each one lived alone, in a dark hut.

great hope that, if they received notice of the true Creator of heaven and earth, they would embrace His holy law with little hesitation.

44·

Treats especially of the affairs of the river, and of the entrances into it.

Up to this point I have spoken, in general terms, of all things touching this great river of Amazons ; it will be well now to descend to particulars, and to describe the entrances into it, to enumerate its ports, to inquire into the waters by which it is fed, to open to view the lands near it, to mark the heights on its banks, to notice the qualities of its various tribes, and, finally, to leave nothing that is worthy to be known, which, as an eye-witness and a person sent by his Majesty on purpose to examine everything, I shall be able to do better than others.

I do not here treat of the principal entrance into this river by the ocean, near the coast of Gran Para ; for this is well known to all who wish to sail to those parts, which are under the equator, at the extreme limits of Brazil. Nor shall I mention that by which the tyrant Lope de Aguirre came out, in front of La Trinidad ; for it is out of the way, and the river is not entered by it, having other streams to give it birth.

It is only my intention to bring out clearly, and to enumer-ate, as with a finger, all the ports by which, from the pro-vinces of Peru, the inhabitants of those conquests may make sure of entering this great river ; with which, as I said before, many others of great volume communicate from both sides of its banks ; on the currents of which it would be necessary to sail, in order to reach this principal river. But as it is not certainly known from what cities or provinces they derive their first origin, neither is it possible to treat positively of their entrances. I am, however, able to do this of some eight, concerning which no one, having a knowledge of this country, can find difficulty. Three of these come from the new kingdom of Granada, which is, with respect to this river, on the north side ; four come from the south, and one from the equator itself.

45.

Of the three ways which lead from the new kingdom.

The first entrance which, on the side of the new kingdom of Granada, is known to lead to this immense sea of fresh water, is by the province of Micòa, which belongs to the Government of Popayan; by following the current of the great river Caquètà, which is the lord and master of all the streams which flow from the side of Santa Fé de Bogota, Timana, and El Caguan, and which are famed, among the natives, for the vast provinces of infidels who live on their banks. This river has many branches flowing through wide districts, and, as it approaches to join the Amazons, it forms a great multitude of islands, all inhabited by many savages. It flows, for a great distance, in the same direction as the Amazons, accompanying that river, though at some distance, and from time to time sending forth branches, which might well be the main streams of any other great river. Finally it collects all its force in 4° of latitude, and surrenders itself.

By one of the branches which is nearest to the province of the *Aguas* or flat-heads, is the way by which it is necessary to come out, in order to enjoy the grandeur of our great river of Amazons; for if any one should attempt those which incline more to the north, the same would happen to him as befell Captain Fernan Perez de Quesada, in times past, who, starting from the direction of Santa Fé, entered this river with three hundred men, and reached the province of Algodonal, but was obliged to retreat faster than he had come.[1]

[1] According to other authorities his name was Francisco Perez de

The second entrance to this river, on the northern side, is by the city of Pasto, also in the jurisdiction of Popayan, whence, traversing the Cordillera with some difficulty owing to the bad road, on foot, for it is impossible on horseback, reaching the Putumayo, and navigating its downward course, explorers would reach the Amazons in 2° 30' south latitude ; at a distance of three hundred and thirty leagues from the port of Napo. By this same road, starting, as I said, from the city of Pasto and crossing the Cordillera, they would approach the *Sucumbios*, who are not far from the river called Aguarico, otherwise the " river of gold". By this river, the Amazons may be reached almost on the line itself, at the commencement of the province of the *Encabellados,* which is ninety leagues from the said port of Napo. This is the third way by which the great river may be entered from the northern side.

46.

Other means of entrance.

The port for this great river, which is on the equator, is in the government of Quijos, near Quito, and in the territory of the *Cofanes;* whence, by the river of Coca, the principal channel of our river of Amazons is traced by the strong current, until it meets with the Napo. The navigation is not so good as it becomes lower down, in the southern part of its course. Of the entrances, the first of all, though not the best, is by the settlement of Avila, in the same government of Quijos; whence, by three days journey on land, the river Payamino is reached, by which the Portuguese fleet approached the jurisdiction of Quito. This river empties itself between the rivers Napo and Coca, at that point which is

Quesada. He explored the territory to the eastward of Popayan in 1557, and was appointed governor of the country of the Cofanes Indians, by the Viceroy of Peru.

12

called " the Confluence of the rivers", distant twenty-five
leagues from the port of Napo. We discovered a better entrance for this fleet, on the return voyage, than that which
they had found on ascending the river, though with much
labour and loss. It was found to be by way of the city of
Archidona, also in the government of Quijos, and jurisdiction
of Quito ; whence, by only one day's journey on foot in
winter (for in summer it may be performed on horse-back),
we reached the port of Napo, on a powerful river, in which
the inhabitants of that province have all their treasure, taking
every year from the shores, in gold, that which they require
for their expenses.[1] Its waters are well supplied with fish,
and its banks with game. The land is good, and with little
trouble would yield plenty of fruit.

This is the road by which, with most ease and least trouble, all persons who wish to navigate the river of Amazons, may descend from the province of Quito. It is also
said that from Quito, at or near the town of Ampato,
which is eighteen leagues from the city itself, on the road to
Riobamba, there is an entrance by a river which is an affluent of the Amazons, without any impediment caused by falls
in its course. This way is very convenient for entering the
said river, about seventy-seven leagues below the port of
Napo, by which the whole of the journey through Quijos is
avoided.[2]

47.

Other entrances into this river.

By the way of the province of Macas, which is under the
same jurisdiction, and from the sierras of which the torrents
which form the river Curaray descend, there is another en-

---

[1] The gold washings of the river Napo are still famous ; and gold is
also obtained in the sands of most of its tributaries.—*Report of Señor
Villavicencio.*

[2] By the river Curaray, which is navigable for a considerable distance.

trance to the Amazons, in 2° of latitude, and one hundred
and fifty leagues from Napo ; the intervening territory being
peopled by various tribes. This is the seventh way to this
river.

The eighth is by " Santiago of the forests", and the province of Maynas ; a land which is drained by one of the largest
rivers which feeds the Amazons, under the name of Marañon, and at its mouth by that of Tumburagua.

This river is such that, for more than three hundred
leagues from the place, in 4°, where it empties itself into the
principal one, its navigation is dreaded, as well on account
of its depth, as for the violent current, and the rumours concerning many savage tribes who infest it. But those who
are zealous for the honour of God, and the welfare of souls,
would overcome greater difficulties. In quest of these objects,
two priests of my order, in the beginning of the year 1638,
entered the country of Maynas ; from whom I received many
letters, in which they did not cease to enhance its grandeur,
and to speak of the innumerable provinces, of which every
day they continued to receive information.[1] This river unites
with the main stream of the Amazons, two hundred and
thirty leagues from the port of Napo.

48.

The river of Napo.

This river of Napo, so frequently mentioned by me, has
its source in the skirts of a mountain called Antezana, eight-
teen leagues from the city of Quito ; and, though so near the
equator, it is wonderful, that, like many other peaks which
rise up above the inhabited parts of these provinces, it is
always covered with snow. The Cordilleras thus serve to
temper the heat which, according to St. Augustine, neces-

---

[1] The intrepid missionaries, named Cujia and Cueva, who reached
Borja, in Maynas, on the 6th of February, 1638. (See Introduction.)

sarily renders these lands of the torrid zone uninhabitable :
but with this cooling process, they become the most temperate and agreeable of all the countries which have been
discovered.

This river of Napo flows from its source, between great
masses of rock, and is not navigable until it reaches the port
where the citizens of Archidona have established the hamlet
for their Indians. Here it becomes more humane, and less warlike, and consents to bear a few ordinary canoes on its shoulders, conveying provisions ; but, from this point, for four or
five leagues, it does not forget its former fury, until it unites
with the river Coca.   The united stream has great depth,
and becomes tranquil, offering a good passage for larger
vessels.   This is the junction of rivers where Francisco de
Orellana, with his party, built the barque with which he
navigated this river of the Amazons.

49.

Here they killed Captain Palacios.

Forty-seven leagues from this union of waters, on the south
side, is Anete, the settlement which captain Juan de Palacios
made, who was killed by the natives, as I said before : and
eighteen leagues from Anete, on the north side, is the mouth
of the river Aguarico, well known, both for its unhealthy
climate, and for the gold which is found in it ; from which
it also takes the name of the " golden river."[1]   At both sides
of its mouth, the great province of the *Encabellados* commences ; which, extending in a northerly direction for more
than one hundred and eighty leagues, and always having
the advantage of the waters which the great river of Ama-

---

[1] The Aguarico takes its rise in the Cayambe mountains, and forms
the boundary between the modern Republics of Ecuador and New
Granada.   It is famous for its productive gold washing.   *Report of
Señor Villaricencio.*

zons spreads into wide lakes ; has, from the first receipt of
information respecting it, excited ardent desires to subject
the whole to the jurisdiction of Quito. Several expeditions
were made with this object, but the last, under captain Juan
de Palacios, met with a disastrous termination, as we have
before seen.

50.

Province of the Encabellados. Here the Portuguese fleet remained.

In this province, at the mouth of the river of the *Encabellados,* which is twenty leagues below that of Aguarico,
forty soldiers of the Portuguese expedition, with more than
three hundred Indian friends, whom they brought in their
company, remained for a space of eleven months. Though
at first they were on friendly terms with the natives of the
country, and received the necessary supplies from them ;
such confidence did not long endure in the breasts of those
who were yet influenced by the rage which led them to shed
the blood of a Spanish captain ; and as they also sought
vengeance against the present invaders, they rebelled with
slight cause, and, killing three of our Indians, placed themselves in an attitude to defend their persons and lands. The
Portuguese were not idle ; and being far from long-suffering,
and still less accustomed to such liberties from Indians, they
desired to commence the work of punishment presently.

They took up their arms, and, with their usual vigour, fell
upon them in such sort that, with few deaths, they collected
more than sixty persons alive, and kept them prisoners until
some being dead, and others escaped, not one was left. The
Portuguese squadron was now placed in such a position that
if they wished to eat, they must seek food from the hands of
the enemy, or perish. They determined to make forays into
the country, and forcibly rid themselves of their difficulty.
Some entered the forest, others remained behind, and both

one and the other party did not cease to be molested by the
enemy, who continued to do them all the mischief in their
power. They attacked their vessels, destroying some, and
breaking up those which were most frail ; nor was this the
least damage that was received from them ; for they also
attacked our friendly Indians in the forests, beheading those
who fell into their hands ; though the Portuguese payed
them with three times the number of their own lives, for one
of ours,—a slight chastisement compared with those which
the Portuguese are accustomed to inflict in similar cases.

The first Spaniard who discovered the *Encabellados*,[1]
called them by that name because of the long hair, worn both
by men and women, which in some instances reached below
the knees. Their arms are darts, their habitations are straw
huts, and their food the same as other tribes on the river.
They are continually at war with the surrounding tribes,
which are the *Seños, Becabas, Tamas,* and *Rumos.* To the
south of this province of the *Encabellados,* are the *Auxiras,
Yurusunes, Zaparas,*[2] and *Yquitos,* whose territory is inclosed
between the rivers Napo and Curaray, down to the point
where they unite in one, which is forty leagues from the
river of the *Encabellados,* and almost in 2° of latitude.

The river Tumburagua.

Eighty leagues from the Curaray, on the same side, the
famous river Tumburagua empties itself ; which, as I said
before, descends from Maynas, with the name of Marañon.
It makes itself respected by the river of Amazons, insomuch
that with its united force it forms for itself a mouth of more
than a league in breadth, by which it enters to kiss the hand
of the greater river, paying it not only the ordinary tribute
of its waters, but another very abundant one of many kinds

---

[1] This was Father Rafael Ferrer, in 1608. See *ante,* p. 52 (note).
[2] See list of Indian tribes, at the end of the volume.

of fish, which were not known in the Amazons, until it reaches the mouth of this river.[1]

51.

Province of the Aguas.

Sixty leagues below the Tumburagua, commences the best and broadest province of any that we met with on this great river, which is that of the *Aguas*, commonly called *Omaguas*. This province is more than two hundred leagues long, with settlements so close together, that one is scarcely lost sight of when another comes in view. Its breadth seems to be small, not more than that of the river; and in the islands, which are numerous and some very large, the Indians have their dwelling places. Considering that all these islands are peopled, or at least cultivated, by these natives, it may be imagined how numerous the Indians are who support themselves from so plentiful a country.

This tribe is the most intelligent and best governed of any on the river. They owe these advantages to those who were living peacefully, not many years ago, in the government of Quijos; who, having been ill-treated, descended the river until they met with the great body of their nation, and, introducing amongst them some of the things they had learned amongst the Spaniards, the tribe became somewhat more civilized. They all go about decently clothed, both men and women; and the latter, from the quantity of cotton they cultivate, weave not only the cloths they require themselves, but much more, which serves as an article of barter with the neighbouring nations, who have good reason to value the work of such cunning weavers. They make very beautiful

---

[1] It is necessary to explain here that this river of Tumburagua (or Marañon) is really the main stream of the Amazons; and that the stream which Acuña called by that name, is merely the lower part of the Napo.

cloths, not only woven in different colours, but also painted with great skill. These Indians are so obedient to their principal chiefs, that a single word is sufficient to make them perform whatever they are ordered to do. They all have flattened heads, which causes ugliness in the men, but the women conceal it better with their abundant tresses. The custom of flattening their heads is so confirmed amongst them, that when the children are born they are placed in a press, a small board being secured on the forehead, and another one at the back of the head, so large as to serve as a cradle, and to receive the whole of the body of the new-born infant. The child is placed with its back upon the larger board, and secured so tightly to the other one, that the back and front of the head become as flat as the palm of the hand ; and, as these tightenings have the effect of making the head increase at the sides, it becomes deformed in such a way, that it looks more like an ill-shaped Bishop's mitre, than the head of a human being.

These *Aguas* are engaged in constant wars on both sides of the river, with strange tribes. On the south, among others, with the *Curinas*, who are so numerous, that not only are they able to defend themselves on the side of the river, against the infinite numbers of the *Aguas*, but at the same time they keep up a war against the other nations, who are continually attacking them from inland. On the north side, these Aguas have for adversaries a tribe called *Ticunas*, who, according to good authority, are not less numerous or less brave than the *Curinas*, for they also wage wars against their neighbours inland.

52.

How they use the slaves they capture.

These *Aguas* supply the slaves they capture in their battles with everything they want, becoming so fond of them that

they eat with them out of one plate, and are much annoyed
if asked to sell them, a thing which we saw by experience
on many occasions. When we arrived at a village of these
Indians, they received us not only peacefully, but with
dances and signs of great joy; they offered all they had, for our
support, with great liberality ; they cheerfully gave us woven
cloths, treating with us also for the hire of those canoes,
which are to them as fleet horses, in which they travel; but
on naming their slaves, and asking them to sell them, " *hoc
opus hic labor est;*" here was the point of disagreement ; here
was the subject which made them sorrowful ; then appeared
arrangements for concealing them, and then it was that they
managed to place them out of our reach.

These are sure signs that they value their slaves more,
and feel the sale of them more, than all the rest of the things
they possess. Let no one say that their dislike to selling these
Indians, their slaves, arises from a desire to eat them in
their drinking bouts, which, though a common saying, has
very little foundation, being invented by the Portuguese to
give a colour to their injustice.

As far as this nation is concerned, I inquired of two
Indians who had come up with these same Portuguese, and
were natives of Para. They had been taken prisoners by these
Aguas, with whom they lived for eight months, and whom
they accompanied in some of their wars (a time long enough
to judge of their habits). These men assured me that they
had never seen them eat their slaves. What they did with
the principal and most valiant prisoners was, to kill them
in their festivals and general meetings, dreading that they
might do them greater injury if they preserved their lives :
and, having thrown the bodies into the river, they preserved the heads as trophies in their houses, which were
those which we often met with throughout the voyage.

I do not wish to deny that there is a race of cannibals on
this river, who, on occasions, do not feel disgust at eating

13

human flesh ; that which I wish to persuade my readers is, that the flesh of Indians is not to be found in every public meat market, as those declare who, on pretence of preventing like cruelty, make slaves of those Indians who are born free.

53.

Of a cold district, in which wheat might be grown.

At a distance of a hundred leagues, (a little more or less), from the first settlements of these *Aguas* (which are 3° from the equator), in about the centre of this wide province, we reached a village where we remained three days, and it was so cold that even those who were born and bred in the coldest parts of Spain, found it necessary to put on additional clothes. Such a sudden change of temperature surprised me, and, having asked the natives if it was an extraordinary thing in their village, they assured me that it was not so, but that every year for a space of three moons (for it is thus that they count), which is the same as to say three months, they experienced this cold weather, which, according to their account, was in June, July and August. But as I was not yet quite satisfied with their account, I desired, with more accuracy, to investigate the cause of such penetrating cold ; and I found that there was a great sierra situated on the south side (inland), whence during all those three months the winds blow, which are frozen by the snow with which the sierra is covered, and which are the cause of this cold in the surrounding country. This being the fact, there can be no doubt that very good wheat might be grown in this place, as well as all the other seeds and fruits which the district of Quito produces, though situated under the equinoctial line ; where similar winds, passing across snowy mountains, produce the like marvellous effects.

54.

The river Putumayo, and of the nations on its banks, and on the banks of the river Yetaù.

Sixteen leagues from these villages, on the north side, is the mouth of the great river Putumayo, well known in the province of Popayan, for being so mighty a river, that, before emptying itself into the Amazons, it receives thirty other great rivers. The natives, in that country, call it the Yza. It descends from the Cordilleras of Pasto, in the new kingdom of Granada ; contains much gold; and, as we are told, its banks are well peopled with Infidels: for which reason the Spaniards who descended it a few years ago, retired with some haste. The names of the tribes who inhabit its banks are the *Yurunas, Guaraicus, Yacariguaras, Parias, Ziyus, Atuais, Cunas,* and those who, nearer its sources, people this river on both sides, like sovereign lords, are the *Omaguas,* whom the *Aguas* of the islands call *Omaguasyeté,* or true *Omaguas.*

Fifty leagues from the mouth of the Putumayo, on the opposite side, we came to the mouth of a fine and powerful river, which, rising in the neighbourhood of Cuzco, empties itself into the Amazons in 3° 30′ of latitude. The natives call it Yetaú,[1] and it is very famous among them as well for its riches, as for the multitude of nations which live near it, such as the *Tipunas, Guanarús, Ozuanas, Moruas, Naunas, Conomomas, Marianas,* and lastly, those who live near the Spaniards of Peru, namely, the *Omaguas,* said to be a people very rich in gold, which they hang in plates from their ears and noses; and, unless I am deceived, according to what I read in the history of the tyrant Lope de Aguirre, this was the province of *Omaguas,* to discover which Pedro de Ursua was sent

[1] Jutay. Castelnau says it is navigable for upwards of five hundred and forty miles.

by the viceroy of Peru, on account of the many notices which fame had published respecting its riches. The reason of their not finding this province arose from their entering the river by a branch which comes out into the Amazons some leagues lower down, and these nations remained so high up that it was impossible to reach them, owing to the danger caused by the impetuosity of the current, but chiefly on account of the little zeal displayed by the vacillating soldiers.

This river of Yetaù is very abundantly supplied with fish and game, and, according to the accounts of the Indians who inhabit its banks, it is easily navigable, being of sufficient depth, and the current moderate.

55.

End of the province of the Aguas ; and of the river of Cuzco.

Following the course of our principal river, after fourteen leagues, we reached the last settlement of this extensive province of the *Aguas*, which ends at a very populous village, with warlike inhabitants, being the first force which, in this direction, is prepared to resist the onslaught of their enemies. From this place, for a space of fifty-four leagues, no Indians people the banks of the river ; for their villages are out of sight, some distance inland, in dense thickets, whence they come forth to seek for anything they require. These Indians are, on the north side, the *Curis* and *Guayrabas*, and on the south, the *Cachiguaràs*, and *Tucuriys*. But though, as I said, we were unable to get a sight of these people, we came to the mouth of a river which may be properly called the river of Cuzco ; for, according to an account of the voyage of Francisco de Orellana, which I saw, its source is near the same city of Cuzco. It flows into the Amazons in 5° of latitude, and twenty-four leagues from the last village of the

Aguas. The natives call it Yurúa.[1] Its banks are well peopled with tribes ; those on the right banks, on entering it, being the same as those of whom I spoke, as inhabiting the banks of the Yetaù. They are isolated between the two rivers. This is the river by which Pedro de Ursua descended from Peru, if my imagination does not deceive me.[2]

56.

A province where they find gold.

Twenty-eight leagues below the river Yurúa, on the same (that is the south) side, in a land full of deep ravines, commences the populous tribe of *Curuziraris,* who extend, always along the banks, for a distance of about eighty leagues, with settlements so close together, that one was scarcely passed before, within four hours, we came upon others; while sometimes, for the space of half a day at a time, we did not lose sight of their villages. Most of these we found to be uninhabited, as the Indians had received false news that we came destroying, killing, and making prisoners ; and they had retired into the forests. These Indians are more ingenious than any others on the river. They do not display less order and civilization, both in the quantity of provisions they possess, and in the ornaments of their houses than any other tribe on the river. They find in the ravines near their dwellings, very good clay for all kinds of hardware, and taking advantage of it, they have large potteries, where they make earthen jars, pots, ovens in which they make their flour, pans, pipkins, and even well formed frying pans. All this diligence is caused by the traffic with the other tribes, who, forced by necessity, (as these things are not made in their country),

[1] Jurua. Castelnau says it may be ascended for seven hundred and eighty miles.

[2] Ursua descended by the river *Huallaga.* The *Jurua* rises many leagues north of the city of Cuzco. The true " river of Cuzco" is the *Purus.*

come for large cargoes of them, giving, in exchange, other things which are wanted by the *Curuziraris*.

The Portuguese, in ascending the river, called the first village of these Indians they came to, " *the town of gold*", having found and procured some there, which the Indians had in small plates, hanging from their ears and noses. This gold was tested in Quito, and found to be twenty-one carats. As the natives saw the desire of the soldiers, and how much they coveted the gold, they were diligent in procuring more of these little plates, and soon collected all they had. We found the truth of this in returning, for, though we saw many Indians, only one brought a very small earring of gold, which I obtained by barter.

57.

Mines of gold.

In the ascent of the expedition, they were unable to make certain of anything respecting what they met with on this river, because they did not know the language by means of which they might make an investigation ; and if the Portuguese thought they understood anything, it was only by means of signs, which were so uncertain, that each one might apply any meaning to them, that happened to enter his own mind. All this ceased on the return voyage, as it pleased our Lord to favour the expedition, by supplying it with good linguists, through which all things were ascertained, which are contained in this narrative.

That which they said to me respecting the mines whence this gold is taken, is what I shall here relate.

Opposite this village, a little higher up, on the north side, is the mouth of a river called Yurupazi, ascending which, and crossing a certain district by land, in three days another river is reached called Yupura, by which the Yquiari is entered, called also ' *the river of gold*'. Here, at the foot of

a hill, the natives get a great quantity ; and this gold is all
in grains and lumps of a good size; so that by beating it,
they make plates, which, as I said before, they hang to their
ears and noses. The natives who communicate with those
who extract the gold, are called *Managùs*, and those who
live on the river and work at the mine, are called *Yumaguaris*,
which means " extracters of metal", for *yuma* is a " metal",
and *guaris* " those who extract". They give every kind of
metal this name of *yuma ;* and thus they called all the
tools, hatchets, mattocks, and knives we had, by this same
word *yuma*.

The entrance to these mines seems difficult, on account of
the obstacles on the rivers, and the necessity of opening a
road by land ; so that I was not satisfied until I had discovered another much easier one, of which I shall speak
presently.

58.

They make holes in their ears and noses.

These savages all go naked, both men and women, their
wealth only supplying them with small ornaments, with
which they adorn their ears and noses, by piercing holes
through them. They affect these holes in the ears so much,
that many have them to cover the whole of the lower part
whence the earrings are hung. These holes are ordinarily
filled with a bundle of leaves.

Opposite all these settlements, the land is flat, and so shut
in by other rivers, branches of the Caqueta, that great lakes
are formed many leagues long, extending until, mingling
with the Rio Negro, they unite with the main stream. Islands
are thus formed, which are peopled by many tribes, but
that which is the largest and most populous, is the island of
Zuanas.

59.

Entrance to the mines of gold.

Fourteen leagues from the village which we called 'golden',
on the north side, is the mouth of the river Jupura, and this is
the most certain and direct entrance, to reach the hill which
so liberally offers its treasures. The mouth of the Jupura is
in 2° 30′ of latitude; as also is a village which is situated
four leagues lower down on the south side, near a great
ravine, and at the mouth of a large and clear river which the
natives call Tafi.[1] It has a great multitude of infidels on its
banks, called *Paguanas*. All this territory, as I said, for a
distance of eighty leagues, is occupied by the nation of
Curuziraris. It is very high, with beautiful plains and
pasture for sheep, groves not very thick, many lakes, and a
promise of many and great advantages to those who may
settle in it.

60.

The golden lake.

Twenty-six leagues from the river Tafi, another river called
the Catuà, falls into the Amazons, forming a great lake of clear
water at its mouth.[2] Its sources are many leagues inland on
the south side, and its banks are as thickly peopled with
barbarians, as the other rivers.

If indeed there be any advantage in a multitude of different
tribes, that advantage is possessed by another river, called

---

[1] Teffé, or Egas. The town of Egas, in the Brazilian territory, is at
the mouth of the Teffé, on the margin of a lake. It now has a population of about a thousand souls ; and there is a thriving trade here, between Peru on the one side, and Para, at the mouth of the Amazons, on
the other.

[2] The lake of *Catuà*, is half way between the mouths of the rivers
Teffe and *Coari*.

the Araganatuba, six leagues lower down, on the north side, which communicates with the Yupura. These tribes are called the *Yaguanais, Macunas, Mapiarús, Aguaynaús, Huirunas, Mariruas, Yamoruas, Terarús, Siguiyas, Guanapuris, Pirás, Mopitirus, Yguaranis, Aturiaris, Masipias, Guayacaris, Anduras, Caguaraús, Maraymumas,* and *Guanibis.* Among these tribes, (who all speak different languages), according to information from the new kingdom of Granada, is the desired ' golden lake ', which keeps all the spirited youths in Peru in a state of unrest. I do not affirm this positively, but some day it may please God to deliver us from our uncertainty.

As there is a river which comes from the north, twenty-six leagues from the Araganatuba, with the same name, it is necessary to state that they are both the same river, which empties itself into the Amazons by two mouths. Twenty-two leagues from this last branch, the territory of the populous and rich tribe of *Curuziraris,* inhabitants of the best soil that we met with in the whole course of this great river, comes to an end.

61.

The province of Yorimàn.

Two leagues lower down commences the territory of the most warlike and renowned tribe on the river of the Amazons, who, on the passage up, daunted the whole Portuguese expedition. It is that of Yorimàn. It is on the south side, occupying not only the main land, but also a great number of the islands ; and, though it is little more than sixty leagues long, yet the islands and main land are used to such advantage, and are so covered with people, that in no other part did we see so many savages collected together.

These Indians are usually handsomer and better made

14

than any others. They go naked, and gave us proofs of their valour, by coming and going amongst us with confidence. Every day more than two hundred canoes came, full of women and children, with fruit, fish, flour, and other things, which they exchanged for glass beads, needles, and knives. The first village of this province is situated at the mouth of a limpid river, which seems to be very large, judging from the great force with which it enters the Amazons. It no doubt, like all the rest, has innumerable tribes on its banks, whose names we did not ascertain, as we passed the mouth without stopping.

62.

A village more than a league in length.

Twenty-two leagues from the first settlement of Yorimàn, is the site of the largest village that we met with on the whole river, its houses covering a length of more than a league and a half. A single family does not live in one house, as is usually the case in Spain, but the smallest number that are contained under one roof are four or five, and very often more, from which circumstance the great number of people in this village may be imagined. These Indians remained peacefully in their houses, giving us all the supplies that were required by our forces. We remained here five days, and got on board, as ship's stores, upwards of five hundred bushels *(fanegas)* of mandioc flour, which lasted during the rest of the voyage. We continued onwards, occasionally touching at the villages of Indians of the same nation. But the place where the greatest numbers of them are congregated together, is thirty leagues lower down, in a large island, near an arm which the great river forms in going in search of another, which approaches to pay it tribute ; and on the banks of this new guest there are so many natives, that, with reason, though it only be on account of their numbers, they are feared and respected by all the others.

63.

The river of Giants.

Ten leagues from the above place the province of Yori-màn ends, and two leagues further on, on the south side, is the mouth of the famous river which the Indians call *Cuch-iguará*.[1] It is navigable. Although there are rocks in some places, it has plenty of fish, a great number of turtle, and abundance of maize and mandioc, and all things requisite for facilitating the entrance of an expedition. This river is peopled by various nations, which, beginning at the mouth and going upwards, are as follows. The *Cuchiguaras*, who have the same name as the river, the *Cumayaris*, *Guaquiaris*, *Cuyari-yayanas*, *Curucurus*, *Quatausis*, *Mutuanis*, and finally there are the *Curiguerès*, who, according to the information of those who had seen them, and who offered to guide us to their country, are giants of sixteen palms in height, very brave, going naked, and having great plates of gold in their ears and noses. To reach their villages, it takes two months continual travelling from the mouth of the Cuchiguarà.

From this river, along the south side of the Amazons, wander the *Caripunás*, and *Zurinas*, the most skilful races on the whole river at working with their hands, without more tools than those which I have mentioned above. They make seats formed in the shape of animals, with such skill, and so well arranged for placing the body in a comfortable position, that nothing could be imagined more ingenious and commodious. They also make *estolicas*, which are their arms, of very handsome wands, so dexterously that they are sought after with good reason by the other tribes. What is more, they carve, from a rough log of wood, small idols so like nature, that many of our sculptors would do well to

---

[1] The *Purus*. This magnificent navigable river, which rises in the mountains east of Cuzco, has never yet been explored.

take a lesson from them. These manufactures not only serve for their own use, but are also of great profit, as articles of exchange with other tribes ; for procuring all that they require.

64.

The river Basururù, and its tribes.

Thirty-two leagues from the mouth of the river Cuchiguara there is another, on the north side, called by the natives Basururu ; which divides the land into great lakes, where there are many islands, which are peopled by numerous tribes. The land is high, and never inundated by the many floods which take place ; very productive both in maize, mandioc, and fruit, as well as in flesh and fish ; so that the natives are well off for food, and multiply rapidly.

In general they call all the natives who inhabit this broad region, *Carabuyanas ;* but, more precisely, the tribes into which they are divided, are as follows :—the *Caraguanas, Pocoanas, Vrayaris, Masucaruanas, Quererùs, Cotocarianas, Moacaranas, Ororupianas, Quinarupianas, Tuinamaynas, Araguanaynas, Mariguyanas, Yaribarus, Yarucaguacas, Cumaruruayanas,* and *Curuanaris.* These Indians use bows and arrows, and some of them have iron tools, such as axes, knives, and mattocks. On asking them carefully, through their language, whence these things came, they answered that they bought them of those Indians who, in this direction, are nearer the sea, and that these received them from some white men like ourselves, who use the same arms, swords, and arquebusses, and who dwell on the sea coast. They added that these white men could only be distinguished from ourselves by their hair, which is all yellow. These are sufficient signs that they are the Hollanders, who have possession of the mouth of the Rio Dulce or Felipe. These Hollanders

in 1638, landed their forces in Guiana, in the jurisdiction of
the new kingdom of Granada, and not only got possession of
the settlement, but the affair was so sudden that our people
were unable to take away the most holy sacrament, which remained captive in the hands of its enemies. As they knew
how much this capture was valued amongst catholics, they
hoped for a large ransom for it. When we left those parts,
the Spaniards were preparing some good companies of
soldiers, who, with Christian zeal, were ready to give their
lives to rescue their Lord, with whose favour they will doubtless attain their worthy desires.

65.

The Rio Negro.

Not quite thirty good leagues below the Basururù, likewise on the north side, in 4° of latitude, there comes forth
to meet the Amazons, the largest and most beautiful river
which, in the space of more than thirteen hundred leagues,
does it homage. It appears that it comes to recognize
another larger one, though it is so powerful that its mouth
is a league and a half broad;[1] and though the Amazons opens
its arms with all its force, the new river does not wish to
become subject to it, without receiving some marks of respect; and it thus masters one half of the whole Amazons,
accompanying it for more than twelve leagues, so that the
waters of the two can be clearly distinguished from each
other.

At last the Amazons, not permitting so much superiority,
forces it to mingle with its own turbulent waves, and recognize for a master, the river which it desired to make a vassal.

The Portuguese, with good reason, called this great river
the Rio Negro, because at its mouth, and for many leagues

---

[1] The mouth of the Rio Negro is really not above a mile across. The
river is navigable for large vessels for a distance of four hundred miles.

higher up, its great depth and the clearness of the water, coming from lakes at the sides, make its waves appear as black as if they really were so, whereas in reality they are clear as crystal.

The early part of its course is from west to east, though it winds so much that its course is frequently changed. For many leagues before entering the Amazons its course is again from west to east. The natives who inhabit it call the river Curiguacurù, while the *Tupinambas*, of whom we shall speak presently, give it the name of *Vruna*, which in their language is as much as to say " black water ": as likewise they call the Amazons, in this country, *Parana-guazù*, which signifies 'great river', to distinguish it from the other smaller yet still very large one which they call *Parana-miri* or ' small river ', and which empties itself on the south side, a league above the Rio Negro. It is said to be thickly peopled by different tribes, the last of which use hats, a sure sign that they are in the neighbourhood of the Spaniards of Peru.

Those who inhabit the banks of the Rio Negro are very numerous; that is to say,—the *Canizuaris, Aguayras, Yacu-ucaraes, Cahuayapitis, Manacurus, Yanmas, Guanamas, Carapanaaris, Guarianacaguas, Azerabaris, Curupatabas,* and *Guaranaquazanas,* who people a branch which this river throws off, whence, according to my information, it comes out in the Rio Grande, at whose mouth, in the north sea, are the Hollanders.[1]

All these tribes use bows and arrows, and many of them tip their weapons with poison. The land near this river is elevated, and has good soil which, if under cultivation, would produce any fruits, even those of Europe in some parts. There are many good pastures, covered with excellent grass, sufficient to afford grazing ground for innumerable flocks.

[1] Acuña here alludes to the Cassiquiari, which unites the Rio Negro with the Orinoco.

The land produces large trees of good timber, of a kind fit
for vessels, or for buildings ; which latter may be constructed not only of timber, but also of very good stone,
in which this spot abounds. The banks of the river
abound in all kinds of game. It is true that the fish are
not so plentiful as in the Amazons, because the water is so
clear, though in the lakes inland they may always be secured
in abundance.

At its mouth there are good positions for a fortress, and
plenty of stones to build it, with which the entrance may be
defended against an enemy, who may desire to pass from
this river to the Amazons.[1]

I am of opinion that, not at this point, but many leagues
further inland, on the branch which joins the Rio Grande,
(the river which I before alluded to as falling into the ocean),
is the place where it would be most advisable to place
all defensive works ; by which the passage into this new
world, which the covetous will doubtless attempt some day,
would be entirely closed to the enemy. I do not hesitate
to affirm, that the Rio Grande, into which this branch of the
Rio Negro empties itself, is either the Dulce or the Felipe,
though I much incline, according to good information, to
believe it to be the latter, as this is the first considerable river
that enters the sea for some leagues north of the Cabo del
Norte ;[2] but that which I can most confidently affirm is that,
under no circumstances, can it be the Orinoco, whose principal mouth is opposite the island of Trinidad, one hundred
leagues from the place where the river Felipe enters the
sea, by which Lope de Aguirre came out ; and surely if he
navigated it, any one else may enter where he has once
opened a road.

---

[1] The present Brazilian town of Barra is built on elevated ground on
the left bank of the Rio Negro, about seven miles from its mouth. It is
fourteen hundred and seventy-five feet above the level of the sea.

[2] The cape on the northern side of the principal mouth of the Amazons.

66.

The Portuguese try to enter the Rio Negro.

On the 12th of October, 1639, the Portuguese fleet, on the return voyage, was stationed at the mouth of the Rio Negro; when the soldiers, considering that they were now, as it were, on the threshold of their homes; and, turning their eyes, not over their gains, which amounted to nothing, but over the losses which they had suffered in the space of more than two years, during which this discovery had lasted; while the services done to his Majesty were, on the other hand, neither small nor incomplete, in effecting these conquests: bethought them that they had received no remuneration for the countries which, on similar occasions, they had watered with their blood; and that they were now consumed and dying of hunger, and were unable to look forward to any one who was able to reward them.

They determined to bring the captain to agree to their desire, persuading him that now their poverty obliged them to seek some remedy; and that the notices of the number of slaves, possessed by the natives up the Rio Negro, offered the occasion close at hand. He should not, they said, permit it to pass without taking some advantage of it, but should give orders for the people to follow this route, so that, with the numerous slaves that they would obtain from this river, even if they brought nothing else, they would be well received by the people of Para. On the other hand, without this, they would doubtless be held very cheap, in having passed so many different nations, and so many slaves, and yet come back with empty hands; the more so, as there are men in those parts who, at the doors of their own houses, know how to make slaves serve them.

The Capitan Mayor gave signs that he would let them have their will, he being one and they were many, and thus he promised that they should set sail, as the wind was abaft, and favourable for the course they wished to take. They were all overjoyed with this determination, and no one promised himself less than a great number of slaves; those who dissented were almost alone, while the other party amounted to three hundred.

This resolution might have given me great concern, had I not known the noble nature of our chief, and had I not been very sure that he would follow, in the first place, what was best for the service of both Majesties. With this assurance, after having said mass, I went apart with my companion, desirous by every means to thwart intentions which were so disastrous, and we drew up the following paper.

67.

Injunction made to the army.

We, the fathers Cristoval de Acuña and Andres de Artieda, priests of the company of Jesus, are persons whom our Lord the King (by a Royal Order issued through his Royal Audience of the city of San Francisco de Quito, in the kingdom of Peru, on the 24th day of the month of January of this present year of 1639) ordered and charged to accompany this Portuguese expedition down all this great river of the Amazons, now discovered; to take as clear notes as we were able of the tribes which inhabit its banks, of the rivers which join it, and of other things; that the Royal Council of the Indies may have a full report of this enterprize; and having done this, to go on to Spain with the greatest dispatch possible, to give an account of all to His Majesty; without any person having authority to impede the execution of the above instructions.

This will be seen more at large in the Royal Order which we have in our possession, and which, if necessary, we are

15

ready to show to all, as we have done to some of the principal officers of this army.

At present, we understand through the conversation of many persons, and by the sails which have been got ready for the navigation, that the captain Pedro Texeira and the other captains and officers of this expedition (in whose company we came, by order of His Majesty), intend to delay the voyage by entering the Rio Negro, in the mouth of which river we now are, with the design of bartering for slaves, to convey them to their estates in Para and Marañon ; as is their custom in all the expeditions which they make from the said Para, among the natives who inhabit the countries adjacent. As, in this, much time must necessarily be wasted, and as many other inconveniences will arise : in order to discharge the duty entrusted to us, and to clear ourselves before the royal person of His Majesty ; in his name, speaking with proper deference, we require captain Pedro Texeira, colonel Benito Rodriguez de Olivera, major Felipe de Matos, captains Pedro de Acosta and Pedro Bayon, and the other officers, who are now in command of the forces at the mouth of the said Rio Negro, to consider that His Majesty has notice, through his Royal Audience of the city of Quito, and through his Viceroy of Peru, of the dispatch of our persons with the above ends in view, and of the short time in which they hoped we should reach the royal presence ; for, according to the word of captain Pedro Texeira, and many others of his company, the said Royal Audience of Quito was assured that we should be in Para within two months and a half, while in six days from this time it will be eight months since we left Quito, and we are yet six hundred leagues from Para.[1] This delay may be the cause of many and great disasters, such as the delay to His Majesty's service in the fortification of this river, which has been an object of his desires for so many years, and concerning which it is

---

[1] Barra de Rio Negro is one thousand miles from Para.

hoped we shall shortly be able to convey information; meanwhile the enemy may get possession of the principal entrances, from which much damage to the crown will result. At the same time such good and gallant officers as are now here, will doubtless cause great damage, by this delay, to the fortress of Para; for, if the enemy should arrive, they being absent, its loss would be inevitable. The Indians of this Rio Negro, into which it is intended to enter, are, in the opinion of all, a very warlike race and able to do us much harm with their bows and poisoned arrows, while, considering the small number of the friendly Indians with us, many of whom are sick, others mere boys without experience in war, and all unwilling to join in this foray; the total loss of the whole army may be the result; besides, as the Indians have no wish to go, it may be that they will escape from us, as most of them came from Para, and are now almost at the doors of their homes.

Here we may add that the slaves, whom it is intended to get, cannot be taken without much difficulty to a good conscience, (except such as may be necessary as interpreters), because this land is new, and though there are *Cedulas* of His Majesty (as it is said), for getting slaves, this only applies to the jurisdiction around Para and Marañon, and according to the other rules laid down, those of this river are not known to belong to that jurisdiction. In case none of the above reasons should have any force, and the end of this undertaking should be attained, that is the procuring of a great quantity of slaves: these very men, owing to our small force to guard them and defend ourselves, may be the total ruin and destruction of us all. For all these reasons, and many others which might be urged respecting the detriment the enterprize will occasion to both Majesties, divine and human, and the prejudice to the salvation of such a vast number of souls, as are in this river:—Once again we repeat our requisition to the said captain Pedro Texeira, the major, captains, and officers of this expedition, that, not giving way to delays which will be disadvantageous to the service of God and His Majesty, they do, with all dispatch, arrange so that we may continue our voyage to Para, and pass from thence to Spain, to complete the ends of our mission: moreover such dispatch may be useful, and as such held as good service by His Majesty, to the salvation of so many souls as have been discovered in this new world, and who now lie miserable in the shadow of death.

And if this be not sufficient to induce all to continue the voyage without delay ; we require again, on the strength of the Royal Order which we have with us, that captain Pedro Texeira, and the other officers of the army, shall give and supply us with all things necessary to protect our persons, and permit us to continue our voyage without delay, which, though there be danger from enemies, we will risk, to accomplish that which His Majesty has commanded us in his Royal Order : and, in case our requisition should not be heeded, we protest against all the evils and inconveniences which may follow from this delay, and we will give an account of it to the Royal Council of the Indies, and to the royal person of the King our Lord, according to our orders; and finally, for the safety of our persons, and as evidence that we desire to comply effectually with our orders; we beg that the notary appointed to this expedition, may give us his testimony of all that is contained in this our requisition, and of the answer we may receive.

68.

The voyage is continued; and of the river Madeira.

Having drawn up this paper, and communicated with the Capitan Mayor; he was rejoiced to have us on his side, and, acknowledging the force of our reasons, he ordered the sails to be taken in at once, the preparations to be discontinued, and everything to be got ready to leave the mouth of the Rio Negro on the following day, so as to continue our voyage down the river of the Amazons.

This we did, and after forty-four leagues we came to the great river of Madeira, so called by the Portuguese, on account of the quantity of large timber which was floating down it, when they passed; but its real name among the natives is Cayari. Its mouth is on the south side of the Amazons, and according to the information we received, it is formed of two great rivers which unite some leagues inland; by which, according to good accounts, and according to the statements of the *Tupinambás*, who descended by it, there is a shorter route than by any other way, to the rivers which are nearest to the province of Potosi.[1]

Of the tribes of this river, which are numerous, the first are named *Zurinas* and *Cayanas*, after which follow the *Vrurihaus, Anamaris, Guatinumas, Curanaris, Erepunacas,* and *Abacatis*. From the mouth of this river, along the banks of the Amazons, are the *Zapucayas*, and *Vrubutingas*, who are very cunning workers in wood. Beyond these follow the *Guaranaguacas, Maraguas, Quimaus, Burais, Punouys, Oreguatus, Aperas,* and others whose names I was unable to ascertain with certainty.

69.

The great Island of the Tupinambàs.

Twenty-eight leagues from the mouth of this river, always continuing on the south side, is a beautiful island which is sixty leagues in length, and consequently more than one hundred in circumference. It is entirely peopled by the valiant *Tupinambds*, à people of the Brazilian conquest, from the territory of Pernambuco. Many years ago they

---

[1] The Madeira is navigable by means of its tributaries, the Mamoré and Beni, into the centre of Bolivia. Lieutenant Gibbon, U.S.N., descended it in 1852.

were subjected, and fled from the severity with which the Portuguese treated them. So great a number left their homes, that eighty-four villages, where they lived, were left uninhabited at one time, there was not a single creature left, out of the whole number, that did not accompany them in their flight. They kept skirting along the Cordilleras which, coming from the Straits of Magellan, run along the whole of America, and they crossed all the rivers which send their tribute to the ocean in that direction. At length some of them reached the Spanish frontiers of Peru, where there were settlers, near the head waters of the river Madeira. They remained with them some time, but, by reason of a Spaniard having flogged one of them for killing a cow, they, taking advantage of the river, all descended by its current, and finally reached the island which they now inhabit.

These Indians speak the " *lingoa geral*" of Brazil, which also prevails amongst nearly all the tribes of the Para and Marañon conquests. They say that there was such a multitude of fugitives, that it was impossible to support them all, and they divided over distant tracks, (at least nine hundred leagues across), some peopling one land, some another; so that all these Cordilleras must doubtless be full of them.

They are a people very valiant in war, and so they showed themselves when they reached those districts which they now inhabit; for though they were without comparison greatly inferior in numbers to the natives of this river, yet they attacked them with such force, that they subjected all those with whom they made war, and entire tribes were obliged to leave their homes, and to seek others in strange lands, from fear of the *Tupinambás*. These Indians use bows and arrows with dexterity. They are noble hearted and of good ancestry, as almost all those now living are sons or grandsons of the first settlers, though they are now becoming addicted to meanness and robbery, like the surrounding tribes; with whose blood they are mixed. They treated us all with great kindness, giving indications that they may soon be reduced to live among the friendly Indians of Para ; a thing which will undoubtedly be of much use in conquering all the other tribes of this river, for there is no tribe that will not surrender, at the very name of the *Tupinambàs*.

70.
Information given by the Tupinambàs.

From these *Tupinambàs* Indians ; as a more intelligent race, and because we did not require interpreters, they speaking the " *lingoa Geral*",[1] which many of the Portuguese know well, having been born and bred in these parts ; we received some information which I will repeat, for, they being a people who have overrun and subdued all the neighbourhood, can speak with certainty.

They say that near their settlement, on the south side, there live, among others, two nations, one of dwarfs as small as little children, whom they call *Guayazis ;*[2] the other of people who all have their feet turned the wrong way, so that a person who did not know them, in following their footsteps, would always walk away from them : they call them *Mutayas*, and they are tributary to these *Tupin-*

---

[1] The basis of the *Lingoa Geral* of the tribes on the Amazons is the *Guarani* language of Paraguay. It is called *Tupi* by the natives, and (with the exception of the Malay, and the Athabascan dialect) is the most widely extended language in the world; reaching from the Rio Negro to the Rio de la Plata, and from Rio de Janeiro to the sources of the Madeira.

The *Guarani* was learned by the Jesuits in Paraguay, and the *Tupi* by the Portuguese traders of the Amazons ; and the two combined to form a sort of Tupi-Guarani (or " Lingua Franca") dialect, known as the *Lingoa Geral*. The languages of the Cocomas, Omaguas, and the Indians of the Napo, are also offshoots of the Guarani.—*Wallace*, p. 531, Appendix.

[2] Castelnau mentions a tribe of dwarfs on the river Jurua, produced by a mixture of Indians and monkeys.

ambàs, having to cut down the trees with stone hatchets, when their masters wish to cultivate the earth. They make these hatchets with great skill, and are continually employed in manufacturing them.

On the opposite or northern shore, they say that there are seven well peopled provinces, adjoining each other; but as the tribes who inhabit them are not worth much, and only live on fruits and little animals of the woods, without ever making war on their neighbours, the *Tupinambàs* take no notice of them. They also say that they have been at peace, with a tribe which borders on these Indians, for a long time, having commerce with them, and each one exchanging what his country most abounds in. The chief commodity required by the *Tupinambàs* is salt, which their friends bring to trade with, saying that it comes from a country not far from their own. This is a thing which, if true, would be of great importance in the conquest and settlement of this river. Even if it is not found here, it has been discovered in great abundance near a large river which descends from Peru; where, in the year 1637, I being then in the city of Lima, two men, having casually gone from those parts to a certain district, and descended one of the rivers which falls into this large one, came upon a great hill, entirely composed of salt.[1] The settlers have the monopoly of this salt, by which they have become rich and opulent, from the payments made by purchasers who come from a distance. Nor is it a new thing for the Cordilleras of Peru to have hills of excellent rock salt; indeed this is a cause of expense, for the salt has to be broken out by bars of steel, in lumps so large as to weigh five or six arrobas[2] each.

---

[1] This is the *Cerro de la Sal*, in the forests to the eastward of Tarma, in Peru. In 1636 Father Jeronimo Ximenes, a Franciscan, built a chapel on this hill; but he was murdered on the river Perene, by the wild Indians in 1637.

[2] One arroba=twenty-five pounds.

This province of *Tupinambàs* is seventy-six leagues in length, and ends in a fine village situated in the same parallel as the first village of the Aguas, of which we have already made mention, namely, in 3° of latitude.

71.

They give information respecting the Amazons.

The discourse of these *Tupinambàs* confirmed the information, which we had heard throughout this river, of the famous Amazons, from whom it took its name, and it is not known by any other, but only by this, to all cosmographers who have treated of it up to this time. It would be very strange that, without good grounds, it should have usurped the name of the river of the Amazons, and that it should desire to become famous, with no other title than a usurped one : nor is it credible that this great river, possessing so much glory at hand, should only desire to glorify itself by a name to which it has no title. This is an ordinary meanness with those who, not caring to obtain the honour they desire by their own merits, acquire it by falsehood. But the proofs of the existence of the province of Amazons on this river are so numerous, and so strong, that it would be a want of common faith not to give them credit. I do not treat of the important information which, by order of the Royal Audience, was collected from the natives during many years, concerning all which the banks of this river contained ; one of the principal reports being that there was a province inhabited by female warriors, who lived alone without men, with whom they associated only at certain times; that they lived in villages, cultivating the land, and obtaining by the work of their hands all that was necessary for their support. Neither do I make mention of those reports which were received from some Indians, and particularly from an Indian woman, in the city of Pasto,

16

who said that she had herself been in the country which was peopled by these women, and her account entirely agreed with all that had been previously reported.

I will only dwell upon that which I heard with my own ears, and carefully investigated, from the time that we entered this river. There is no saying more common than that these women inhabit a province on the river, and it is not credible that a lie could have been spread throughout so many languages, and so many nations, with such an appearance of truth. But the place where we obtained most information respecting the position of the province of these women, their customs, the Indians with whom they communicate, and the roads by which their country may be entered, was in the last village of the *Tupinambàs*.

72.

River of the Amazons.

Thirty-seven leagues from this village, and lower down the river, on the north side, is the mouth of that of the Amazons, which is known among the natives by the name of Cunuris. This river takes the name of the first Indians who live on its banks, next to whom follow the *Apantos*, who speak the " *lingoa geral*" of Brazil. Next come the *Taguaus*, and the last, being those who communicate and traffic with the Amazons themselves, are the *Guacaràs*.

These manlike women have their abodes in great forests, and on lofty hills, amongst which, that which rises above the rest, and is therefore beaten by the winds for its pride, with most violence, so that it is bare and clear of vegetation, is called Yacamiaba. The Amazons are women of great valour, and they have always preserved themselves without the ordinary intercourse with men; and even when these, by agreement, come every year to their land, they receive them with arms in their hands, such as bows and arrows, which they brandish about for some time, until they are satisfied that the Indians come with peaceful intentions. They then drop their arms and go down to the canoes of their guests, where each one chooses the hammock that is nearest at hand (these being the beds in which they sleep) ; they then take them to their houses, and, hanging them in a place where their owners will know them, they receive the Indians as guests for a few days. After this the Indians return to their own country, repeating these visits every year at the same season. The daughters who are born from this intercourse are preserved and brought up by the Amazons themselves, as they are destined to inherit their valour, and the customs of the nation, but it is not so certain what they do with the sons. An Indian, who had gone with his father to this country when very young, stated that the boys were given to their fathers, when they returned in the following year. But others, and this account appears to be most probable, as it is most general, say that when the Amazons find that a baby is a male, they kill it. Time will discover the truth, and if these are the Amazons made famous by historians, there are treasures shut up in their territory, which would enrich the whole world. The mouth of this river, on which the Amazons live, is in $2\frac{1}{2}°$ of latitude.[1]

---

[1] This story of the existence of a race of Amazons is also believed by MM. de la Condamine and Humboldt. Sir R. Schomburgk, though he says that all the Caribs believe in the existence of a tribe of Amazons, treats the whole thing as a fable. Wallace suggests that Orellana and others might have mistaken the young men, with long hair, eardrops, and necklaces, for female warriors.

Mr. Southey, in his *History of Brazil*, discusses the whole question, and decides, with Acuña, Condamine, and Humboldt, in favour of the probability of their existence.

73.

The narrrowest part of the river.

Passing the mouth of this river, where the Amazons live, and descending the great stream for twenty-four leagues, another moderate sized river empties itself on the north side, called Vrixamina,[1] which comes out at that port where, as I before said, this great river narrows to a breadth of little more than a quarter of a league. Here a convenient position is presented, for planting two fortresses on each side, which would not only impede the passage of an enemy, but would also serve as custom houses, where all things might be registered, which were sent down this river of the Amazons, from Peru. From this point, which is more than three hundred and sixty leagues from the sea, we began to feel the tides, discerning the ebb and flow every day, though not so clearly as we did a few leagues lower down.

74.

River and tribe of the Tapajosos.

Forty leagues from this narrow part, on the south side, is the mouth of the great and beautiful river of the *Tapajosos*, taking the name from the tribe who live on its banks, which are well peopled with savages, living in a good land full of abundant supplies. These *Tapajosos* are a brave race, and are much feared by the surrounding nations, because they use so strong a poison in their arrows, that if once blood is drawn, death is sure to follow. For this reason the Portuguese themselves avoided any intercourse with them for some time, desiring to draw them into friendly relations.

However, they received us very well, and lodged us together in one of their villages, containing more than five hundred families, where they never ceased all day from barter-

---

[1] This is the *Trombetas* of modern maps.

ing fowls, ducks, hammocks, fish, flour, fruit, and other
things, with such confidence that women and children did
not avoid us ; offering, if we would leave our lands, and
come to settle there, to receive and serve us peacefully all
their lives.

75.

Oppression of the Portuguese.

The humble offers of these *Tapajosos* did not satisfy a set
of people so selfish as are those of these conquests, who only
undertake difficult enterprizes from a covetous desire to
obtain slaves, for which object the *Tapajosos* were placed in
a convenient position. Suspecting that this nation had many
slaves in their service, they treated them as rebels, and came
to attack them. This was going on when we arrived at the
fort of Destierro, where the people were assembled for this
inhuman work, and though, by the best means I could, I
tried, as I could not stop them, at least to induce them to
wait until they had received new orders from the King ; and
the Sargente Mayor and chief of all, who was Benito Maciel,
son of the governor, gave me his word that he would not
proceed with his intended work, until he had heard from
his father ; yet I had scarcely turned my back, when, with
as many troops as he could get, in a launch with a piece of
artillery, and other smaller vessels, he fell upon the Indians
suddenly with harsh war, when they desired peace. They sur-
rendered, however, with good will, as they had always offered to do, and submitted to all the Portuguese desired. The
latter ordered them to deliver up all their poisoned arrows,
which were the weapons they most dreaded. The unfortunate Indians obeyed at once ; and, when they were dis-
armed, the Portuguese collected them together like sheep, in
a strong enclosure, with a sufficient guard over them. They
then let loose the friendly Indians, each one of them being

an unchained devil for mischief, and in a short time they had gutted the village, without leaving a thing in it, and, as I was told by an eye-witness, cruelly abused the wives and daughters of the unfortunate captives, before their very eyes. Such acts were committed, that my informer, who is a veteran in these conquests, declared he would have left off buying slaves, and even have given the value of those he possessed, not to have beheld them.

The cruelty of the Portuguese, excited by the desire of these slaves, did not cease until they had obtained them. They threatened the captive Indians with fresh outrages if they did not produce their slaves, assuring them that if they obeyed, they should not only be free, but be treated with friendship, and supplied with tools and linen cloths, which they should receive in exchange.

What could the unfortunates do? themselves prisoners, their arms taken, their homes pillaged, their wives and children ill-treated; but yield to everything their oppressors desired? They offered to give up a thousand slaves whom, when they were attacked, they had placed in concealment; and not being able to find more than two hundred, they collected them and delivered them up, giving their words that the remainder should be found, and even offered their own children as slaves.

All these were sent down to Marañon and Para, and I saw them myself. The Portuguese, delighted with their captures, presently prepared for others on a larger scale, in another region more inland, where doubtless the cruelties will be greater, because fewer persons of valour accompany the expedition, to superintend the conduct of the rest. Thus the river is now in such a disturbed state that when your Majesty desires to restore peace, there will be much difficulty, though, if it had been in the state I left it, that object might have been effected with very little trouble.

Such are the conquests of Para, such the method by which

they are retained, and such the most just cause for which the
conquerors are forced to endure so much suffering, without
having even a loaf of bread to eat. If it were not for the
services they have performed for both Majesties divine and
human, in bravely resisting the Dutch enemy whom they
have vanquished several times in this land, our Lord would
have destroyed them utterly.

Returning, however, to the subject of the *Tapajosos*, and
to the famous river which bathes the shores of their country ;
I must relate that it is of such depth, from the mouth to a
distance of many leagues, that in times past an English ship
of great burden ascended it, those people intending to make a
settlement in this province, and to prepare harvests of tobacco.
They offered the natives advantageous terms, but the latter
suddenly attacked the English and would accept no other,
than the killing of all the strangers they could get into their
hands, and the seizure of their arms, which they retain to
to this day. They forced them to depart from the land much
quicker than they had come, the people who remained in the
ship declining another similar encounter, (which would have
destroyed them all), by making sail.[1]

[1] The English appear to have made several attempts to settle on the
banks of the Amazons. In 1615 Caldeira, the Portuguese founder of
Para, was informed by the Indians, that there was a colony of English,
with their wives and children, one hundred and fifty leagues up the
river ; and both Dutch and English continually sent vessels to those
parts, to form settlements for cultivating tobacco. In 1630 the English
endeavoured to settle on the island of Tocujos, and about two hundred
fortified themselves on the island of Felipe, at the mouth of the Amazons.
Coelho, the governor of Para, sent a force against them under Jacome
de Noronha, who massacred them all, and razed their fort. Another
English party, under one Roger Frere, was overpowered and cut to
pieces by Coelho's son. The Portuguese perpetrated atrocious cruelties
on these occasions.

76.

Curupatuba.

At a distance of a little more than forty leagues from the mouth of this river of the *Tapajosos*, is that of Curupatuba, which is on the north side of the Amazons, and gives a name to the first settlement or village which the Portuguese hold in peace, and subject to their crown. This river does not appear to be very large, but is rich in treasures, if the natives did not deceive us. They affirm that, after ascending by this river, which they call Yriquiriqui, for six days, a great quantity of gold is found, which they gather on the shores of a small rivulet, which bathes the skirts of a moderate sized hill, called Yaguaracu. They also say that near this hill there is another place, the name of which is Picuru; whence they have often taken another metal, harder than gold and of a white colour, which is doubtless silver, and of which they formerly made axes and knives, but finding they were no use, and that they were soon notched, they made no more of them. In the same district there are two hills, the one, according to the signs made by the Indians, being of sulphur; while of the other, which is called Paraguaxo, they assured us, that when the sun shone on it, and also at night, it glitters so as to appear enamelled with rich jewels, while from time to time it resounds with great noises, a certain sign that stones of much value are enclosed within it.

77.

The river Ginipape.

The river Ginipape, according to common report, does not promise less treasure. It falls into the river of Amazons on the north side, sixty leagues below the village of Curupatuba. The Indians say so much of the quantities of gold that might be collected on its banks, that, if all they say is true, this river would leave the most famous in Peru far behind. The territory bathed by this river belongs to the captaincy of Benito Maciel the father, governor of Maranon, a province which is larger than all Spain put together, and there are many notices of mines in it. The greater part of it consists of good soil, fit to produce more fruits and other provisions than any other part of this immense river of the Amazons.

All this territory, on the north side, contains vast provinces of Indians, and, what is of more consequence, it encloses, within its jurisdiction, the famous and extensive land of Tucujù, so much coveted, and so often occupied, though to their own damage, by the Dutch enemies, who, recognizing in it the greatest advantages in the world for enriching its inhabitants, are never able to forget it. It is not only suitable for great harvests of tobacco, capable of sustaining, better than any of the other discoveries, numerous sugar estates, and of producing all kinds of provisions ; but it also has excellent plains, which would supply pasture for innumerable flocks and herds.

In this captaincy, six leagues from the mouth of the Ginipape, there is a fort belonging to the Portuguese, which they call "El Destierro", with a garrison of thirty soldiers and some pieces of artillery, which are useless for defending the river, but merely serve to keep up the authority of the captaincy, and to awe the vanquished Indians. Benito Maciel abandoned this fort, with the consent of the governor of Curupa, which is thirty-six leagues lower down, and where he was established for many years in a very good position ; as the ships of the enemy usually come to reconnoitre, in that direction.

78.

The river Paranaiba.

Ten leagues below the river Ginipape, on the south side,

is the mouth of a very beautiful and mighty river, two leagues in breadth. The natives call it Paranaiba, and there are some settlements of friendly Indians on its banks, who, making a treaty with the Portuguese on their first arrival, still obey their orders. More in the interior there are many other tribes, of whom we did not obtain any satisfactory information.

79.

Of the river Pacaxa.

Two leagues below the river Ginipape, the river of the Amazons begins to divide itself into great arms, which form a multitude of islands, continuing down to the place where it discharges itself into the ocean. All these islands are peopled by different tribes, speaking various dialects, though most of them understand the " *lingoa Geral* ". These Indians are so numerous that it would be necessary to write a new history, to describe them fully. I will, however, enumerate some of the best known, such as the *Tapuyas, Anaxiases, Mayanases, Engaïbas, Bocas, Juanes*, and the valiant *Pacaxàs*, who have their habitations on the banks of the river from which they take their name, which empties itself into the Amazons eighty leagues from the Paranaiba, and on the same side. These islands are so full, both of villages and inhabitants, according to the Portuguese, that no other part of the river is equal to them.

80.

The settlement of Conmutà.

Forty leagues from the Pacaxà is situated the village of Conmutà, which, in times past, was very famous in these conquests, as much for the number of its inhabitants, as for being the place where they usually collected their vessels, when they were about to make an inroad. But now there are left neither people, all having removed to other lands, nor provisions, there being no one to cultivate the ground, nor anything besides the ancient site, and a few natives. It is a good position, and, with its pleasant climate and beautiful view, seems to drink in loveliness, and offers advantages to any one wishing to settle there.

81.

The river of the Tocantins.

Near Conmuta is the mouth of the river of the Tocantins, which has the name of being rich, and apparently with reason, though no one has seen its treasure, except a Frenchman, who, when these coasts were peopled with settlers, loaded ships with the earth which he took from its banks, to take advantage of its riches in his own land, without ever daring to shew his treasures to the barbarians who inhabit that country, fearing that if they should find out its real value, they would doubtless defend it with their arms, that they might not be dispossessed of such riches. Certain Portuguese soldiers, with a priest in their company, arrived in search of new conquests at the sources of this river, by skirting the Cordilleras; and, wishing to navigate its downward course to the end, they fell into the hands of the Tocantins; in whose possession, not many years ago, the chalice was found with which the good father said mass to them, in their journeys.

82.

Parà.

Thirty leagues from Conmutà is the site of the fortress of Gran Parà, peopled and governed by the Portuguese. Here there is a Capitan Mayor, who is superior to all the officers

of this captaincy, and to whom all the other captains of
infantry, who usually assist with their companies for the
defence of this place, are subject; while they, as well as the
Capitan Mayor, obey the governor of Marañon, who resides
more than one hundred and thirty leagues off, on the
coast of Brazil.   From this arrangement great inconvenience
arises in Para; and if this river were peopled, the province would necessarily remain lord of it, as one who holds
in his hand the key of all.   Though it is true that, in
the opinion of many, the site on which it is now built is
not the best that could have been chosen; it would be easy,
if this discovery should be followed up, to remove it to the
Island of the Sun, fourteen leagues nearer the sea, a place on
which every one has his eye, owing to the conveniences
it offers for human life, both on account of the fertility and
capability of the soil to sustain people, and for the conveni-
ence of vessels anchoring off it.   Vessels can lie in a cove, safe
from all danger, as long as they may desire; and when they
get under weigh, with the first high tide, they would be left
clear of all the arms of the river, which make these ports
dangerous; and this is no small advantage.

This island is more than ten leagues round, with good
water, plenty of fish both from sea and river, a great multitude of crabs, the ordinary food of the poor people; and it is
now the principal place to which the people of Para usually
resort, to hunt the beasts which are necessary for their sustenance.

83.

The river of the Amazons enters the sea.

Twenty leagues from the Island of the Sun, under the
equinoctial line, spread out into eighty-four mouths, having
the Zaparará on the south side, and the north cape opposite;
the largest sea of fresh water, that has been discovered,

empties itself into the ocean ; the most powerful river in the whole world, the phœnix of rivers, the true Marañon so longed for and never attained by the people of Peru, the ancient Orellana, and to sum up all at once, the great river of the Amazons.

After having bathed with its waters a distance of thirteen hundred and fifty-six leagues of longitude, after sustaining on its banks an infinite number of barbarous tribes, after fertilizing vast territories, and after having passed through the centre of Peru, and, like a principal channel, collected the largest and richest of all its affluents, it renders its tribute to the ocean.

Such is the sum of the new discovery of this great river, which excludes no one from its vast treasures, but rewards all who wish to take advantage of them. To the poor it offers sustenance, to the labourer a reward for his work, to the merchant employment, to the soldier opportunities to display his valour, to the rich an increase to his wealth, to the noble honours, to the powerful estates, and to the King himself a new empire.

But those who are most interested in this discovery, are the zealous men who seek the honour of God, and the good of souls ; for a great multitude of them are here waiting for faithful ministers of the Holy Gospel, that, by its brightness, they may dispel the shadow of death in which these miserable people have lain for so long a time. No one need excuse himself from this undertaking, for there is a field for all ; this new vineyard will always require fresh and zealous labourers to cultivate it, until it is made entirely subject to the keys of the Roman church.

For this object our great and catholic King, Philip IV, whom may God preserve many happy years, will doubtless assist in the support of these ministers, with the liberality which distinguishes him in temporal things; while His Holiness our very holy father Urban VIII, as present father and

head of the church, will show himself no less liberal and
benignant in spiritual things : holding it to be a great
saying that in his time a wide door was opened,
to bring into the fold of the church, at
one time, more numerous and more
populous nations, than have
been met with since the
first discovery of
America.

LAUS   DEO   VIRGINIQUE   MATRI.

MEMORIAL

PRESENTED TO THE ROYAL COUNCIL OF THE
INDIES, ON THE SUBJECT OF THE ABOVE DIS-
COVERY, AFTER THE REBELLION OF
THE PORTUGUESE.

A.D. 1641.

SIRE,

Cristoval de Acuña, a priest of the company of Jesus, who
proceeded, by order of your Majesty, to the discovery of the
great river of the Amazons; always anxious for the greater
increase of your royal crown, and fearful that less favourable
circumstances, seen at our own doors, may strangle and impede
the advance of your gracious service : declares that though
it is true that the principal opening of that newly-discovered
world, by which it might most easily be entered, to enjoy
the advantages and the rich fruits which it freely offers, is
the mouth where the river empties itself into the ocean, which
is now subject to the Portuguese, and therefore less suitable, at
present, to be used; yet this ought not to induce your Majesty,
either to desist from, or to delay the occupation of this
great river, seeing that with greater ease, and much less. expense, it may be entered by the province of Quito, in the
kingdom of Peru, by the same road that he and his companions descended it.   By this means good service will doubtless be done for God our Lord, and for your Majesty; and
many inconveniences will be got rid of; . . . . .   This
may easily be effected, without great expense to the royal

treasury, by merely sending an order to the Audience of
Quito, to organize expeditions to the rivers which drain their
province, composed of some of the many persons who are
ready to undertake these conquests, solely for the sake of
the advantages to be gained; such as the charge over
Indians, the acquirement of land, of offices, and the like. At
the same time the spiritual part should be committed to
priests of the company of Jesus, to have charge of the conversion and education of the Indians; their institution being
for these objects, and they having no small title to this particular discovery. For their sons have not only dispelled, at
the price of much labour and treasure, the shades from a
new and extensive empire, which, bathed by this great river,
offers increased riches to the royal crown of your Majesty;
but they have also acquired the right of possession, for the last
forty years, through the blood of the good father Rafael Ferrer, who was killed by the natives, to whom he preached, near
the sources of this river. Continuing the possession of this
right, the fathers of the company, some years ago, began to
instruct the natives on the Santiago de las Montañas, and the
other rivers of this new conquest; but to proceed with this
work it will be necessary to send new labourers from
Europe to this province of Quito, to aid them in so plentiful a
harvest.

Doubtless your Majesty will grant aid, with your unfail-
ing piety, and with the liberality which the extreme necessity of these numerous tribes requires:—from which will
result the following advantages.

First, and that which is always in the christian bosom of
your Majesty, it will give, without further delay, a beginning to the conversion of a new world of infidels, who now
lie miserable in the shadow of death; a work of such service
to God, that none could be offered which would please Him
more, and such that it will of necessity establish the perpe-
tuity of the crown of your Majesty.

Second. It will save the great outlay which must be made, if these conquests were undertaken, as was intended, by the mouth of the river; in conveying soldiers, supplying vessels, collecting arms and ammunition, and providing all requisites to form new settlements, which will doubtless be numerous. All these things will be avoided, if this conquest is commenced by way of Quito, seeing that those to whom it would be entrusted, would cheerfully incur the expense; and would only require, for the religious work, labourers and apt ministers of the gospel, whom your Majesty would send from Spain,—considering the extreme want of them, in those parts.

Third. Your Majesty will at length enjoy and possess the territory which all the Kings your predecessors, from the time of the emperor Charles V (the worthy great grandfather of your Majesty), have desired, and, with no small outlay and diligence, have attempted to subject to the royal crown. For this purpose, in the year 1549, the same emperor Charles V ordered three ships, with the necessary men and stores, to be given to Francisco de Orellana, that he might take possession of this great river of the Amazons (which the same man had navigated nine years before), with a view to the many advantages which were expected from the enterprize: but misery, and the death of nearly all the soldiers, forced them to retreat to Margarita, having been reduced to one small vessel. Here, owing to this mischance, ended the hopes of the good which would have accrued to Spain, if they had met with better fortune. Your Majesty, from the beginning of your reign,—and may it last many most happy years,—has committed the execution of this discovery to various persons, as is shown by the royal orders, drawn up with this object, in the years 1621, 26, and 34.

That of 1621, was dispatched to the Royal Audience of Quito, that they might arrange the conditions on which the said discovery might be undertaken, with Sargente

18

Mayor Vincente de Reyes Villalobos, captain general and governor, at that time, of Quijos, in the jurisdiction of Quito ; but it never took effect, as a successor arrived to supersede him. That of 1626 was sent to Benito Maciel, the father,[1] a native of Portugal, that he might commence the discovery by way of the provinces of Marañon, and Gran Parà, which are at the mouth of this river, but this also came to nothing, as he was ordered to go to the war of Pernambuco. That of 1634 was sent to Francisco Coello de Caravallo, a Portuguese, and then governor of Marañon and Para, with express orders that, with all dispatch, he should send trust-worthy persons, and if necessary he should go himself, to commence, by those parts, the discovery which was so much desired : but neither did this take effect. Now, however, your desires will be happily gratified, and henceforth greater benefits will each day be seen to arise, from that which our ardent desires promise.

Fourth. By this means the door will be opened, so that those in Peru can send down their treasures by the current of this river, and pay the same duties which they now con-tribute to your Majesty's revenue at Carthagena, while they will avoid the risk of pirates, who almost always frequent those parts.

Fifth. It will impede the communication and intercourse which the Portuguese, in the mouth of this river, desire so much to establish with those of their nation in Peru, which in these times would be very prejudicial. They would in no wise dare to attempt this, if they presently became aware that their evil intentions had been anticipated, and that the entrances were occupied. That the Portuguese of this coast of Marañon and Para intend to attempt this communication, I can positively affirm, and, having heard it discussed among them many times, I can assert it to be an undoubted fact.

---

[1] As distinguished from Maciel, the son, who rivalled his father, in atrocious cruelty to the unhappy Indians.

Sixth. In reducing to obedience to your Majesty, the principal tribes of this river, and especially those who inhabit its banks and islands, who are very warlike, and would valorously assist those whom they had once acknowledged as their masters, there would be little or no resistance, owing to the many wars which they continually wage amongst themselves; so that one being made subject, the others would be easily reduced. Thus, by descending the river, all others who, with bad titles, now possess its banks, may be driven out at its mouth; and the very rich fruits, and that which we hope from them, which only requires to be seen to be enjoyed, may be secured by this road. In this manner, as we hope, a bridle will shortly be put on the insolence of the Portuguese, and they will be driven from the mouth of this river, from which place they now prosecute their conquests. This project having been already commenced by the way of Quito, it will thus be made more easy, and will necessitate less outlay, to bring it to a successful termination.

Seventh. It ought here to be noticed particularly, that the Indians in all Peru, and in almost all the discovered country, especially where there are mines, or other important works, which depend on their personal labour, are rapidly diminishing, as we are able to affirm, who have been in those parts; and each day they decrease in such a way that, in a few years, they will be extinct, or at least so reduced, that the many interests which depend on their existence will suffer great damage. Your Majesty assuredly ought to interfere in time, and remedy this evil, by every possible means, which those cannot but apprehend who take deep interest in the conquest and conversion of this new world, where the natives who inhabit it are so numerous, that they might people afresh the uninhabited parts of Peru. If they could be subjected to the yoke of the holy Evangelists, and, with a general peace, the continual wars which are now consuming them might cease, they would increase in such a way that, breaking the narrow limits which now enclose them, they would spread themselves over wider kingdoms. When, by their means alone, the mines, and the other riches, which the fertility of the soil offers in those countries, are made productive; another new Peru would be ready for occupation, and with greater facility than was found in the first conquest.

Eighth. If the Portuguese who are in the mouth of this river (which may be fairly presumed, from their small amount of Christianity, and less of loyalty) should desire, with the aid of some warlike tribes which are subject to them, to penetrate by the river as far as Peru, or the new kingdom of Granada; though it is true that in some parts they would meet with resistance, yet in many others there would be very little, as there are few people in the towns; and, in short, these disloyal vassals of your Majesty would pillage those lands, and cause very great damage. If, on the other hand, the people of Brazil, united with the Hollanders, should attempt the like audacity, it is clear that much care is required to oppose them. The Hollanders have desired possession of these countries for many years; and it is quite certain that they covet the lordship of this great river, as Juan Laeth,[1] a Dutch author, did not hesitate to publish in a book entitled *Utriusque Americæ*, which appeared in the year 1633. In the 16th book, 15th chapter, are these words :—" Verum tamen, tan hi (scilicet Angli et Hiberni) quam nostri (scilicet Belgi) a Portugalis, e Para venientibus, in opinato oppressi et fugati, non leve damnum fuerunt perpessi ad quod referciendum et acceptas injurias

---

[1] John de Laeth was also the author of a little book, in Latin, called *Hispania, sive de Regis Hispaniæ Regnis et opibus Commentarius ;"* published in 1629, and dedicated to Sir Edward Powell, Bart., containing a full description of Spain and its dependencies, of Portugal, and of the Royal families and peerages of both countries.

vindicandas majori conatu et viribus, institutum repetere, et urgere fatigant."

And in the same book, 2nd chapter, he says :—" Post annum autem 1615 Portugali ad Paræripam, qui sine dubio hujus magni fluminis ramus est, cœperunt incolere, ut ante diximus, et animum ad cætera fortè adjicient, nisi ab Anglis et Belgis nostris impediantur."

From these passages it is clear, that the reason the Hollanders have not attempted the conquest of this great river of the Amazons, is because they had not the power, and not because they wanted the desire, and the knowledge of how much there was to gain in its execution. Your Majesty should prevent such great damage, which this your faithful subject . . . . . ,[1] and not permit the possibility of some day having to lament over losses, in that land which now offers increasing advantages.

Finally, if in future the passages to this great river are subjected and explored, and the entrances which lead to them from all parts of Peru are discovered ; and if it is found how much these countries will enrich Spain ; I shall glory in having done one of the greatest and most advantageous services to your Majesty, that a subject could hope to do ; by which not only will a great sum of money be saved, which is unavoidably expended, while the passage by way of Panama and Carthagena continues to be used, but which would be economized by this route (which is by water, and with the help of the currents would be very easy) ; but also (which is a thing of more importance), it will secure your Majesty's fleets from the fear of pirates, and will place your treasure in safety, at least until it reaches Para : whence in twenty-four days, on the high sea, galleons built on the same river may at all times reach Spain. Moreover an enemy could not watch the entrance, because the coast of Para is such that

---

[1] Illegible.

ships, outside the river, cannot resist the force of the current for two days together.

Thus the continual anxiety which is every day caused, by the long and dangerous voyage by way of Carthagena, would cease to exist.

All these things might be remedied, Sire, by the proposals contained in this Memorial; to which I will only add, that the chief part of the success of this undertaking depends on the celerity of its execution: and if I can be of any use in furthering it, I shall always be at the feet of your Majesty.

FINIS.

A LIST

OF

THE PRINCIPAL TRIBES

OF THE

VALLEY OF THE AMAZONS.

A LIST

OF

THE   PRINCIPAL   TRIBES

OF THE

VALLEY   OF   THE   AMAZONS.

THE following alphabetical list is intended to contain every tribe
on the main stream of the great river of the Amazons, and on its
Peruvian and Ecuadorian tributaries, including all that are mentioned in this volume; and, to that extent, I believe it to be nearly
complete. A great number of tribes, inhabiting the "Gran Chacu,"
and the banks of the Brazilian rivers, will also be found; and many
hundreds which wander along the banks of the Tapajos, Xingu,
Tocantins, and other great Brazilian streams, might have been added,
had they been connected with the subject of the present volume.

I have inserted short notices of the more important tribes, taken
from various sources; and a few words of explanation will make
this list, which I trust will be found useful for purposes of reference in connexion with the voyages of Orellana and Acuña, suffi-
ciently clear.

It is essential, in the first place, to pay attention to the *date*
when each authority wrote; because many of the names of tribes
may since have disappeared, either from their having been changed,
or from the tribe having merged into some other larger tribe, or
from its having entirely disappeared, and become extinct. For
this purpose the following list of authorities, referred to in the list,
with the time when each wrote, will be necessary :

Garcilasso de la Vega (" Commentarios Reales "), 1609-16.

Antonio de Herrera(" Hist. General de las Indias," etc.), 1601-15.

Cristoval de Acuña (" Nuevo Descubrimiento del Rio de las Amazonas), 1639.

Manuel Rodriguez (" Amazonas y Marañon"), 1684.

Samuel Fritz's Map, published at Quito, 1707.

Stocklein's Reise-Beschreibungen, 1726.

Lozano's Descripcion del " Gran Chacu", 1733.

La Condamine's Voyage, 1737.

Ribeiro, (" from Southey's History of Brazil, vol. iii."), 1774.

Dobrizhoffer's History of the Abipones, 1784.

Velasco's Historia del Reino de Quito, 1789.

" Mercurio Peruano", 1791-95.

Von Martius and Spix, Voyage up the Amazons, 1820.

Maw's Voyage down the Huallaga and Amazons, 1827.

Poeppig's Voyage down the Huallaga, 1830.

Smyth's Journey from Lima to Para, 1835.

General Miller's Journeys to Sta. Anna and Paucartambo, 1835.

Castlenau's expedition, 1847.

Herndon's and Gibbon's " Valley of the Amazon", 1852.

Wallace's Travels on the Amazon and Rio Negro, 1853.

Villavicencio's Geografia del Ecuador, 1858,

Commercio de Lima ⎱ modern newspapers.
Heraldo de Lima   ⎰

Velasco has given the fullest list of Indians of the Marañon missions ; and he divided the period during which the wild tribes were preached to by the Jesuits, into three missionary epochs,—namely

1st, from 1638 to 1683 ;

2nd, from 1683 to 1727 ;

3rd, from 1727 to 1768.

This includes a period of one hundred and thirty years ; and I have, therefore, thought it of importance to notice during which of these epochs any tribe, mentioned by Velasco, was preached to by the missionaries ; as the names of many of them have now disappeared.

The references to Orellana and Acuña, refer to the pages of this volume.

Many of the larger tribes, extending their wanderings over vast tracts of country, are divided into numerous branches, each with a distinct name; and I have inserted the branches into the list, with a reference to their parent tribes.

ABACTIS. A tribe of the river Madeira. *Acuña*, p. 117.

ABIGIRAS, AVIJIRAS, AUXIRAS, or ABIRAS. A tribe of the rivers Napo, and Marañon; marked on Fritz's map (1707), near the banks of the Napo. They were preached to between 1638 and 1683, and they murdered Father Pedro Suarez in 1667. They wander in the forests to the south of the *Encabellados* (which see). *M. Rodriguez; Velasco; Acuña,* p. 94; *Fritz's map.*

At the present day, the *Avijiras* are met with on the south side of the Napo, near its mouth. They have the same language and customs as the *Iquitos*. They live by fishing, and the chace. *Villavicencio,* p. 173.

ABIPONES, or CALLAGAES, a large tribe of the "Gran Chacu"; on the banks of the Paraguay, Bermejo, and Rio Grande (the latter being a tributary of the Mamorè). I have therefore included these Indians, and several other tribes of the Chacu, in this list of Indian tribes of the Amazonian valley.

The Abipones have no fixed abode, nor any boundaries; they roam extensively in every direction. In the seventeenth century their homes were on the northern shore of the river Bermejo; but they removed to avoid the war carried on by the Spaniards of Salta, against the Indians of the Chacu; and settled in a valley further to the south. At the beginning of this century their wanderings extended from the Bermejo to the Paraguay; whence they made frequent desolating incursions into the country settled by the Spaniards. They are well formed, and have handsome features, black eyes, and aquiline noses. In symmetry of shape they yield to no other nation in America. They have thick, raven black hair, and no beards. As soon as they wake in the morning, the Abiponian women, sitting on the ground, dress, twist, and tie their husbands' hair. They pluck out their hair from the forehead to the crown of the head, accounting this baldness as a religious mark of their nation. The women have their faces, breasts, and arms covered with black figures of various shapes; thorns being used as pencils, and ashes mixed with blood, for paint. The *Abipones* also pierce their lips and ears.

They are taught to swim before they can walk, and no little child is without his bow and arrow. They live on game, generally roasted. In Dobrizhoffer's time they did not number more than five thousand people; having been thinned by intestine feuds, small-pox, and the cruelty of mothers towards their offspring. They are subdivided into hordes, each commanded by a chief called "Nelareyrat"; but these chiefs have little authority, except in time of war.

Dobrizhoffer devotes two chapters to a very interesting account of the language of the *Abipones*.

Their chief weapons are the bow and spear, the latter of great length; which they fix at the threshold of their huts. Their bow strings are made of the entrails of foxes; and their quivers are made of rushes, adorned with woollen threads of various colours. Their arrows are made of wood, and sometimes of bone. In battle they use a kind of armour, made of the hide of a tapir, over which a jaguar skin is sewn. Their victories are celebrated by songs, dancing, and drinking parties. In 1641 they first became possessed of horses, and were soon very dexterous in the management of them. The Jesuits established some mission villages amongst these Indians. *Dobrizhoffer's Abipones.*

The Abipones are excellent swimmers, of tall stature, and they paint their faces and bodies, and hang rings on their lower lips.

For five months in the year, when the floods are out, they live on islands, or even in trees. When a mother is brought to bed with a child, the father also takes to his bed for some days. They do not bring up more than two children in a family, the others being killed to save trouble. *Lozano*, p. 90.

ABIRAS (see *Abigiras*).

ACAMORIS. A branch of the *Simigaes* (which see). *Velasco.*

ACANEOS. A branch of the *Aguaricos* (which see).

ACHOUARIS. A tribe of the river Teffé. *Ribeiro.*

ACHUALES. A branch of the *Jeberos* (which see). *Villavicencio.*

AGAPICOS. A branch of the *Jeberos* (which see). *Villavicencio.*

AGOYAS. A tribe of the " Gran Chacu." *Lozano*.

AGUANOS. A tribe of the Huallaga, and Marañon. The men have beards, and are very fierce; the women have fair hair, like Flemings. *M. Rodriguez*.

AGUANACOS. A branch of the *Chepeos* (which see). *M. Rodriguez ; Velasco*.

AGUARICOS. A tribe on a river of the same name, a tributary of the Napo. *Velasco*.

AGUARUNAS. A powerful and encroaching modern tribe, on the Marañon. *Heraldo de Lima*.

AGUAS. (Same as *Omaguas*.)

AGUAYRAS. A tribe of the Rio Negro. *Acuña*, p. 110.

AGUILOTES. A tribe of " Gran Chacu." *Lozano*.

AICORES. A branch of the *Iquitos* (which see). *Velasco*.

AISUARIS. A tribe of the Marañon, 1683-1727. *Velasco*.

AJUANAS or CHAMICURAS, a tribe of the Pampa del Sacra-mento, living one day's journey east of Laguna ; in a large village called Chamicura. *Smyth*, p. 204.

ALABONOS. A branch of the *Yameos* (which see). *Velasco*.

AMAJUACAS. A tribe of the Ucayali, next to the *Remos* (which see), and extending as far as the Vuelta del Diablo. They have been repeatedly converted to Christianity, but have more than once murdered their priests, and returned to their barbarous state. From their apparently quiet and docile manner, the missionaries conceived great hopes of them, but they found themselves most cruelly deceived. They are short and have beards. They are hunters, and live in the interior, seldom coming down to the river. *Smyth*, p. 232 ; *Herndon*, p. 199.

AMAONAS, a branch of the *Yameos* (which see). *Velasco*.

AMAZONS, a tribe of female warriors. *Orellana*, p. 34; *Acuña*, p. 122.

AMULALAES, a tribe of the " Gran Chacu." *Lozano*, p. 51.

ANAXIASES, a tribe of the Pacaxa river. *Acuña*, p. 130.

ANAMARIS, a tribe of the Madeira river. *Acuña*, p. 117.

ANCUTERES. A branch of the *Encabellados* (which see) *Velasco*.

ANDOAS. A tribe of the Marañon, (see *Muratos*). Preached to from 1683 to 1727. They are placed, on Fritz's map (1707) between the rivers Pastaza and Tigre. According to Villavicencio they are a branch of the *Zaparos*. There is a small village, called Andoas, on the Pastaza. *Velasco, Samuel Fritz, Villavicencio*.

ANDURAS. A tribe of the Araganatuba. *Acuña*, p. 105.

ANGUTERAS. A tribe on the east bank of the Napo, below the junction of the Aguarico, according to Villaviencio, a branch of the *Putumayus*. They cultivate the ground. *Villavicencio*.

ANJENGUACAS. A branch of the *Campas* (which see). *Velasco*.

ANTIS. A great and powerful tribe, in the forests east of Cuzco ; especially in and near the valleys of Santa Anna and Laris. They are mentioned in the ancient Incarial Drama of Ollantay ; and the eastern division of the Empire of the Incas was called, after them, *Anti-suyu*. *G. de la Vega*, lib. ii, cap. ii.

They are the same as the *Campas*. They are renowned for their ferocity, and are said to be cannibals. They wear a long robe, secured round the waist, with a hole for the head, and two others for the arms. Their long hair hangs down over their shoulders, and the beak of the toucan, or a bunch of feathers, is suspended as an ornament round their necks. Their arms consist of clubs, bows and arrows.

The *Antis* or *Campas*, are identical with, or closely allied to the *Chunchos* (which see). They wander in the forests, about the head waters of the Ucayali, and its tributaries. *Castelnau*, iv. p, 290-1.

The *Antis* have good features, and pleasant countenances. They live in huts, and wear a cotton robe, reaching to the heels. They occupy the banks of the Ucayali, forty leagues below Santa Anna. *General Miller, R. G. S. Journal*, vi.

ANTIVES. A branch of the *Putumayus*, (which see) *Velasco*.

AOMAGUAS. Same as the *Omaguas*, (which see) *Orellana*, p. 27.

APANTOS. The second tribe, from the mouth of the river Cunuris, the head waters of which were said to be occupied by the Amazons. *Acuña*, p. 122.

APARIA. An Indian chief, in whose territory Orellana built his brigantine. The Spaniards left the village of Aparia on the 4th of April, and reached the mouth of the Putumayu on the 12th of May, going down stream. *Aparia* was possibly the name of a tribe, but I have not met with it elsewhere. *Orellana*, p. 27.

APERAS. A tribe of the Amazons, below the mouth of the Madeira. *Acuña*, p. 117.

APIACAS. A tribe of the "Gran Chacu". *Lozano*.

ARAGUANAYNAS, (see *Carabayanas*).

ARAYCUS, (see *Uaraycus*).

ARAZAS. A branch of the *Simigaes*, (which see) *Velasco*.

ARDAS. A branch of *Yameos* (which see) between the rivers Napo and Nanay. *Velasco, Villavicencio*.

AREKAINAS. A tribe on the Rio Negro; and on the upper waters of some of its tributaries. They make war against other tribes, to obtain prisoners, for food. In their religious ideas they resemble the *Uaupés* (see *Uaupés*). *Wallace*, p. 508.

ARIQUENAS; according to Von Spix, a tribe of the Putumayu; probably the same as the *Arekainas*. *Spix und Martius*, iii, p. 1136.

ARUBAQUIS. Marked on Fritz's map (1707) near the north side of the Amazons, and below the mouth of the Rio Negro.

ATAGUATES. A tribe of the Marañon, preached to between 1638 and 1683. *M. Rodriguez, Velasco*.

ATUAIS. A tribe on the Putumayu. *Acuña*, p. 99.

ATURIARIS. A tribe on the Araganatuba. *Acuña*, p. 105.

AUNARES. A branch of the *Ugiaras* (which see) *Velasco*.

AUXIRAS or AVIJIRAS (see *Abigiras*).

AVANATEOS. A tribe marked on Fritz's map (1707) between the rivers Ucayali and Yavari.

AVIJIRAS, (see *Abigiras*).

AYACARES. A branch of the *Iquitos* (which see). *Velasco*.

BARBUDOS (see *Mayorunas*).

BAURES. A tribe near the Itenez, to the eastward of the territory of the *Moxos   Baraza, in " Reise Beschreibungen."*

BECABAS. A tribe on the Napo, a branch of the *Aguaricos* (which see), *Acuña*, p. 94., *Velasco*.

BETOCUROS. A branch of the *Papaguas*, (which see) *Velasco*.

BILELAS. A tribe of the " Gran Chacu". *Lozano*.

BLANCOS. A branch of the *Iquitos*. *Velasco*.

BOCAS. A tribe on the river Pacaxa. *Acuña*, p. 130.

BURAIS. A tribe on the Amazons, below the mouth of the Madeira. *Acuña*, p. 117.

BUSQUIPANES. (see *Capanahuas*).

CACHICUARAS. A tribe on the south side of the Amazons, evidently the same as the *Cuchiguaras*. *Acuña*, p. 55.

CAGUARAUS. A tribe of the Araganatuba. *Acuña*, p.105.

CAHUACHES. A branch of the *Jeveros* (which see). *Velasco*.

CAHUAMARES, (same as the *Cahuaches*).

CAHUAYAPITIS. A tribe of the Rio Negro. *Acuña*, p. 110.

CALLISECAS, (see *Cashibos*).

CAMAVOS. A tribe of the Marañon, preached to between 1683 and 1727. *Velasco*.

CAMBEBAS, (see *Omaguas*).

CAMPAS, (see *Antis*). They are said by Velasco to be descended from Inca Indians. They are marked on Fritz's map (1707) near the head waters of the Ucayali.

CAMPEVAS, (see *Omaguas*).

CANAMARIES. A tribe of the river Jurua. *Spix u. Martius*, iii, p. 1183.

CANIZUARIS. A tribe of the Rio Negro. *Acuña*, p. 110.

CAPANAHUAS. A tribe on the Ucayali, between the *Sencis* and the *Mayorunas*, with whom they are always at war. They go quite naked, and are said to be a bold race; but they have no canoes, and are not numerous, consequently not much feared.

Dr. Girbal made two unsuccessful expeditions from Sarayacu, in search of them, in the early part of 1793. They are marked on

Fritz's map (1797) between the rivers Ucayali and Yavari. *Mercurio Peruano*, 1794, No. 381 ; *Smyth*, p. 225; *Fritz's map*.

CARABUYANAS. A tribe of the Amazons, below the mouth of the Basururu, a branch of the Japura. They are divided into the following branches :—

Caraguanas	Quererús	Quinarupianas	Yaribarus
Pocoanas	Cotocarianas	Tuinamaynas	Yarucaguacas
Vrayaris	Moacaranas	Araguanaynas	Cumaruruayanas
Masucaruanas	Qrorupianas	Mariguyanas	Curuanaris.

They used the bow and arrow, and had iron tools obtained from other tribes, who communicated with the Dutch in Guiana. *Acuña*, p. 108.

CARAGUANAS (see *Carabuyanas*).

CARAPACHES (see *Cashibos*).

CARAPANAS. A tribe of the Rio Negro, and a branch of the larger tribe of *Uaupés* (which see). *Acuña*, p. 110.

CARCANAS. A race of dwarfs on the Jurua. *Castelnau*. (See *Cauanas*).

CARIPUNAS. A tribe on the Madeira, near the falls. They swell themselves out by eating earth, but are otherwise strong and healthy. The men wear beads of hard wood round their necks, and bands tight round the arms and ankles. They are not numerous. (See the account of them, given by Acuña.) *Acuña*, p. 107; *Gibbon*, p. 295. According to Spix, they are met with on the river Jurua, iii, p. 1183.

A chief of this name is mentioned by Orellana, near the mouth of the Amazons. *Orellana*, p. 36. Marked in Fritz's map (1707) on the Rio Branco.

CASHIBOS, or CALLISECAS, or CARAPACHES. A tribe on the west side of the Ucayali, as far as the head waters of the rivers Pisqui and Aguatya. In 1651 Father Cavallero resided some time in their country, but the priests left there by him were murdered. In 1661 they drove Father Tineo away, and in 1704 they killed and ate Father Geronimo de los Rios. In 1744 they joined Juan Santos, and destroyed all the missions of the Cerro de la Sal.

20

No one dare venture among them; and they live scattered about in the forests, like wild beasts. The greatest number of them live on the Pachitea, which they navigate on rafts. They are said to be cannibals. The men have beards, and wear long frocks. The women go naked till they are married, when they wear a waist cloth. The men are very dexterous in hunting. When one of them is pursuing the chase in the woods, and hears another hunter imitating the cry of an animal, he immediately makes the same cry to entice him nearer, and, if he is of another tribe, kills him if he can, and eats him. They are in a state of deadly hostility with all their neighbours. They have large houses, and live in the interior during the rainy season; but in the dry time they resort to the banks of the rivers. Their weapons are clubs, lances, bows, and arrows. *Smyth, Herndon.*

CATAUXIS. A tribe on the river Purus, sixteen to thirty days voyage up. They have houses, sleep in hammocks, and cultivate mandioc. They go naked, wearing a ring of twisted hair on their arms and legs. They use bows and poisoned arrows. Their canoes are made of the bark of a tree. They eat forest game, tapirs, monkeys, and birds; and they are cannibals, eating Indians of other tribes. *Acuña,* p. 107, who calls them *Quatausis; Wallace,* p. 515.

CATAUUIXIS. A tribe of the river Jurua, according to Von Spix. Evidently the same as the *Catauxis. Spix und Martius,* iii, p. 1183.

CATUQUINAS. A tribe of the river Jurua. They use the blow-pipe and poisoned arrows, as well as bows and arrows, and live on snakes, fish, and monkeys. *Spix und Martius,* iii, p. 1184.

CAUANAS. A race of dwarfs on the river Jurua, only four or five spans high. One of them was seen by Von Spix at Para. *Spix,* iii, p. 1183 (see *Carcanas*).

CAUXANAS. A tribe between the Iza and Japura; who are said to kill all their first-born children. They eat alligators. *Wallace,* p. 511; *Spix und Martius,* iii, p. 1185.

CAYANAS. A tribe of the river Madeira. *Acuña,* p. 117.

CAYUBABAS. A tribe to the eastward of the *Moxos* (which see).

Their chief was named "Paytiti." *Baraza ; Reise Beschreibungen.*

CHAIS. A branch of the *Chepeos* (which see). *Velasco.*

CHAMICURAS (see *Ajuanas*).

CHAPAS. A branch of the *Roamaynas* (which see). They wander along the banks of the Pastaza river, between that river and the Morona. *M. Rodriguez ; Velasco ; Villavicencio's Map.*

CHAVELOS. A branch of the *Aguaricos* (which see). *Velasco.*

CHAYAVITAS. Indians of the Upper Marañon, of the first missionary epoch (1638-83). Chayavitas is a village containing about three hundred and twenty inhabitants. *M. Rodriguez ; Velasco.*

CHEPENAGUAS. A branch of the *Chepeos* (which see). *Velasco.*

CHEPEOS. A numerous tribe of the Marañon, of the first missionary epoch. *M. Rodriguez ; Velasco.*

CHICHAS OREJONES. A tribe of the "Gran Chacu." They are met with between the *Chiriguanas* and *Guaycurus ;* in a very inaccessible country. They dress in cloth made from llama wool, and are said to work in silver mines. The Incas employed them in this work ; and it seems probable that they composed one of the *Mitimaes,* or colonies of the Incas. They live peaceably with another tribe of Indians, called *Churumatas.* They cultivate the land, and come down to the river Bermejo, to fish ; but are very careful to prevent the Spaniards from discovering a road into their country. They are called *Orejones,* because they are believed to be descended from the *Orejones nobles del Cusco,* "officers of the Incarial court." *Lozano,* pp. 72-3.

CHIQUITOS. A numerous tribe in the province of Santa Cruz de la Sierra, in Bolivia ; and between the head waters of the rivers Mamoré and Itenez. They are considered as minors by the Bolivian government ; and they cultivate cotton, and sugar cane. Their produce is sold for the benefit of the community, and a fund is formed for the relief of the infirm and aged. They speak seven different languages, called *tapacuraca, napeca, paunaca, paiconeca, quitemoca, jurucariquia,* and *moncoca,* which is the common language of the *Chiquitos.* The word *Chiquito* means *small* or *little ;* a name which was given to these Indians by the early Spaniards for the following reason. When they first invaded this country, the Indians fled into the forests; and the Spaniards came to their abandoned huts, where the doorways were so exceedingly low, that the Indians who inhabited them were supposed to be dwarfs.

Their houses are built of *adobes*, and thatched with coarse grass. For manufacturing sugar, they fabricate their own copper boilers; and they understand several trades. They also weave ponchos and hammocks, and make straw hats. They are very fond of singing and dancing, and seldom quarrel amongst themselves. They are a peaceful race. When he takes a fancy to wear striped trousers, the Chiquito Indian plants a row of white and a row of yellow cotton. Should he wish for blue, he adds a row of indigo. The heart-leaved *bixa* grows wild around him, the vanilla bean scents the doorway of his hut, while the coffee and chocolate trees shade it. *Castelnau*, iii, p. 217; *Gibbon*, p. 164.

CHIRIGUANAS. A tribe of the " Gran Chacu", nearest to the confines of Peru; speaking the *Guarani* language, and supposed to be a branch of that wide spread nation. When Inca Yupanqui conquered them, they were indiscriminate cannibals; and in 1571 they repulsed an invasion of Spaniards, led by the viceroy Toledo in person. *G. de la Vega; Lozano; Dobrizhoffer.*

CHIRIPUNOS. A tribe, on the head waters of the Curaray. *Villavicencios's map.*

CHOLONES. A tribe of the Huallaga, on the left bank. They were first met with by the Franciscans in 1676, in the forests near the Huallaga, who established them in mission villages.

They are now found in the mission villages of Monzon, Uchiza, Tocache, and Pachiza, on the Huallaga. Their skin is a dark brown, they have shiny black hair, and scarcely any beard; nose arched, and cheek bones high. They consider themselves great doctors, and are very superstitious. They are proud, perverse, and fond of a wild life; but are possessed of courage, and great self-possession in danger. They are good-tempered, cheerful, and sober.

They use the blow gun, called by the Spaniards *cerbatana*, by the Portuguese *gravatana*, and by the Indians *pucuna*. It is made of a long straight piece of the wood of the Chonta palm; about eight feet long, and two inches in diameter, near the mouth end, tapering to half an inch at the extremity. The arrow is made of any light wood, about a foot long. A marksman will kill a small bird at thirty or forty paces, with the *pucuna*. *Mercurio Peruano*, No. 51 ; *Poeppig Reise*, ii, p. 320 ; *Herndon*, p. 138-9.

CHUDAVIÑAS. A branch of the *Andoas* (which see). *Velasco*.

CHUFIAS. A branch of the *Aguaricos* (which see). *Velasco*.

CHUNCHOS. A numerous and formidable group of tribes, in the forests to the eastward of Cuzco, and Tarma : first reduced to subjection by the Inca Yupanqui. They are said, by Velasco, to be descended from Inca Indians.

Those to the eastward of Cuzco are divided into three branch tribes, the *Huachipayris*, *Tuyuneris*, and *Sirineyris*. They call their chiefs "Huayris". General Miller, in 1835, saw a chief of the *Huachipayris*, and some of his tribe, in the plains of Pancartambo, where the great river Purus takes its rise. Their hut was well built, on a rising ground, wall six feet high, with a good pointed straw roof. The chief was about five feet ten inches in height, well made, of a good cast of features, and a jovial disposition. These Indians are afraid to be in utter darkness, at any time, for fear of evil spirits. They cultivate corn, yucas, plantains, and pineapples. They live in long huts, twenty people in each, and wander for leagues through the matted forests, in search of game. They have no religion whatever, and bury their dead in the huts. They are fierce, cruel, and untameable.

The Chunchos of the forests of Tarma are quite independent, very fierce, and formidable. *G. de la Vega*, i, lib. vii, cap. xiv; *Velasco; General Miller, R. G. S. Journal*, vi, p. 182; *Van Tschudi*, p. 466; *Gibbon, p.* 51; *Markham's "Cuzco and Lima"*.

CHUNIPIES. A tribe of the "Gran Chacu"; between the Rio Grande, and the Bermejo. They are said to be descended from Spaniards, and are very peaceful and courteous; and, besides food obtained from hunting and fishing, they cultivate maize. They go quite naked; and are constantly at war with the *Tobas* and *Mocovies*, but live in friendship with four other tribes, who appear to be of the same origin, and who resemble each other closely, namely the *Tequetes, Guamalcas, Yucunampas,* and *Velelas. Lozano,* p. 85-7.

CHUNTAQUIROS (see *Pirros*).

CHURITUNAS. A branch of the *Jeberos* (which see). *M. Rodriguez; Velasco.*

CHUZCOS. A tribe of the Huallaga, established in a mission village, by the Franciscan Father Lugando, in 1631. *Mercurio Peruano.*

CINGACACHUSCAS. A tribe supposed to have been descended from the Inca Indians; now disappeared. *Velasco.*

CIURES. A tribe of the river Pastaza. *M. Rodriguez.*

COATA TUPUÜJAS. A tribe of the river Jurua, reported to have short tails. *Von Spix,* iii, p. 1183 ; *Castelnau.*

COBEUS (see *Uaupés*).

COCOMAS. A tribe of the Marañon and Lower Huallaga; of the first missionary epoch, 1638-83. Their province was called, by the missionaries, "La Gran Cocoma." They built their huts round a beautiful lake, near the mouth of the Huallaga, where Father Lucero established a mission. In 1681 they were still in the habit of eating their own dead relations, and grinding their bones, to drink in their fermented liquors. They said "that it was better to be inside a friend, than to be swallowed up by the black earth." In 1830 they moved from Laguna to Nauta, at the mouth of the Ucayali. They are bolder than most of the civilized Indians, and carry on war with the savage *Mayorunas. M. Rodriguez; Velasco; Poeppig Reise,* ii, p. 449; *Herndon,* p. 195.

COCAMILLAS. A branch of the *Cocomas,* settled at Laguna, on the Huallaga. They are lazy and drunken, but capital boatmen. *M. Rodriguez; Herndon,* p. 176.

COCRUNAS. A tribe of the river Teffé. *Ribeiro.*

COERUNAS. A tribe of the river Japura. They are, in general, small, strong, and dark, with nothing agreeable in their faces. Their language, spoken through their noses, sounds disagreeable. *Spix und Martius,* iii, p. 1201.

COFANES. A tribe in the forests sixty leagues east of Quito, on the head waters of the river Aguarico, near the foot of Mount Cayambe. They are much reduced in numbers, and have lost their fierce character. They speak a harsh guttural language. *Velasco*, iii, p. 136 ; *Villavicencio*, p. 173.

COHIDIAS (see *Uaupés*).

COHUMARES. A tribe of the Marañon, preached to between 1727 and 1768. *Velasco.*

COLCHAQUIES. A tribe of Tucuman, and in the southern part of the " Gran Chacu." They resisted the invasions of the Spaniards of Salta and Jujuy very bravely, and were not entirely subdued until 1665. *Lozano*, p. 92 ; *Dobrizhoffer.*

COMACORIS. A branch of the *Simigaes* (which see). *Velasco.*

COMAVOS. A tribe, said by Velasco to be descended from the Inca Indians ; preached to between 1683 and 1727. *Velasco.*

CONAMBOS. A tribe on the head waters of the river Tigre. *Villavicencio's map.*

CONEJORIS. A branch of the *Simigaes* (which see). *Velasco.*

CONOMOMAS. A tribe of the river Jutay. *Acuña*, p. 99 ; *Von Spix*, iii, p. 1185.

CONIBOS or MANOAS. A tribe of the Pampa del Sacramento, and the banks of the Ucayali. It was first visited by missionaries, between 1683 and 1727. In 1685 some Francisans descended the Pachitea, and formed a mission amongst them, but the good Friars were killed by the *Cashibos* Indians (which see). Father Ricter was killed by the *Conibos* in 1695. At present most of them profess christianity, thanks to the labours of the indefatigable Fathers Girbal and Plaza. They are quiet, tractable people.

They paint their faces in red and blue stripes, with silver rings in their lips and noses. They are good boatmen and fishermen, and are employed by the traders to collect salt fish, and sarsaparilla. *Velasco* ; *Mercurio Peruano* ; *Castlenau* ; *Smyth*, p. 235 ; *Herndon*, p. 202-9.

They are marked on Fritz's map (1707) on the east side of the Ucayali.

COPATASAS. A branch of the *Jeberos* (which see). *Villavicencio.*

COROCOROS,—*(see Uaupés)*

CORONAS. A tribe of the river Teffé. *Ribeiro.*

CORONADOS. A tribe of the river Pastaza. *M. Rodriguez.*

COTOCARIANAS, (see *Carabuyanas*).

COUAS. (See *Uaupés*).

CUCHIGUARAS. A tribe of the river Purus. *Acuña*, p. 107; *Spix und Martius*, iii, p. 1175.

CUCHIVARAS. A tribe of the river Coari. *Southey's Brazil*, iii.

CUINUAS. A branch of the *Camavos* (which see). *Velasco.*

CUIRES. A branch of the *Roamaynas* (which see). *Velasco.*

CUIYACUS. A tribe of the river Aguarico. *Villavicencio's Map.*

CUIYAYOS. A tribe between the Aguarico and Putumayu. *Villavicencio's Map.*

CUMARURUAYANAS (see *Carabuyanas*).

CUMAYARIS. A tribe of the river Purus. *Acuña*, p. 107; *Spix und Martius*, iii, p. 1175.

CUMBASINOS. A tribe of the Santa Catalina, in the Pampa del Sacramento. *Smyth*, p. 204.

CUNAS. A tribe of the Putumayu. *Acuña*, p. 99.

CUNJIES. A branch of the *Avijiras* (which see). *Velasco.*

CUNURIS. A tribe living at the mouth of a river, up which the Amazons are said to live. *Acuña*, p. 122.

CURANAS. A tribe of the Ucayali, said to be a branch of the *Campas* (which see). *Velasco.*

CURANARIS. A tribe of the river Madeira. *Acuña*, p. 117.

CURARAYES. A branch of the *Zaparos* (which see). *Villavicencio.*

CURETUS. A tribe inhabiting the country between the rivers Japura and Uaupès. They are short, but very strong, wear their hair long, and paint their bodies. The men wear a girdle of woollen thread, but the women go entirely naked. Their houses are circular, with walls of thatch, and a high conical roof. They reside in small villages, governed by a chief; and are long lived, and peaceable. They cultivate maize and mandioc. They have no idea of a Supreme Being. Their language is very guttural, and difficult to understand, as they keep their teeth close together, when speaking. A tribe, of the same name, is met with on the river Teffè. *Ribeiro; Von Martius*, iii, p. 1222; *Wallace*, p. 509.

CURIATES. A tribe marked on Fritz's map (1707) between the rivers Madeira and Tapajos.

CURIGUERES. A race of giants, on the Purus. *Acuña*, p. 107.

CURINAS. A tribe living south of the *Omaguas*. *Acuña*, p. 96; *Spix und Martius*, iii, p. 1187.
Marked on Fritz's map (1707) between the rivers Yavari and Jutay.

CURIS. A tribe of the river Amazons. *Acuña*, p. 100.

CURIVEOS. A tribe said to have been subject to the Gran Paytiti. *M. Rodriguez.*

CURUANARIS (see *Carabuyanas*).

CURUCURUS. A tribe of the river Purus. *Acuña*, p. 107.

CURUPATABAS. A tribe of the Rio Negro. *Acuña*, p. 110.

CURUZIRARIS. A very populous tribe, on the south side of the Amazons, twenty-eight leagues below the mouth of the Jurua. *Acuña*, p. 101.

CUSABATAYES. A branch of the *Manamabobos* (which see). *Velasco.*

CUSTINIABAS. A branch of *Pirros* (which see). *Velasco.*

CUTINANOS. A branch of the *Jeberos*. Father Cujia preached to them in 1646. *Velasco.*

DESANNAS (see *Uaupès*).

ENCABELLADOS. A tribe of the Napo, so called by Father Rafael Ferrer, in 1600, from their long hair. They were preached to from 1727 to 1768. Marked on Fritz's map (1707) between the rivers Napo and Putumayu.

Villavicencio places them on the lower part of the Aguarico. They are much reduced in numbers, and live chiefly on fish, and the manatee. *Acuña,* p. 92-4 ; *Velasco; Villavicencio.*

 EREPUNACAS. A tribe of the river Madeira. *Acuña,* p. 117.

ENGAIBAS. A tribe of the river Pacaxa. *Acuña,* p. 130.

ENJEYES. A branch of the *Itucales* (which see). *Velasco.*

ERITEYNES. A branch of the *Iquitos* (which see). *Velasco.*

FRASCAVINAS. A branch of the *Andoas* (which see). *Velasco.*

GAES. A tribe of the Marañon, with a language similar to that of the *Jeberos.* In 1707 they killed Father Durango. Placed in Fritz's map, on the upper waters of the rivers Tigre and Pastaza. *M. Rodriguez ; Velasco.*

GINORIS. A branch of the Simigaes (which see). *Velasco.*

GIS (see *Uaupés*).

GIVAROS (see *Jeberos*).

GUACARAS. A tribe living next to the race of Amazons, with whom they had intercourse. *Acuña,* p. 122.

GUACHIS. A tribe of the " Gran Chacu". *Lozano.*

GUAJAYOS. A tribe of the Marañon : preached to between 1727 and 1768. *Velasco.*

GUALAQUIZAS. A branch of the *Jeberos* (which see). *Villavicencio.*

GUAMALCAS (see *Chunipies*).

GUANAS. A tribe of the " Gran Chacu". *Lozano.*

GUANAMAS. A tribe of the Rio Negro. *Acuña,* p. 110.

GUANAPURIS. A tribe of the Araganatuba. *Acuña,* p. 105.

GUANARUS. A tribe of the river Jutay : marked on Fritz's map (1707) between the rivers Jurua and Teffé. *Acuña,* p. 99.

GUANIBIS. A tribe of the Araganatuba. *Acuña,* p. 105.

GUAQUIARIS. A tribe of the river Purus. *Acuña,* p. 107.

GUARAICUS. A tribe of the Putumayu (see *Uaraycus*). *Acuña,* p. 99.

GUARANACUAZANAS. A tribe between the Rio Negro and the Orinoco. *Acuña*, p. 110.

GUARANAGUACUS. A tribe of the Amazons, below the mouth of the Madeira. *Acuña*, p. 117.

GUARAYOS. A tribe, on the head waters of the Mamoré, and its tributaries. This tribe, and that of the *Sirionos*, are believed to be descended from Spaniards, who, in former days, went into the forests in search of the "Gran Paytiti." They are bearded and florid, but also have some characteristics of their Indian maternal ancestry. The *Guarayos* are kind and hospitable; the *Sirionos* fierce. *Dalence.* "*Bosquejo estadistico de Bolivia.*"

GUARIANACAGUAS. A tribe of the Rio Negro. *Acuña*, p. 110.

GUASITAYAS. A tribe of the Marañon, preached to between 1727 and 1768. *Velasco.*

GUATINUMAS. A tribe of the river Madeira. *Acuña*, p. 117.

GUAYABAS. A tribe on the north side of the Amazons. *Acuña*, p. 100.

GUAYACARIS. A tribe of the Araganatuba. *Acuña*, p. 105.

GUAYAZIS. A race of dwarfs, of whom credulous Acuña heard, from the Tupinambas Indians. *Acuña*, p. 119.

GUAYCURUS. A tribe of the "Gran Chacu"; between the rivers Pilcomayu and Yaveviri. In the wet season their country is so marshy, and full of swamps, that they cannot walk; and in the dry season it is so parched up, that there is great scarcity of water. It was found almost impossible to penetrate this territory; and the *Guaycurus* remained independent, and made frequent attacks on the Spaniards in Paraguay. They go quite naked, without shame, but the women wear a short petticoat. Lozano gives a long and interesting account of them. *Lozano*, p. 59-72.

GUAZAGAS. A branch of the *Andoas* (which see). *Velasco.*

GUENCOYAS. A tribe of the Marañon, preached to between 1727 and 1768. *Velasco.*

GUEVAS. A tribe which was already extinct in Velasco's time. *Velasco.*

HAGUETIS.   A branch of the *Manamabobos* (which see). *Velasco.*

HIBITOS.   (See *Jibitos*).

HIMUETACAS.   A branch of the *Iquitos* (which see).   *Velasco.*

HUACHIPAYRIS.   (See *Chunchos*).

HUAHUATALES.   A tribe marked on Fritz's map (1767) near the sources of the Yavari.

HUAIROUS.   A tribe marked on Fritz's map, between the rivers Jurua and Teffé.

HUAMBISAS.   A fierce tribe of the Upper Marañon, and Santiago rivers.   In 1841 they drove all the civilized Indians from the upper missions.   In 1843 they murdered all the inhabitants of a village called Santa Teresa, between the mouths of the Santiago and Morona.   They encroach more and more on the few settled villages, which remain on the Upper Marañon.   *Heraldo de Lima,* Sept. 13th, 1855.

HUASIMOAS.   A branch of the *Iquitos del Nanay,* preached to between 1727 and 1768.   *Velasco.*

HUIRUNAS.   A tribe of the Araganatuba.   *Acuña,* p. 105.

HUMURANAS.   A branch of the *Maynas,* preached to between 1727 and 1768.   *Velasco.*

IBANOMAS.   A branch of the *Jeberos* (which see.)   Marked on Fritz's map (1707) between the rivers Teffé and Purus.   *Velasco.*

IBITOS.   (See *Jibitos*.)   *Herndon,* p. 150.

ICAHUATES.   A tribe of the Marañon, preached to between 1683 and 1727.   *Velasco.*

ILURUS.   A branch of the *Jeberos* (which see.)   *Velasco.*

IMASCHAHUAS.   A branch of the *Maynas.*   *Velasco.*

INCURIS.   A branch of the *Simigaes* (which see).   *Velasco.*

INUACAS.   A branch of the *Camavos* (which see).   *Velasco.*

IPAPUISAS.   A branch of the *Maynas,* identical with the *Coronados* (which see).   *Velasco.*

IPILOS.   A branch of the *Piros* (which see).   *Velasco.*

IPECAS. (See *Uaupés*).

IQUITOS. An extensive tribe, divided into numerous branches; some living on the river Tigre, others on the Nanay. The latter is a stream which flows into the Marañon, near Omaguas, and the village of Iquitos is at its mouth. The Iquitos were preached to between 1727 and 1768. Villavicencio places them on the east side of the lower course of the Napo. *Velasco. Villavicencio.*

ISANNAS or PAPUNAUAS. A tribe on the river Isanna, a tributary of the Rio Negro. They cut their hair; the women wear a cloth, instead of being naked, and adorn themselves with bracelets. Their huts are collected together in little scattered villages. They bury their dead inside the huts, and mourn for them a long time, but make no feast on the occasion. *Wallace*, p. 507-8.

ITREMAJORIS. A branch of the *Simigaes* (which see) *Velasco.*

ITUCALES. A tribe of the Upper Marañon. *Velasco.*

IZAS. A tribe believed to be extinct in Velasco's time. *Velasco.*

IZIBAS. A branch of the *Itucales* (which see). *Velasco.*

IZUHALIS. A branch of the *Urarinas* (which see). *Velasco.*

JACAMIS (see Uaupés).

JACARES. A tribe near the junction of the Beni and Mamoré; few in number, and scattered over the country. Quite savages. *Gibbon*, p. 287-8.

JAMAMARIS. A tribe on the west side of the Purus, but living some distance inland. There is no information concerning them, except that, in their customs and appearance, they resemble the *Catauxis* (which see). *Wallace*, p. 516.

JANUMAS. A tribe of the river Teffé. *Ribeiro.*

JAPUAS. A tribe of the Marañon; preached to between 1727 and 1768. *Velasco.*

JAUANAS. A tribe of the river Teffé. *Ribeiro.*

JAWABUS. A branch of the *Panos* (which see). *Velasco.*

JEBEROS or JIVARAS. A tribe of the Upper Marañon, the first fruits of the Jesuit Missions. Velasco, who divides them into three branches, says they are the most faithful, noble, and amiable of all the tribes. Villavicencio divides them into ten branches, all speaking the same language; which is sonorous, clear, and harmonious, easy to learn, and energetic. The Jeberos wander in the forests between the rivers Chinchipe and Pastaza, and on both sides of the Marañon. The branch tribes are constantly at war with each other, but they unite against a common enemy. On the conquest of Peru, the Spaniards reduced these Indians, and founded colonies in their country; but, in 1599, a general insurrection of the *Jeberos* destroyed all these settlements in one day. The Jeberos have muscular bodies, small and very animated black eyes, aquiline noses, and thin' lips. Many have beards and fair complexions, and it is said that this arises from the number of Spanish women whom they captured, in the insurrection of 1599. The Jeberos love liberty, and can tolerate no yoke; they are warlike, brave, and astute. They have fixed homes, cultivate yucas, maize, frijoles, and plantains; and their women wear cotton cloth. They live in well built huts, and sleep in standing bed places, instead of hammocks. They are very jealous of their women, and keep them apart. Their lances are made of the chonta palm, the head being triangular, thirty or fifty inches long, and ten to fifteen broad. They all take a strong emetic every morning (an infusion of leaves of the *guayusa*) for the sake of getting rid of all undigested food, and being ready for the chace, with an empty stomach. At each village they have a great drum called *tunduli*, to call the warriors to arms, and it is repeated from village to village, as a signal. Their hair hangs over their shoulders, and they wear a helmet of bright feathers. When they are engaged in war, their faces and bodies are painted, but during peace they wear breeches down to the knees, and a shirt without sleeves.

In September, 1855, the Jeberos are reported to have destroyed the ancient town of San Borja, and the villages of Sta. Teresa and Santiago. *Samuel Fritz's map* (1707); *Velasco*; *Villavicencio*, pp. 169 and 375; *Heraldo de Lima*, September 1855.

JIBITOS. A tribe first met with by the Franciscans in 1676, in the forests near the Huallaga, on the eastern borders of the province of Caxamarquilla. They were converted, and settled in villages on the western bank of the Huallaga. Their women wear a dress of cotton, confined round the waist by a girdle. They bathe in the river, for their health, very early in the morning. They are only distinguished from the *Cholones* by their dialect (see *Cholones*). *Mercurio Peruano*, 1791, No. 51; *Poeppig Reise.* They are less civilized than the *Cholones*, and paint their faces, not with any fixed pattern, but each man according to his fancy; using the blue of *Huitoc*, and the red "*Achote.*" They are met with on the Huallaga, at Tocache, and Lamasillo. *Herndon*, p. 150.

JUANAS. A tribe of the river Pacaxa. *Acuña*, p. 130.

JUBIRIS. A tribe on the Purus. They are little known, but their bodies are spotted and mottled like the *Purupurus* (which see). *Wallace*, p. 516.

JUMAS. A tribe of the river Coari. *Southey's Brazil*, vol. iii.

JUMANAS (see *Ticunas*).

JURIS. A tribe of the Amazons, between the rivers Içá and Japura. Many of them have settled on the Rio Negro. Their huts are formed of a circle of poles, with others woven in, and a roof of palm leaves in the shape of a dome.

The *Juris* are nearly related to the *Passes* (which see); and, in former days, they were undoubtedly one tribe. Their language, manners, and customs are the same; but the *Juris* have broader features and chests. In ancient times they were the most powerful tribe between the Içá and Japura; but in 1820 their whole number did not exceed two thousand. *Von Martius*, iii, p. 1235; *Von Spix*, iii, p. 1184.

The *Juris* tattoo in a circle round the mouth, and hence they are called *Juripixunas* (black *Juris*). They are good servants for canoe or agricultural work, and are the most skilful of all in the use of the *gravatána* or blow pipe. *Wallace*, p. 510.

In 1775 there was a settlement of *Juris* on the Japura, near its mouth, ruled by a chief called *Machiparo*, or *Macupari*. *Southey*, vol. iii, p. 721; *Orellana*, p. 29, note.

Their hair is curled so closely as to resemble the African woolly head. The women have both cheeks tattooed. *Smyth*, p. 278.

JUTIPOS. A tribe, preached to between 1683 and 1727. Velasco says that the *Manoas, Panos,* and *Pelados,* are branches of the *Jutipos;* but this must be a mistake. *Velasco.*

LAMAS. Said to be extinct. Probably the same as the *Lamistas.*

LAMISTAS or MOTILONES. A tribe of the Huallaga, civilized by the Franciscans in 1676. They are settled at Lamas, Moyo-- bamba, and Tarapoto. They are industrious, and are employed chiefly in agriculture, and the preparation of cotton. They also inhabit Chasuta; but there they have retained, to a great extent, the mode of life of the wild hunting Indians. They are of a mild disposition, and have polite friendly manners. *Poeppig Reise.*

LECOS. A tribe on the Tipuani, a tributary of the Beni ; settled in the mission villages of Mapiri and Guanay, where they are half civilized. They have agreeable expressions, high foreheads, mouths comparatively small, and horizontal eyes. Guanay was founded in 1802. *Weddell,* p. 453.

LLIQUINOS. A tribe on the head waters of the Curaray. *Villavicencio's map.*

LOGROÑOS. A tribe on the western side of the Morona. *Villa- vicencio's map.*

LULES. A tribe of the "Gran Chaco." First visited by San Francisco Solano, and afterwards by Father Alonzo de Barzana. Their language is very deficient in words to express abstract ideas, and they are described as a very savage race. *Lozano,* pp. 94 and 380.

Father Machoni, and other Jesuits, laboured amongst the Lules Indians, between 1711 and 1729.

MACAGUAS. A tribe of the Araganatuba. *Acuña,* p. 105.

MACAVINAS. A branch of the *Andoas* (which see). *Velasco.*

MACUNAS. A tribe of the Araganatuba. *Velasco.*

MACUS. One of the lowest and most uncivilized tribes of the Amazonian valley, inhabiting the forests near the Rio Negro. They have no houses, and no clothing. They stitch up a few leaves at night, to serve as a shed, if it rains. They make a most deadly kind of poison to anoint their arrows. They eat all kinds of birds and fish roasted. They often attack the houses of other Indians, and murder all the inhabitants. They have wavy and almost curly hair. *Wallace*, p. 508.

MAISAMES. A tribe between the Nanay and Napo. *Villavicencio's map.*

MANACURUS. A tribe of the Rio Negro. *Acuña*, p. 40.

MANAHUAS. A tribe of the Ucayali, living between that river and the Yavari; mentioned by Father Girbal, in 1793, as being met with near the *Capanahuas. Mercurio Peruano.* No. 381.

MANAMABOBOS. A tribe of the Ucayali, visited by Father Lucero in 1681. They are marked on Fritz's map (1707) on the east side of the Ucayali. *M. Rodriguez. Velasco. Mercurio Peruano.*

MANAMABUAS. A branch of the *Manamabobos.* They were preached to between 1683 and 1727. *Velasco.*

MANAOS. A tribe of the river Teffé. Also met with on the banks of the Rio Negro. The whole of them are now civilized, and their blood mingles with that of some of the best families in the province. *Ribeiro. Wallace.*

MANATINABAS. A branch of the *Pirros* (which see). *Velasco.*

MANAGUS. A tribe employed in procuring gold, near the river Amazons. *Acuña*, p. 103.

MANOAS. (See *Conibos*).

MANUES. A branch of the *Campos* (which see). *Velasco.*

MAPARINAS. A tribe of the Upper Marañon, which joined the *Cocomas* in their rebellion against the Missionaries in 1664. *M. Rodriguez; Velasco.*

MAPARIS or MAPIARUS. A tribe of the *Araganatuba,* according to Acuña. Smyth mentions such a tribe in the "Pampa del Sacramento." *Acuña*, p. 105; *Smyth*, p. 235.

MARAGUAS. A tribe on the river Amazons, below the mouth of the Madeira. *Acuña*, p. 117.

MARANHAS (see *Marianas*).

MARAYMUMES. A tribe of the *Araganatuba. Acuña*, p. 105.

MARIANAS or MARANHAS.   A tribe of the river Jutay.   *Acuña,* p. 99.

They wear small pieces of wood in their ears and lips, but are not tattooed.   The boring of the lips of a child is celebrated by a feast.   When a boy is twelve years old, the father cuts four lines near his mouth, and he must then fast for five days.   The elder lads scourge themselves, with a small girdle, which operation is considered as proving their manhood.   *Spix und Martius,* iii, p. 1185.

MARIGUYANAS (see *Carabuyanas*).

MARIRUAS.   A tribe of the Araganatuba.   *Acuña,* p. 105.

MASAMAES.   A branch of the *Yameos* (which see).   Preached to between 1727 and 1768.   *Velasco.*

MASIPIAS.   A tribe of the Araganatuba.   *Acuña,* p. 105.

MASUCARUANAS (see *Carabuyanas*).

MATAGENES.   A branch of the *Zaparos* (which see).   *Villavicencio.*

MATAGUAYOS.   A tribe of the "Gran Chacu".   *Lozano,* p. 51-73.

They occupy the country on the west bank of the river Bermejo, for a space of eighty-two leagues in length.   Their chief food is fish, which they catch with nets, and with arrows.   They are not warlike, and have few horses.   Their dress is the skin of animals.   *Mercurio Peruano,* No. 583.

MAUTAS.   A branch of the *Zaparos,* between the Nanay and Napo.   *Villavicencio's map.*

MAYANASES.   A tribe of the river Pacaxa.   *Acuña,* p. 130.

MAYNAS.   A general name for tribes on the upper Marañon : placed on Fritz's map (1707) between the rivers Santiago and Pastaza.   *Velasco.*

MAYORUNAS or BARBUDOS.   A tribe between the Ucayali, Marañon, and Yavari.   They have thick beards and white skins, more like English than even Spaniards.   They wander through the forests, hunting, and do not go much to the rivers.   *Manuel Rodriguez; Velasco,* iii, p. 108.

They are supposed to be descended from Spanish soldiers of Ursua's expedition. They have a strange and painful way of pulling out their beards. They take two shells, which they use as tweezers, and pull out the hairs one by one; making such grimaces that the sight of it moves to laughter, and at the same time to compassion. *Mercurio Peruano*, No. 76.

They are sometimes called *Barbudos*, and are very numerous. They are of a light olive complexion, taller than most of the other tribes, and go perfectly naked. They are very warlike, and are in amity with no other tribe. They do not use bows and arrows, but only spears, lances, clubs, and *cerbatanas* or blow pipes; and the poison they make is esteemed the most powerful of any. They are well formed, the women particularly so in their hands and feet; with rather straight noses, and small lips. They cut their hair in a line across the forehead, and let it hang down their backs. Their cleanliness is remarkable, a quality for which this tribe alone is distinguished. *Smyth*, p. 223-4.

Very little is known of this tribe, as they attack any person who goes into their territory, and boatmen are careful not to encamp on their side of the Ucayali. *Herndon*, p. 218.

MAZANES. A tribe between the rivers Nanay and Napo. *Villavicencio's map.*

MIGUIANAS. A branch of the *Yameos* (which see): they were preached to between 1727 and 1768. *Velasco.*

MIRANHAS. A race of cannibals, between the rivers Içá and Japura, in the neighbourhood of the Juris. *Wallace*, p. 510.

MIRITIS (see *Uaupés*).

MOACARANAS (see *Carabuyanas*).

MOCHOVOS. A branch of the *Pirros* (which see). *Velasco.*

MOCOVIES or MOCOBIOS. A tribe of the "Gran Chacu". They are a savage tribe, allied to the *Tobas*. In 1712 the Spaniards, from Tucuman, invaded their country. They are an insolent and turbulent race, very cruel, and given to rapine and robbery. They possess horses. *Lozano.*

MOPITIRUS. A tribe of the Araganatuba. *Acuña*, p. 105.

MORONAS. A branch of the *Jeberos* (which see). *Villavicencio.*

MORUAS. A tribe of the river Jutay. *Acuña*, p. 99.

MOTILONES. A tribe of the Huallaga, mentioned by Simon and Velasco; probably the same as the *Lamistas* (see *Lamistas*).

MOXOS. A numerous tribe on the river Mamoré. They submitted to the dominion of the Inca Yupanqui, more through persuasion than by force. The Inca sent a colony into Moxos. In 1564, Don Diego Aleman started from La Paz, with a few followers, in search of the gold of Moxos, but he was defeated by the Indians, and taken prisoner. *G. de la Vega*, ii, cap. 14 and 15.

During the inundations of the rivers, the Moxos live on rising grounds, surrounded by the flood. When the dry season arrives, the sun, acting on the stagnant waters, generates pestilence. The climate is unhealthy. The *Moxos* are divided into twenty-nine sub-tribes or branches, speaking thirteen different languages, besides sundry dialects. *Southey's Brazil*, vol. iii.

Moxos is now a province of the Bolivian Department of Beni; separated from Brazil, by the rivers Itenez and Madeira. *Dalence, Bosquejo de Bolivia.*

The *Moxos* Indians are quite under the dominion of the Bolivians. They are a grave, sedate, and thoughtful people; and are fond of cultivating the soil. They have set aside the bow and arrow, and have taken up the lasso, which they handle well. They are civil, quiet, peaceable, and seldom quarrel amongst themselves. The Bolivians treat them worse than slaves. The *Moxos* manufacture cotton, and are expert carpenters. The various tribes in Moxos speak nine different languages. *Gibbon*, p. 235; *See also Introduction*, p. xxxix.

MUEGANOS. A branch of the *Zaparos* (which see) *Villavicencio*.

MUNDRUCUS. One of the most powerful tribes on the Amazons, and Tapajos. In 1788 they entirely vanquished their ancient enemies the *Muras* (which see). *Southey's Brazil*, vol. iii.

When a *Mundrucu* is hopelessly ill, his friends kill him, and children consider it a kindness to kill their parents, when they can no longer enjoy hunting, dancing, and feasting. They are very dirty. They are a broad chested, and very muscular people; with broad, strongly developed, good natured, but rough features.

Their glossy black hair is cut close across the forehead, and the whole body is tattooed in small lines. They are very warlike, and are the Spartans among the Indians of North Brazil, as the *Guaycurus* (which see) are of the South. The *Mundrucus* are a numerous tribe, numbering from twenty to forty thousand. Since 1803, they have been at peace with the Brazilians. There are many *Tupi* words in their language, as well as many traits in their manners, which make it likely that they once belonged to that great family of tribes, which, some centuries ago, being split up into hordes, appears to have spread over the whole of Brazil. The *Mundrucu*, like the *Tupi* language, is not harsh, but is pronounced with much modulation. The *Mundrucus* do not believe in immortality. *Von Martius*, iii, p. 1235.

The *Mundrucus* dwell on the river Tapajos, and extend far into the interior, towards the rivers Madeira and Purus. They are a very numerous tribe, and portions of them are now civilized. *Wallace*, p. 479.

MUNICHES. A tribe of the Huallaga, preached to between 1638 and 1683. There is a village of the same name. *M. Rodriguez; Velasco; Maw*, p. 141.

MUPARINAS : supposed to be extinct. *Velasco.*

MURAS. A powerful tribe on the Amazons, who were very formidable to the Portuguese, at the time of Ribeiro's tour of inspection in 1775, and until they were vanquished by the *Mnndrucus*, when they began to settle in the Portuguese villages. They used a bow six feet long. *Southey's Brazil*, iii, p. 723.

A populous tribe, partly civilized, about the mouths of the Madeira and Rio Negro; but in the interior, and up the river Purus, many still live in a perfectly uncivilized state. They are rather a tall race, with beards, and the hair of the head is slightly crisp and wavy. They used to go naked, but now they all wear trousers and shirts, and the women have petticoats. Their houses are grouped together in small villages, and scarcely ever consist of more than a roof supported on posts, without walls. They live on fish, game, and fruit; and cultivate nothing. They have bows and arrows, and spears, and construct very good canoes. Each village has a Tashauá or Chief; the succession is hereditary, but the chief has little power. They trade with the Brazilians, in sarsaparilla, turtle oil, Brazil nuts, etc., in exchange for cotton goods, spear and arrow heads, knives, etc. *Wallace*, p. 479 and 511-13. They were all dressed decently, and the women wore calico shirts. *Gibbon*, p. 306.

MURATOS. A branch of the *Andoas* (which see). They were preached to between 1727 and 1768. They have lately been very troublesome, and in September 1856 they pillaged and burnt the villages of Santander and Andoas. They do not fight with bows and arrows, but with iron lances, and a few muskets obtained from Ecuador. *Velasco ; Commercio de Lima.*

MURIATES. A tribe of the river Putumayu. Directly their children are born they hide them in the depths of the forests, that the moonlight may not cause them any harm. *Von Spix*, iii, p. 1186.

MUSQUIMAS. A branch of the *Urarinas* (which see). *Velasco.*

MUTAYAS. A tribe whose feet are shipped with the toes pointing aft, according to the credulous Jesuit. *Acuña*, p. 119.

MUTUANIS. A tribe of the river Purus. *Acuña*, p. 107.

NANERUAS. A branch of the *Campas* (which see). *Velasco.*

NAPEANOS. A branch of the *Yameos* (which see). *Velasco.*

NAPOTOAS. A branch of the *Simigaes* (which see). *Velasco.*

NAUNAS. A tribe of the river Jutay; marked on Fritz's map (1707) between the rivers Ucayali and Yavari. *Acuña*, p. 99.

NEGUAS. A branch of the *Aguaricos* (which see). *Velasco.*

NEOCOYAS. A branch of the *Encabellados* (which see). *Velasco.*

NEPAS. A branch of the *Simigaes* (which see). *Velasco.*

NERECAMUES. A branch of the *Iquitos* (which see). *Velasco.*

NESAHUACAS. A branch of the *Campas* (which see). *Velasco.*

NEVAS. A branch of the *Avijiras* (which see). *Velasco.*

NUSHINOS. A branch of the *Zaparos* (which see). *Villavicencio.*

OAS. A branch of the *Simigaes* (which see); on the banks of the Napo; preached to between 1638 and 1683. *M. Rodriguez; Velasco.*

OJOTAES. A tribe of the "Gran Chacu." *Lozano*, p. 51.

OMAGUAS. Orellana mentions a chief named *Aomagua* at Machiparo, near the mouth of the Putumayu river. *Orellana*, p. 27.

The fabulous stories, respecting the wealth of the *Omaguas*, led to the famous expedition of Ursua in 1560. *Padre Simon*, p. 402, *et seq. Acuña*, p. 48.

In 1645 the Jesuit missionaries arrived in their country, on the banks of the river Marañon. "The Omaguas are the Phœnicians of the river, for their dexterity in navigating. They are the most noble of all the tribes; their language is the most sweet and copious; and these facts indicate that they are the remains of some great monarchy, which existed in ancient times." After eight years of labour, Father Cujia succeeded in collecting them into villages. In 1687 Father Fritz came amongst them, and established forty villages; and Father Michel lived amongst them for twenty-seven years, until 1753. The Portuguese carried on hostilities against these mission villages, and took many Omaguas away for slaves. San Joachim de Omaguas, a village on the Marañon, was the residence of the Vice Superior of the Missions. *Velasco*, iii, p. 197, *et seq.*

Of all the savages who inhabit the banks of the Marañon, the Omaguas are most civilized, notwithstanding their strange custom of flattening their heads. *La Condamine*, p. 189.

From the Omaguas, the Portuguese first obtained the caoutchouc or Indian rubber. In the Tupi language they are called *Cambebas*, a name which, equally with *Omaguas*, signifies "flatheads." *Southey's Brazil*, iii.

The Ouvidor Ribeiro, in his official progress in 1774, came to the village of Olivença, on the Marañon, thirteen leagues below Tabatinga; where he found the chief remnant of the *Omaguas*. They were fairer and better shaped than the other Indians, and were considered to be the most civilized and intelligent tribe. They had left off the practice of flattening their heads.

Maw says, the *Omaguas* appeared to be more active and industrious than the other Indians, and their huts were cleaner; Smyth, that they appeared to be a finer race than any he had hitherto seen ; and Herndon, that the number of inhabitants in the village of San Joachim de Omaguas (in 1852) was about two hundred and thirty-two. *Maw*, p. 185 ; *Smyth*, p. 259 ; *Herndon*, p. 218.

Von Spix calls the *Omaguas* by their Portuguese name of *Cambebas* or *Campevas*. He says that they are very good natured and honest, and that their language has many Tupi words in it. They, like many other Amazonian tribes, have a custom of proving the fortitude of the youths by scourging them, and of the maidens by hanging them in a net, and smoking them. After a death the family shut themselves up for a month, with continual howling ; and their neighbours support them by hunting. The dead are buried in large earthen jars, beneath the floor of their huts. *Spix und Martius*, iii, p. 1187.

OREGUATUS. A tribe on the south side of the Amazons, below the mouth of the Madeira. *Acuña*, p. 117.

OREJONES. A tribe on the north side of the mouth of the Napo, so called from the practice of inserting a stick into the lobes of their ears. Their language is guttural, nasal, and spoken with great velocity. Their faces are very broad, with thick lips. They are very fierce ; and trade with hammocks, poisons, and provisions, in exchange for tools and trinkets. *Villavicencio's Geographia del Ecuador*.

ORITOS. A tribe of the Napo, on the east side, and below the mouth of the Aguarico. *Villavicencio*.

OROUPIANAS (see *Varabuyanas*).

ORYSTINESIS. A tribe of the " Gran Chacu."

OTANAVIS. A branch of the *Muniches* (which see). *Velasco*.

OZUANAS. A tribe of the river Jutay. *Acuña*, p. 99.

PACAXAS. A tribe of the river Pacaxa. *Acuña*, p. 130.

PACHICTAS. A branch of the *Manamabobos* (which see). *Velasco*.

PAMBADEQUES. A tribe of the Marañon, preached to between 1638 and 1683. *M. Rodriguez*.

PANAJORIS. A branch of the *Simigaes* (which see). *Velasco.*

PÁNATAGUAS. A tribe of the Huallaga, visited by Padre Lugando in 1631. *Mercurio Peruano.*

PANOS. A tribe of the Huallaga, Marañon, and Ucayali. In 1670 Father Lucero collected some of them, in the village of Sant-- iago de la Laguna, near the mouth of the Huallaga. In 1830 they joined the mission of Sarayacu, on the Ucayali. At Sarayacu they wear a short frock, which reaches down to the waistband of the trousers, dyed red or blue. Both sexes are very much addicted to intoxication. Smyth and Castlenau say that the *Panos*, of Sarayacu, belong to the tribe of *Setebos* (which see). When Smyth was at Sarayacu, the population amounted to about two thousand. Their canoes are thirty or forty feet long, and three to five feet wide. Their manners are frank and natural, showing, without any disguise, their affection or dislike, their pleasure or anger. They have an easy courteous bearing, and seem to consider themselves on a perfect equality with every body.

In the last century a missionary, among the Panos, found manu- scripts written on a species of paper made of the leaves of the plan- tain, containing, according to the statements of the Indians, a his- tory of the events in the days of their ancestors. *Smyth*, p. 213 ; *Castelnau*, iv, p. 378 ; *Rivero, Antiq. Per.* p. 102.

PAPAGUAS. A tribe of the Marañon, preached to between 1683 and 1727. *Velasco.*

PAPUNAUAS (see *Isannas*).

PARANAPURAS. A branch of the *Chayavitas* (which see). Preached to between 1638 and 1683. *M. Rodriguez.*

PARATOAS. A branch of the *Encabellados* (which see). *Velasco.*

PARRANOS. A branch of the *Yameos* (which see). Preached to between 1727 and 1768. *Velasco.*

PASSES. The most numerous tribe on the river Japura. They believe the sun to be stationary, and that the earth moves. They call rivers the great blood vessels of the earth, and small streams its veins. They pay great respect to their conjurors. Their dead are buried in circular graves.

The pleasing features and slight figures of the *Passes*, confirm the opinion that they are the most beautiful Indians of this region. Their whiter colour and finer build distinguishes them from their neighbours. Their hands and feet are smaller than those of the other Indians; their necks longer, and their appearance more resembles the Caucasian type. Their features are agreeable, and the women are sometimes beautiful; but the men are wanting in the manly ornament of a beard. Their eyes are more open, finer, and further from each other, than those of other Indians; the nose finely formed and arched. The *Passes* have a tattooed mark, beginning under the eyes, and continuing along the face to the chin. The men cut the hair close, but the women wear it long. They are very clean: the women usually wearing a shirt with short arms, and the men a kind of cloak. The *Passes* are clever, gentle, open, peaceful, and industrious. (See *Juris*). *Von Spix*, iii, p. 1186. *Von Martius*, iii, p. 1201-3. *Southey's Brazil*, iii, p. 722.

PASTAZAS. A branch of the *Jeberos* (which see). *Villavicencio*.

PASTIVAS. A tribe of the Marañon, preached to between 1727 and 1768. *Velasco*.

PAVAS or PEVAS. A branch of the *Andoas*, according to Velasco, preached to between 1727 and 1768. They are met with between the rivers Napo and Putumayu. *Velasco; Villavicencio's map*.

PAUTES. A branch of the *Jeberos* (which see). *Villavicencio*.

PAYAGUAS. A tribe on the north side of the Napo, near its mouth. *Villavicencio*.

PELADOS. A tribe of the Huallaga, preached to between 1683 and 1727. They are probably the same as the *Jitipos* (which see); but are marked on Fritz's map (1707) between the rivers Ucayali, and Yavari. *Velasco; Samuel Fritz; Introduction*, p. xliii.

PEQUEYAS. A branch of the *Encabellados* (which see). Preached to between 1727 and 1768. *Velasco*.

PEVAS. A tribe between the rivers Napo and Putumayu. *Villavicencio's map*.

PINCHES. A branch of the *Andoas*, preached to between 1683

and 1727. Met with between the rivers Tigre and Pastaza. *Velasco* ; *Villavicencio.*

PINDOS. A branch of the *Jeberos* (which see). *Villavicencio.*

PIRAS (see *Uaupés*).

PIRROS or CHUNTAQUIROS. A tribe of the Ucayali, preached to between 1683 and 1727. They wander from place to place in canoes, and are good boatmen and fishermen. They are employed by traders to procure sarsaparilla, and make oil from the fat of the manatee. They navigate nearly the whole length of the Ucayali, and trade with the *Antis* (which see) within a short distance of Cuzco. Velasco says that they are descended from the Inca Indians. They are marked on Fritz's map (1707), on the east side of the Ucayali. *Velasco; Smyth; General Miller ; Castelnau.*

POCOANAS (see *Carabuyanas*).

PUINAUS or MAFIARUS. A tribe in the centre of the Pampa del Sacramento, near the northern part of it. Not numerous, and rarely seen by the mission Indians. *Smyth, p. 235.*

PUNOUYS. A tribe on the south side of the Amazons, below the mouth of the Madeira. *Acuña, p. 117.*

PURUPURUS. A tribe of the river Purus, from sixteen to thirty days voyage up. They are almost all afflicted with a peculiar disease. The body is spotted with white and brown patches of irregular size and shape. Men and women go perfectly naked ; and their huts are very small and of the rudest construction. Their canoes are flat bottomed, with upright sides ; mere square boxes, quite unlike those of any other Indians. They use neither the blow-pipe, nor bow and arrows, but have an instrument called *palheta,*—a piece of wood, with a projection at the end, to secure the base of a dart, the middle of which is held with the handle of the *palheta* in the hand, and thus thrown as from a sling. They have surprising dexterity in the use of this weapon, and readily kill game and fish with it. They construct earthen pans for cooking. In the wet season, when the beaches are flooded, they make rafts of the trunks of trees bound together with creepers, and erect their huts upon them, thus living till the waters subside again. Their skin disease perhaps arises from sleeping naked on the sands, without hammocks. *Spix und Martius*, iii, p. 1174 ; *Castelnau ; Wallace*, p. 514.

PUTUMAYOS. A general name for the tribes of that river. *Velasco.*

QUATAUSIS (see *Catauxis*). A tribe of the Purus. *Acuña*, p. 107.

QUERERUS (see *Carabuyanas*).

QUILIVITAS. Supposed to be extinct in Velasco's time. *Velasco.*

QUIMAUS. A tribe on the south side of the Amazon, below the mouth of the Madeira. *Acuña*, p. 117.

QUINARUPIANAS (see *Carabuyanas*).

QUIRIVINAS. A branch of the *Andoas* (which see). *Velasco.*

REMOS. A tribe of the Ucayali, considered by Velasco as a branch of the *Campas*. They are a numerous and courageous race, and occupy a large tract of inland country, seldom coming down to the river. They are very savage, and wage war against all foreigners. They are fair, their faces rounder than those of other tribes of the Ucayali, their eyes like Chinese, and their stature very short. *Velasco ; Smyth.*

RIMACHUMAS. A branch of the *Maynas*. *Velasco.*

ROAMAYNAS. A tribe of the river Pastaza, preached to between 1638 and 1683. Marked on Fritz's map (1707) between the rivers Pastaza and Tigre. Villavicencio places them between the Morona and Pastaza. *Velasco ; M. Rodrigeuz ; Villavicencio.*

ROTUNOS. A branch of the *Zaparos* (which see). *Villavicencio.*

RUANABABAS A branch of the *Camavos* (which see) *Velasco.*

RUMOS. A tribe of the river Napo. *Acuña*, p. 94.

SENCIS. A bold, warlike, and generous tribe of the Ucayali, inhabiting a hilly country N.E. of Sarayacu. They are on friendly terms with the Indians of the missions, though not converted themselves. Father Plaza was well received by them, and describes them as the greatest warriors of the Ucayali. They have bows and arrows, lances, clubs, and *kowas* (a short spear pointed at one end, the other in the shape of a club, with stag's antlers fixed down its sides). They are agriculturists, and are very industrious. Those who are idle are killed, as useless members of society. They have knowledge of the properties of medicinal herbs, and apply them with skill and success. They wear orna-ments on the ears, nose, neck, and arms. They use canoes, and live on fish during the dry season. *Mercurio Peruano*, No. 381; *Smyth*, p. 225.

" I saw no difference in appearance between the *Sencis*, and the other tribes of the Ucayali." Lieutenant Herndon seems inclined to throw some doubt on the account given by Smyth, from inform-ation supplied by Father Plaza. *Herndon*, p. 209.

SEÑOS. A tribe of the river Napo. *Acuña*, p. 94.

SEPAUNABAS. A branch of the *Campas* (which see). *Velasco.*

SETEBOS. A tribe of the Ucayali, living north of the *Cashibos* (which see). They are said to be quiet, tractable, and well disposed towards the Missions. Since 1651, the Franciscans have occasionally visited them, but were generally murdered. Father Girbal, when he founded Sarayacu, in 1792, induced some of them to settle there. They trade up and down the Ucayali in canoes. *Mercurio Peruano*, No. 51; *Herndon.*

SHIPIBOS. A tribe of the Ucayali, coupled with the Setebos, by Smyth and Herndon. The Franciscans visited them from time to time, since 1651. In 1736 they routed and almost destroyed the Setebos in a bloody battle. In 1764 the good Franciscans brought about a reconciliation. They were collected into a village on the river Pisqui in 1764, by Father Fresneda, but in 1767, all the Missionaries were massacred. After that fatal time, Father Girbal was the first who visited them, in 1790. *Mercurio Peruano*, No. 51.

SHIRIPUNAS. A branch of the *Zaparos* (which see). *Villa-vicencio*, p. 171-3.

SIGUIYAS. A tribe of the Araganatuba. *Acuña*, p. 105.

SIMARRONES. A branch of the *Maynas*. *Velasco.*

SIMIGAES. A group of tribes living on the banks of the

Curaray and Tigre. They were preached to between 1683 and
1727. *Velasco ; Villavicencio ; Fritz's Map.*

SIRINEYRIS (see *Chunchos.*)

SIRIONOS (see *Guarayos.*)

SOLIMOENS. A tribe on the Amazons, formerly powerful, from
which the Portuguese gave the name of the river.

SORIMOENS. A tribe of the rivers Teffé and Coari. In 1788
Ribeiro reported that the chief remains of this once numerous
tribe, was settled at the mouth of the Coari. They are probably
identical with the *Solimoens. Southey's Brazil,* iii.

SUCHICHIS. A tribe supposed to be extinct, in the time of
Velasco. *Velasco.*

SUCUMBIOS. A tribe to the eastward of Quito. *Velasco.*

TABALOSOS. A branch of the *Jeberos* (which see). *M.
Rodriguez.*

TAGUACUAS. A branch of the *Manamabobos* (which see).
Velasco.

TAGUAUS. A tribe dwelling on the river, up which the race of
Amazons were said to live. *Acuña,* p. 122.

TAMAS. A tribe of the river Napo. A branch of the *Aguaricos*
(which see.) *Acuña,* p. 94 ; *Velasco.*

TAMUANAS. A tribe of the river Teffé. *Southey's Brazil,* iii.

TAPAJOSOS. A tribe of the river Tapajos. *Acuña,* p. 124.

TAPURAS (see *Uaupés.*)

TAPUYAS. A tribe of the river Pacaxa (see *Tupis.*) *Acuña,*
p. 130.

TASIAS. A branch of the *Campas* (which see) *Velasco.*

TARIANES (see *Uaupés.*)

TATUS (see *Uaupés.*)

TAUNIES. A tribe of the "Gran Chaco." *Lozano,* p. 75.

TENIMBUCAS (see *Uaupés.*)

TEQUETES (see *Chunipies.*)

TERARUS. A tribe of the Araganatuba. *Acuña*, p. 105.

TIASSUS (see *Uaupés.*)

TICUNAS or JUMANAS. A tribe of the Marañon, neighbours of the Omaguas, preached to between 1683 and 1727. They people Tabatinga, the frontier Brazilian post on the Marañon. They go naked, and have a tattooed oval round their mouths, which the men wear broader than the women, and a line from the corners of the mouth to the ears.

They believe in a good and an evil spirit, named Nanuloa and Locazy. They fear the evil spirit, and believe of the good one that, after death, he appears to eat fruit with the departed, and to take them to his home. Their dead bodies are arranged, with the extremities placed together, and the face towards the rising sun, with broken weapons and fruit placed in the bosom; they are then buried in a great earthen jar; and the ceremony is concluded by a drinking festival.

Wives are obtained by presents to the parents, and it is said that the chief has the "jus primæ noctis." As soon as a child can sit up, it is sprinkled with a decoction from certain leaves, and receives the name of one of its forefathers.

Next to the *Passes* and *Juris*, the *Ticunas* are the best formed Indians of this region. They are not so well built as the former, though slighter than most of the tribes. Their faces are round, nose thin and sharp, and expression generally good humoured and gentle. Their disposition is open and honest. They are darker than most of the Indians of the Marañon, and beardless. *Velasco; Acuna*, p. 96; *Von Spix*, iii, p. 1182; *Von Martius*, iii, p. 1206; *Castelnau; Herndon*, p. 234.

TIJUCOS (see *Uaupés.*)

TINGANESES. A tribe of the Huallaga, preached to by Father Lugando in 1631. Possibly identical with the *Cholones* (which see) *Velasco; Mercurio Peruano.*

TIPUNAS. A tribe of the river Jutay. *Acuña*, p. 99.

TIPUTINIS. A branch of the *Jeberos* (which see) according to Velasco, but Villavicencio places them under the *Zaparos.* They were visited by missionaries between 1727 and 1768. *Velasco; Villavicencio.*

TIVILOS. A branch of the *Jeberos* (which see). *M. Rodriguez.*

TOBAS. A savage tribe of the " Gran Chacu," on the banks of the rivers Pilcomayu and Bermejo. *Lozano*, p. 51 ; *Dobrizhoffer ; Gibbon*, p. 164.

TONOCOTES. A tribe of the " Gran Chacu." *Lozano*, p. 51.

TOQUISTENESES. A tribe of the " Gran Chacu." *Lozano*, p. 51.

TREMAJORIS. A branch of the *Simigaes* (which see). *Velasco.*

TUCALES. A tribe, between the rivers Tigre and Pastaza. *Villavicencio's Map.*

TUCANOS (see Uaupés.)

TUCUNDERAS (see Uaupés.)

TUCURIYS. A tribe living on the south side of the river Amazons. *Acuña*, p. 100.

TUINAMAYNAS (see *Carabuyanas.*)

TULUMAYUS. A tribe on a river of the same name, a tributary of the upper Huallaga. They were first visited by Father Lugando in 1631. *Mercurio Peruano.*

TUPINAMBAS. A powerful Brazilian tribe, settled on a great island, at the mouth of the Madeira, in the time of Acuña. *Acuña*, p. 119.

TUPIS. These Indians people Para, and the shores of the lower Amazons. They have long been civilized, and the Brazilians corruptly call them *Tapuyas.* They are stout, short, and well made. They learn all trades quickly and well; and are a quiet, good natured, inoffensive people. They form the crews of most of the Para trading canoes. *Wallace*, p. 478.

TUPITIMIS. A branch of the *Zaparos* (which see). *Villavicencio.*

TUYUNERIS (see *Chunchos.*)

UAENAMBEUS or " Humming Bird" Indians. A tribe on the

lower part of the Japura. They much resemble the *Curetus* (which see), but are distinguished from other tribes by a small blue mark on the upper lip. The women always wear a small apron of bark. *Wallace*, p. 510.

UAMANIS. A tribe of the river Coari. *Southey*, iii, from *Ribeiro*.

UARAYCUS. A tribe of the river Jutay, and also on the Amazons. To try the fortitude of their maidens, they hang them in a net, in the roof of a hut, exposed to continual smoke, where they fast as long as they can possibly bear it; and the youths are flogged, for the same purpose. A youth must hunt and work for his bride, to whom he is engaged from a child, long before he can marry her. They burn their dead, and bury the ashes in their huts (see *Guaraicus*). *Spix und Martius*, iii, p. 1187-90.

UAUPÉS. An extensive group of tribes, inhabiting the shores of the river Uaupés, a tributary of the Rio Negro. Two of them, the *Piras* and *Carapanas*, are mentioned by Acuña. *Acuña*, p.105. The other sub-divisions of the Uaupésare the

Queianas	*Tucunderas* (ant)	*Tucanas* (toucan)
Tarianas	*Jacamis* (trumpeter)	*Uacarras* (heron)
Ananas (pine apples)	*Miritis* (palm)	*Desannas*
Cobéus (cannibals)	*Omauas*	*Ipecas* (duck)
Piraiurus (fish's mouth)	*Mucuras* (opossum)	*Gis* (axe)
	Macunas	*Coua* (wasp)
Pisas (net)	*Taiassus* (pig)	*Corocoro* (green ibis)
Tapuras (tapir)	*Tijucos* (mud)	*Banhunas*
Uaracus (fish)	*Arapassos* (wood-pecker)	*Tatus* (armadillos)
Cohidias		*Tenimbueas* (ashes)

They are tall, stout, and well-formed. Hair jet black and straight, worn in a long tail down the back, often to the thighs; very little beard; skin a light glossy brown. They are an agricultural people, cultivating mandioc, sugar cane, yams, maize, tobacco, and camotes. Their weapons are bows and arrows, lances, clubs, and blow-pipes. They are great fishermen. Many families live together in one house, a parallelogram one hundred

24

and fifteen feet long by seventy-five, and thirty feet high. The roof is supported on fine cylindrical columns, formed of the trunks of trees, smooth and straight. At the gable end is a large doorway, eight feet high, with a palm mat to serve as a door. The furniture consists of net hammocks, earthen pots, pitchers, and baskets. Their canoes are all made of a single hollowed tree, often forty feet long, paddles about three feet long, with an oval blade. The men wear a cloth round the loins, but the women go quite naked. The men use many ornaments, and a circlet of feathers round the head. A cylindrical white quartz stone is invariably carried on the breast, as a charm, suspended by a chain of black seeds. The dead are buried inside the houses. Every house has its *Tushaúa* or chief, the office being hereditary. They have sorcerers called *Payés*, but do not believe in a God. *Wallace*, pp. 480-506.

UAYUPÉS. A tribe of the river Coari. *Ribeiro.*

UCAYALES. A branch of the *Omaguas* (which see). *M. Rodriguez.*

UCHUCAS. A tribe between the rivers Tigre and Pastaza. *Villavicencio's Map.*

UEREQUENAS. A tribe on the river Isanna, a tributary of the Rio Negro. They are said by Ribeiro (1775) to have Jewish names, such as Jacob, David, Joab, etc. They are cannibals; and use the *quipus*, for keeping their accounts. *Southey's Brazil*, iii, p. 723.

UGIARAS. A tribe of the Marañon, below the mouth of the Huallaga. *M. Rodriguez.*

UMAUAS. A tribe of the river Japura; who are said to be cannibals. *Von Martius*, iii, p. 1243.

UNGUMANAS. A branch of the *Maynas*. *Velasco.*

UNIBUESAS. A tribe of the Ucayali, visited by Father Lucero in 1681, and also by other missionaries, between 1683 and 1727. *Velasco.*

UÑONOS. A branch of the *Ugiaras* (which see). *Velasco.*

UPANAS. A tribe on the east side of the river Morona. *Villavi-cencio's Map.*

UPATANINABAS. A branch of the *Pirros* (which see). *Velasco.*

URARINAS. A tribe of the Pastaza; preached to between 1727 and 1768. *Velasco.*

URAYARIS (see *Carabuyanas*).

URUBATINGAS. A tribe on the south side of the Amazons, below the mouth of the Madeira. *Acuña,* p. 117.

USPAS. A tribe supposed to be extinct, in the time of Velasco. *Velasco.*

VELELAS, A tribe of the "Gran Chacu" (see *Chunipies*). *Lozano,* p. 85.

XAMAS. A tribe of the river Teffè. *Ribeiro.*

XIMANAS. A tribe between the rivers Putumayu and Japura; who kill their first-born children. They are esteemed for willing industry. They burn the bones of their dead, and mingle the ashes in their drink. *Southey's Brazil,* iii, p. 722 ; *Wallace,* p. 511.

YACARIGUARAS. A tribe of the river Putumayu. *Acuña,* p. 99.

YACUCARAES. A tribe of the Rio Negro. *Acuña,* p. 110.

YAGUANAIS. A tribe of the Araganatuba. *Acuña,* p. 105.

YAGUAS. A tribe of the Marañon, preached to between 1683 and 1727. In 1852 they had a village, below Omaguas. *Velasco.* (*Herndon,* p. 226).

YAMEOS. A tribe of the Marañon, preached to between 1683 and 1727. Marked on Fritz's map, between the mouths of the Tigre and Napo. *Velasco.*

YAMORUAS. A tribe of the Araganatuba. *Acuña,* p. 105.

YANMAS. A tribe of the Rio Negro. *Acuña,* p. 110.

YAPUAS. A branch of the *Encabellados* (which see). *Velasco.*

YARAPOS. A branch of the *Yameos* (which see). *Velasco.*

YARIBARUS (see *Carabuyanas*).

YARUCAGUACAS (see *Carabuyanas*).

YASHEOS.   A branch of the *Encabellados* (which see).   *Velasco.*

YASUNIES.   A branch of the *Zaparos;* between the rivers Curaray and Napo.   *Villavicencio.*

YEQUEYOS.   A branch of the *Putumayus* (which see.)   *Velasco.*

YETES.   A branch of the *Putumayus* (which see).   *Velasco.*

YGUARANIS.   A tribe of the Araganatuba.   *Acuña*, p. 105.

YNURIS.   A branch of the *Simigaes* (which see).   *Velasco.*

YQUITOS (see *Iquitos*).

YUCUNAS.   A tribe living some distance up the river Japura. The chief lives in a conical pyramid.   Their shields are covered with tapir skins.   They have poisoned spears.   They cultivate mandioc, which they use in the form of tapioca.   *Southey's Brazil,* iii, p. 721.

. YUCUNAMPAS.   A tribe of the " Gran Chacu" (see *Chunipies*). *Lozano*, p. 85.

YUMAGUARIS.   A tribe of Indians, near the river of Amazons, who are employed in washing for gold.   *Acuña*, p. 103.

YUPIUAS.   A tribe of the river Teffé.   *Ribeiro.*

YURACARES.   A tribe in the Bolivian department of Beni, along the base of the Andes, in a province of which Chimoré is the capital.   They are not numerous.   *Gibbon*, p. 202.

YURIMAGUAS.   A tribe of the Marañon, preached to between 1683 and 1727.   The village of Yurimaguas is situated on the Huallaga, above Laguna.   It has about two hundred and fifty inhabitants.   *Velasco ; Herndon*, p. 171.

YURUNAS.   A tribe of the Putumayu.   *Acuña*, p. 99.

YURUSUNES.   A tribe of the Napo, living to the south of the *Encabellados* (which see).   *Acuña*, p. 94 ; *Velasco.*

YXISTENESES.   A tribe of the " Gran Chacu."   *Lozano*, p. 51.

ZAMORAS.   A branch of the *Jeberos* (which see).   *Villavicencio.*

ZAPAS.   A branch of the *Simigaes* (which see).   *Velasco.*

ZAPAROS. A tribe of the river Napo; according to Velasco, a branch of the tribe of the "*Simigaes del Curaray,*" but Villavicencio considers them to be an important parent tribe. *Acuña,* p. 94; *Velasco.*

They are less numerous than the *Jeberos,* and wander between the river Pastaza and Napo. Villavicencio divides them into ten branches, all speaking the same language, which is copious, simple in grammatical construction, somewhat nasal, and guttural. This family of tribes is more pacific than that of *Jeberos,* but more dexterous in hurling the lance. The *Zaparos* are docile, hospitable, obliging, and ready to mix with Europeans. They are indolent, live by the chace, and are clothed in the bark of a tree called *llanchama,* beaten out. They cultivate a few maize, yuca, and banana plantations. They live in small collections of huts, and sleep in hammocks. Their physiognomy resembles that of the Chinese : of short stature but robust, round faces, small angular eyes, broad noses, thick lips, and little beard. Those who live by fishing on the banks of the rivers are of a copper colour; but those who live in the shade of the forests have whiter skins. The women have agreeable expressive countenances, black, animated, beautiful eyes, humane and sensible hearts, generous and hospitable dispositions. Polygamy is in general use. The *Zaparos* believe that the souls of good and valorous men enter beautiful birds, and feed on delicious fruits ; while cowardly souls become dirty reptiles. They also believe in a good and an evil spirit. *Villavicencio,* pp. 171 and 370.

In war they use a spear made of the chonta palm, a blow pipe, and poisoned arrows, which they carry in bamboo tubes, slung across their shoulders. *Dr. Jameson's Journey,* 1857.

ZAPITALAGUAS. A tribe of the "*Gran Chacu.*" *Lozano,* p. 51.

ZEOQUEYAS. A branch of the *Papaguas* (which see). *Velasco.*

ZEPAS. A branch of the *Camavos* (which see). *Velasco.*

ZEPUCAYAS. A tribe living on the Amazons, below the mouth of the Madeira. *Acuña,* p. 117.

ZEUNAS. Supposed to have been extinct, in the time of Velasco. *Velasco.*

ZIAS or ZIYUS. A tribe of the river Putumayu. *Acuña,* p. 99.

ZIBITOS (see *Jibitos*).

ZUCOYAS (same as *Zeoqueyas*).

ZURINAS. A tribe on the banks of the Amazons, below the mouth of the Purus. They are very expert in making comfortable seats, and in carving images. *Acuña,* p. 107.

FINIS.

For EU product safety concerns, contact us at Calle de José Abascal, 56–1°,
28003 Madrid, Spain or eugpsr@cambridge.org.

www.ingramcontent.com/pod-product-compliance
Ingram Content Group UK Ltd.
Pitfield, Milton Keynes, MK11 3LW, UK
UKHW010343140625
459647UK00010B/785